HARROW

COUNTLESS HAINTS

COUNTY

Script
CULLEN BUNN

Art and Lettering
TYLER CROOK

DARK HORSE BOOKS

President and Publisher
MIKE RICHARDSON

Editor
DANIEL CHABON

Assistant Editor
IAN TUCKER

Designer
KEITH WOOD

Digital Art Technician
RYAN JORGENSEN

NEIL HANKERSON *Executive Vice President*
TOM WEDDLE *Chief Financial Officer* · **RANDY STRADLEY** *Vice President of Publishing*
MICHAEL MARTENS *Vice President of Book Trade Sales* · **SCOTT ALLIE** *Editor in Chief*
MATT PARKINSON *Vice President of Marketing* · **DAVID SCROGGY** *Vice President of Product Development*
DALE LaFOUNTAIN *Vice President of Information Technology* · **KEN LIZZI** *General Counsel*
DAVEY ESTRADA *Editorial Director* · **CHRIS WARNER** *Senior Books Editor*
CARY GRAZZINI *Director of Print and Development* · **LIA RIBACCHI** *Art Director*
CARA NIECE *Director of Scheduling* · **MARK BERNARDI** *Director of Digital Publishing*

Published by Dark Horse Books
A division of Dark Horse Comics, Inc.
10956 SE Main Street
Milwaukie, OR 97222

First edition: December 2015
ISBN 978-1-61655-780-5

International Licensing: (503) 905-2377
Comic Shop Locator Service: (888) 266-4226

This volume collects *Harrow County* #1–#4.

3   5   7   9   10   8   6   4   2
Printed in China

HARROW

COUNTLESS HAINTS

COUNTY

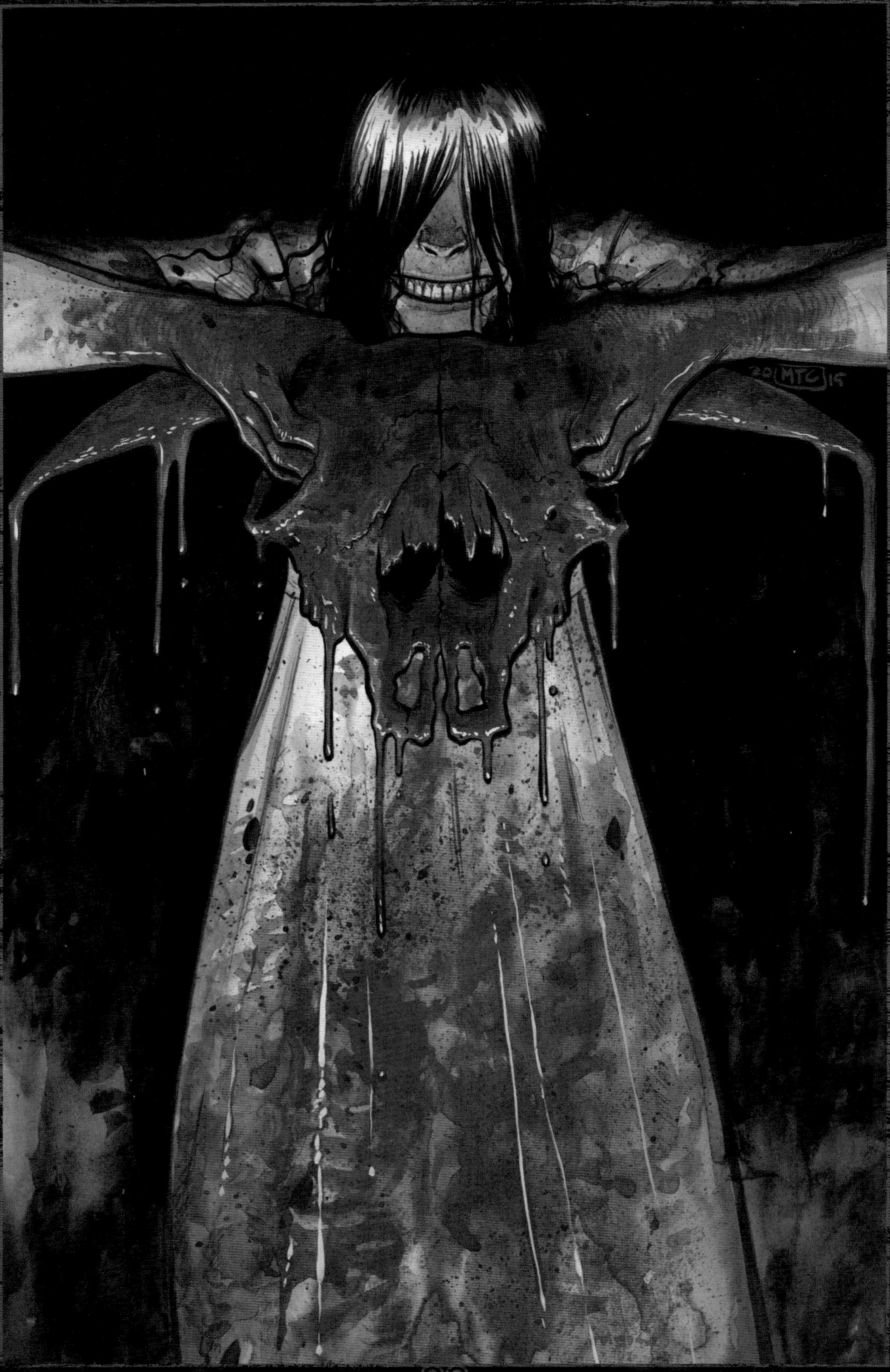

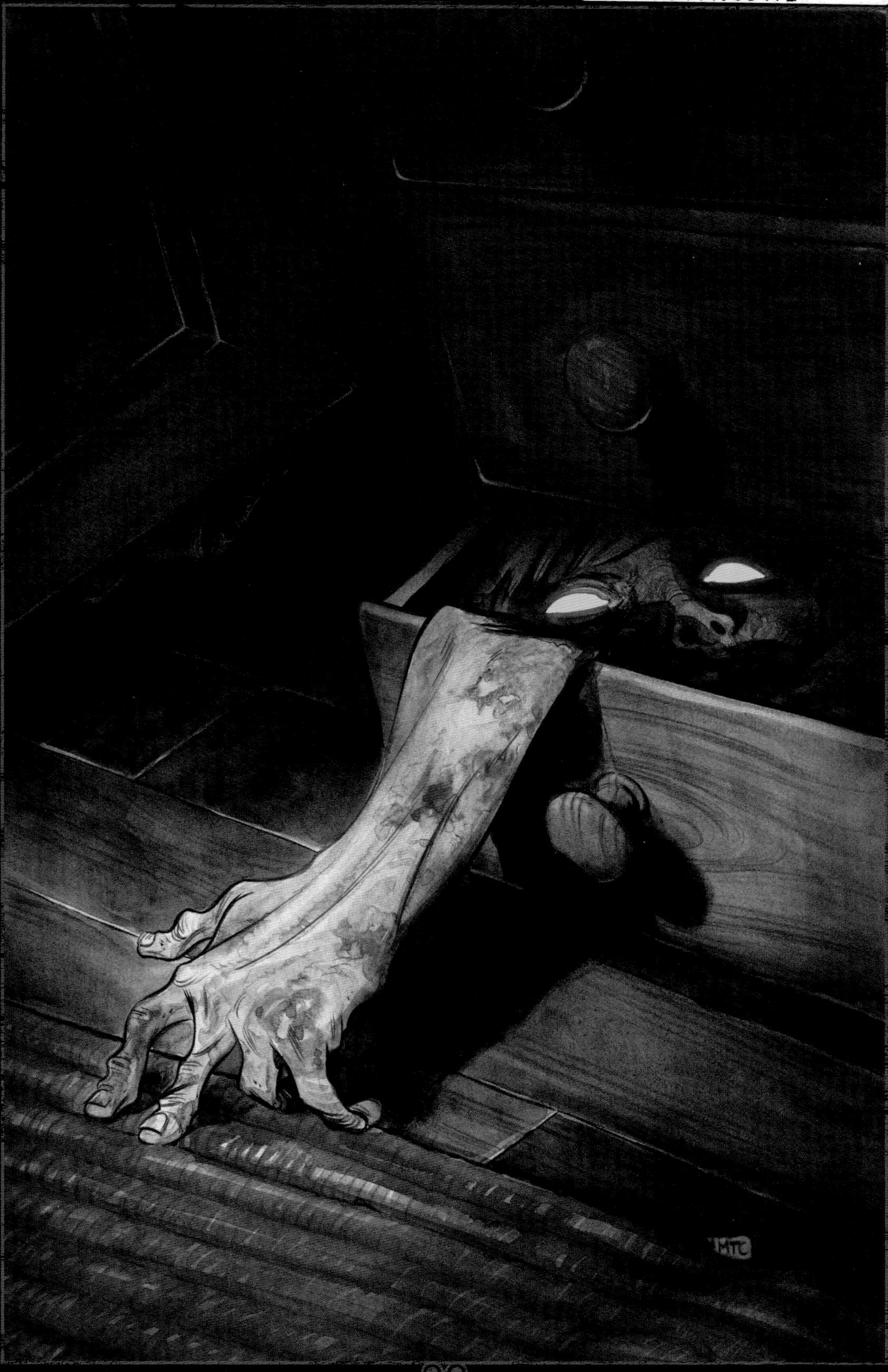
MTC

ONE

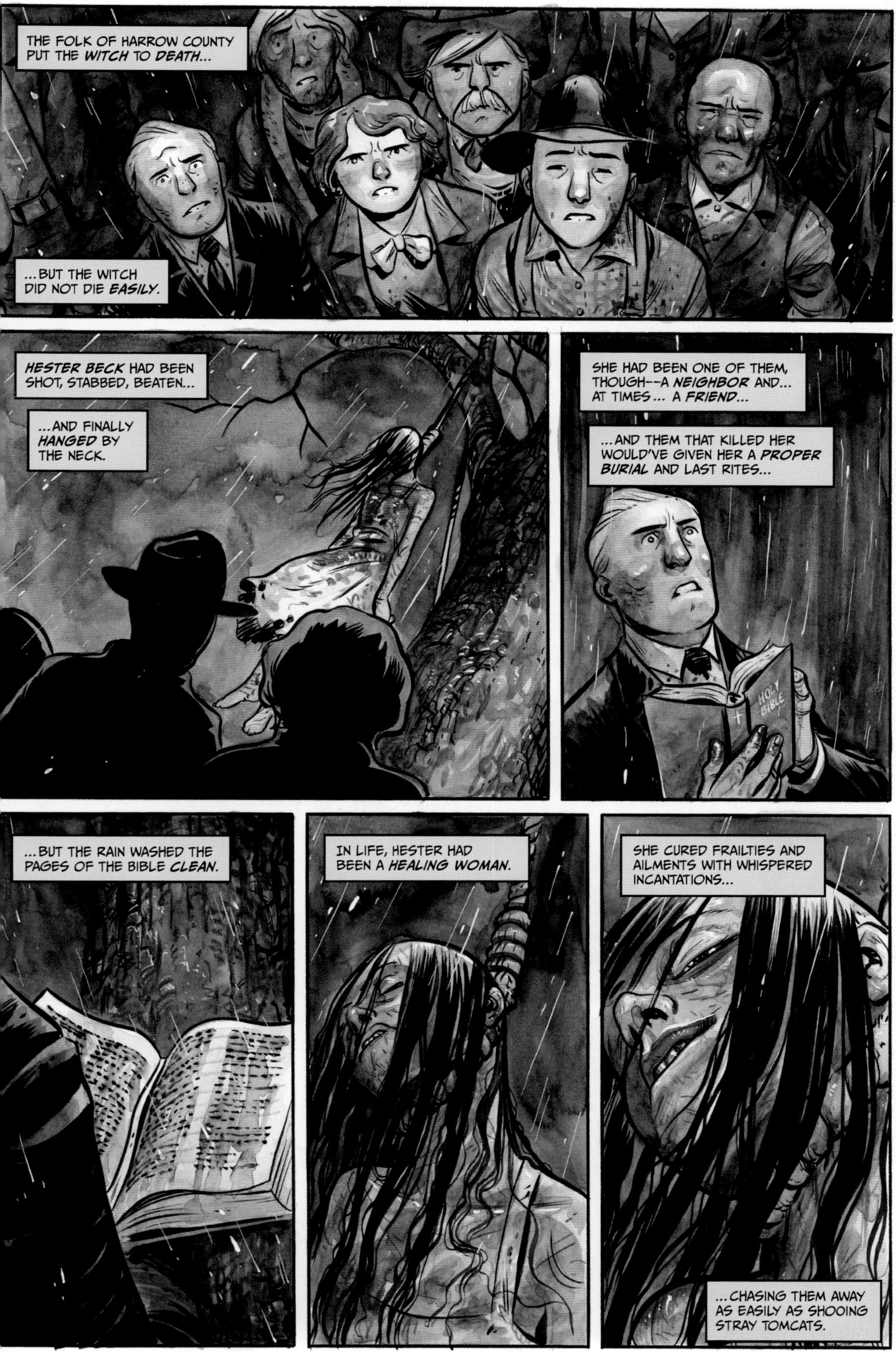
THE FOLK OF HARROW COUNTY PUT THE WITCH TO DEATH...
...BUT THE WITCH DID NOT DIE EASILY.
HESTER BECK HAD BEEN SHOT, STABBED, BEATEN...
...AND FINALLY HANGED BY THE NECK.
SHE HAD BEEN ONE OF THEM, THOUGH--A NEIGHBOR AND... AT TIMES... A FRIEND...
...AND THEM THAT KILLED HER WOULD'VE GIVEN HER A PROPER BURIAL AND LAST RITES...
HOLY BIBLE
...BUT THE RAIN WASHED THE PAGES OF THE BIBLE CLEAN.
IN LIFE, HESTER HAD BEEN A HEALING WOMAN.
SHE CURED FRAILTIES AND AILMENTS WITH WHISPERED INCANTATIONS...
...CHASING THEM AWAY AS EASILY AS SHOOING STRAY TOMCATS.

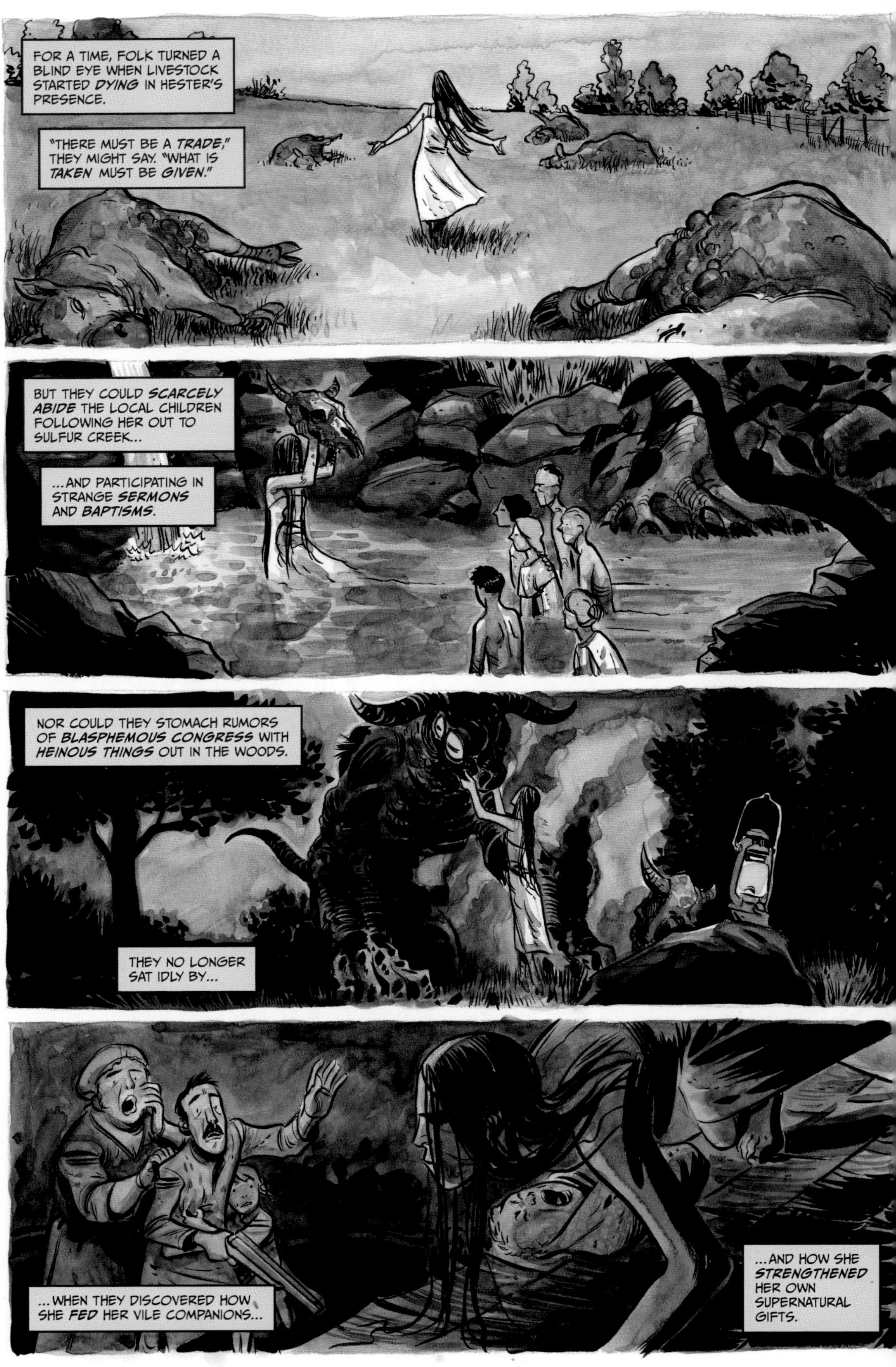

FOR A TIME, FOLK TURNED A BLIND EYE WHEN LIVESTOCK STARTED *DYING* IN HESTER'S PRESENCE.
"THERE MUST BE A *TRADE*," THEY MIGHT SAY. "WHAT IS *TAKEN* MUST BE *GIVEN*."
BUT THEY COULD *SCARCELY ABIDE* THE LOCAL CHILDREN FOLLOWING HER OUT TO SULFUR CREEK...
...AND PARTICIPATING IN STRANGE *SERMONS* AND *BAPTISMS*.
NOR COULD THEY STOMACH RUMORS OF *BLASPHEMOUS CONGRESS* WITH *HEINOUS THINGS* OUT IN THE WOODS.
THEY NO LONGER SAT IDLY BY...
...WHEN THEY DISCOVERED HOW SHE *FED* HER VILE COMPANIONS...
...AND HOW SHE *STRENGTHENED* HER OWN SUPERNATURAL GIFTS.

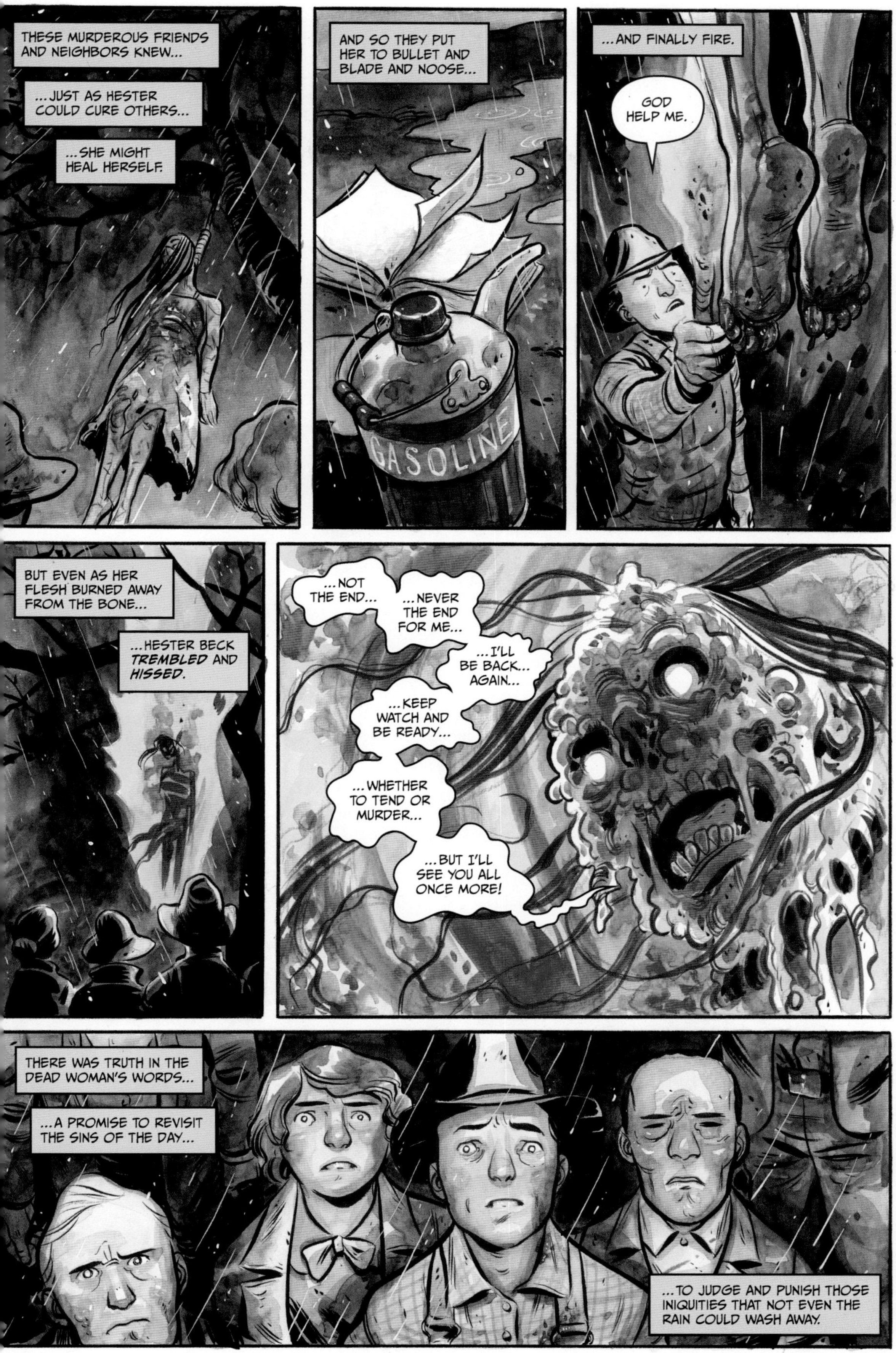
THESE MURDEROUS FRIENDS AND NEIGHBORS KNEW...
...JUST AS HESTER COULD CURE OTHERS...
...SHE MIGHT HEAL HERSELF.
AND SO THEY PUT HER TO BULLET AND BLADE AND NOOSE...
GASOLINE
...AND FINALLY FIRE.
GOD HELP ME.
BUT EVEN AS HER FLESH BURNED AWAY FROM THE BONE...
...HESTER BECK *TREMBLED* AND *HISSED*.
...NOT THE END...
...NEVER THE END FOR ME...
...I'LL BE BACK... AGAIN...
...KEEP WATCH AND BE READY...
...WHETHER TO TEND OR MURDER...
...BUT I'LL SEE YOU ALL ONCE MORE!
THERE WAS TRUTH IN THE DEAD WOMAN'S WORDS...
...A PROMISE TO REVISIT THE SINS OF THE DAY...
...TO JUDGE AND PUNISH THOSE INIQUITIES THAT NOT EVEN THE RAIN COULD WASH AWAY.

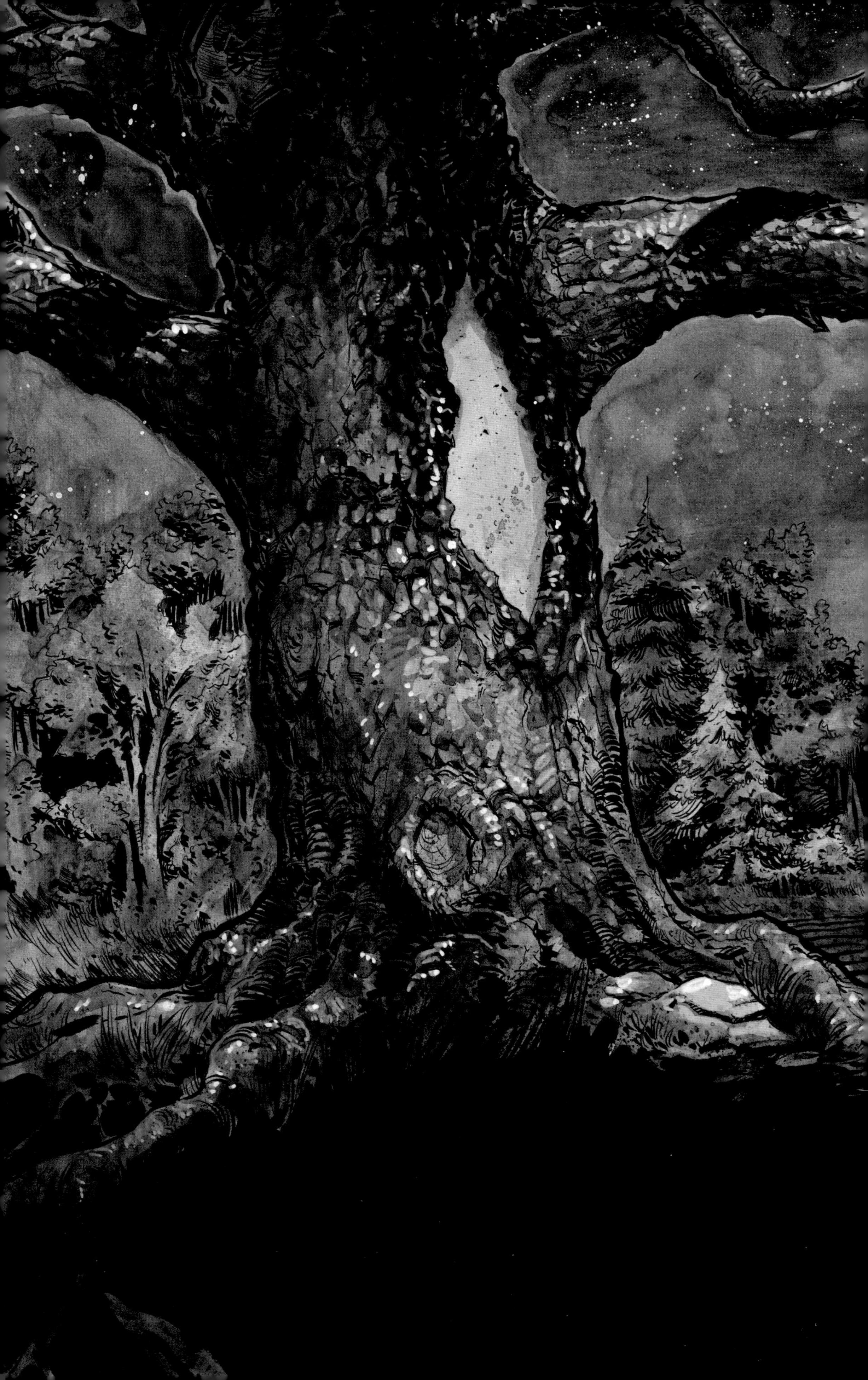

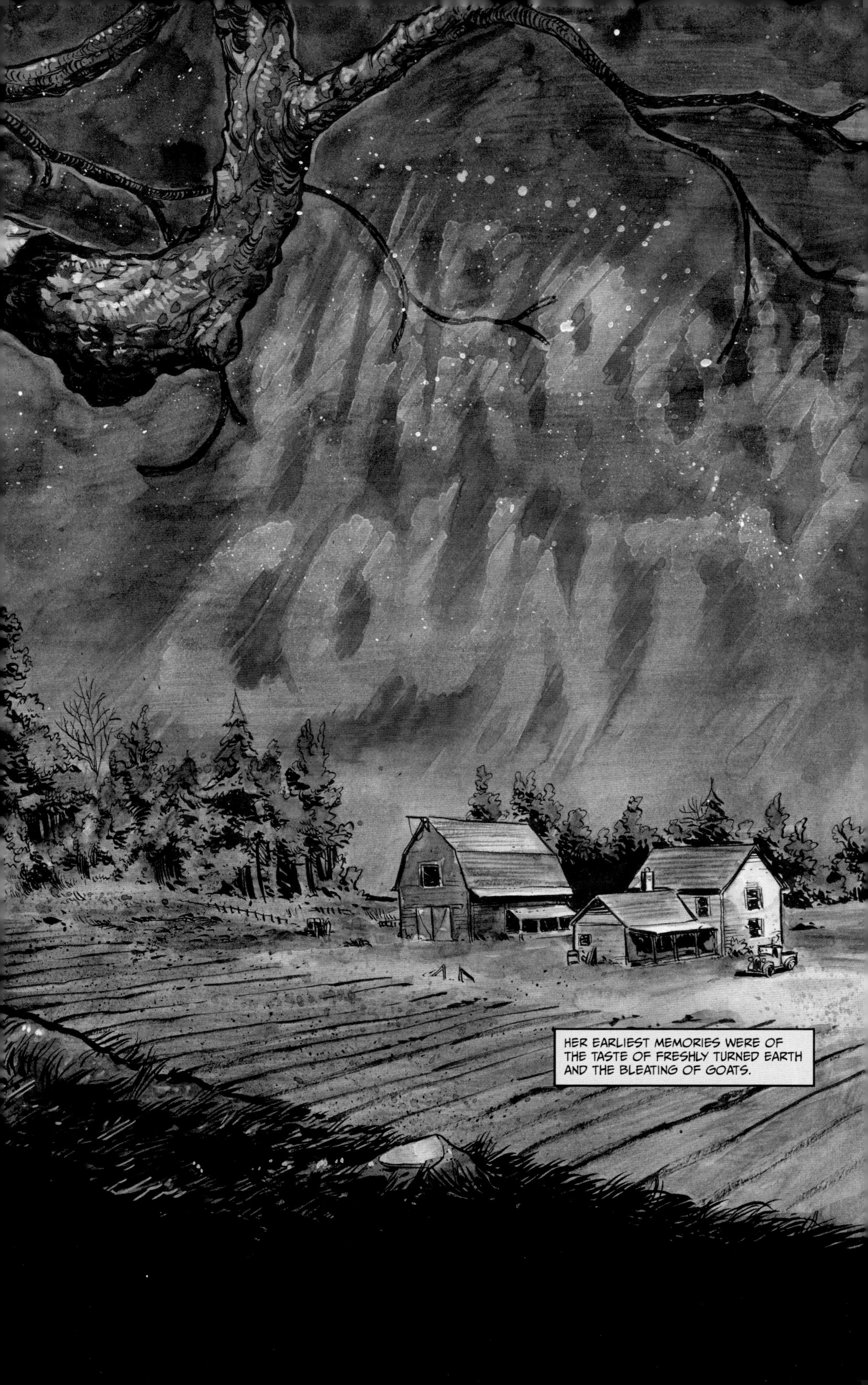
HER EARLIEST MEMORIES WERE OF THE TASTE OF FRESHLY TURNED EARTH AND THE BLEATING OF GOATS.

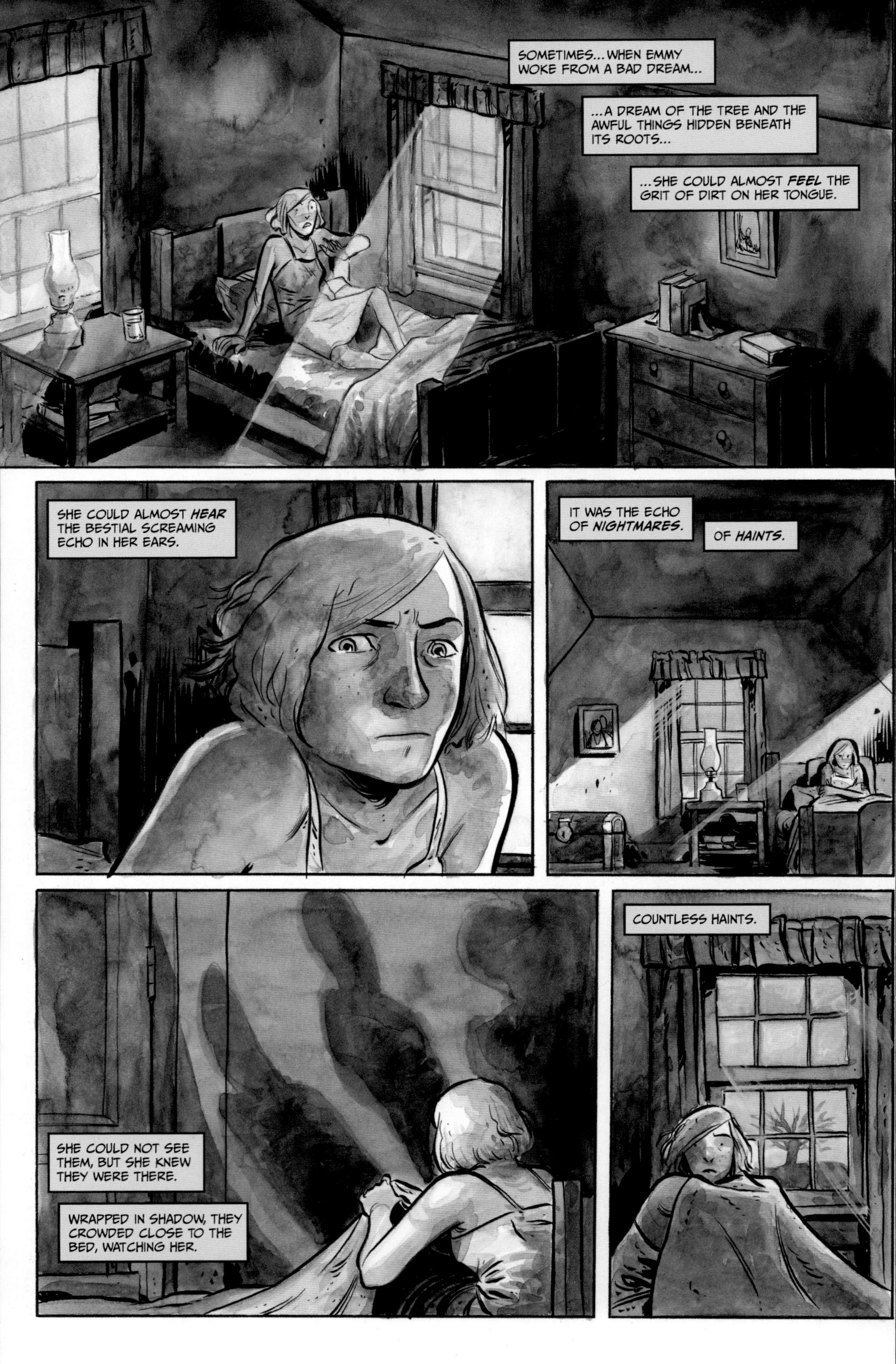
SOMETIMES... WHEN EMMY WOKE FROM A BAD DREAM...
...A DREAM OF THE TREE AND THE AWFUL THINGS HIDDEN BENEATH ITS ROOTS...
...SHE COULD ALMOST *FEEL* THE GRIT OF DIRT ON HER TONGUE.
SHE COULD ALMOST *HEAR* THE BESTIAL SCREAMING ECHO IN HER EARS.
IT WAS THE ECHO OF *NIGHTMARES*.
OF *HAINTS*.
SHE COULD NOT SEE THEM, BUT SHE KNEW THEY WERE THERE.
WRAPPED IN SHADOW, THEY CROWDED CLOSE TO THE BED, WATCHING HER.
COUNTLESS HAINTS.

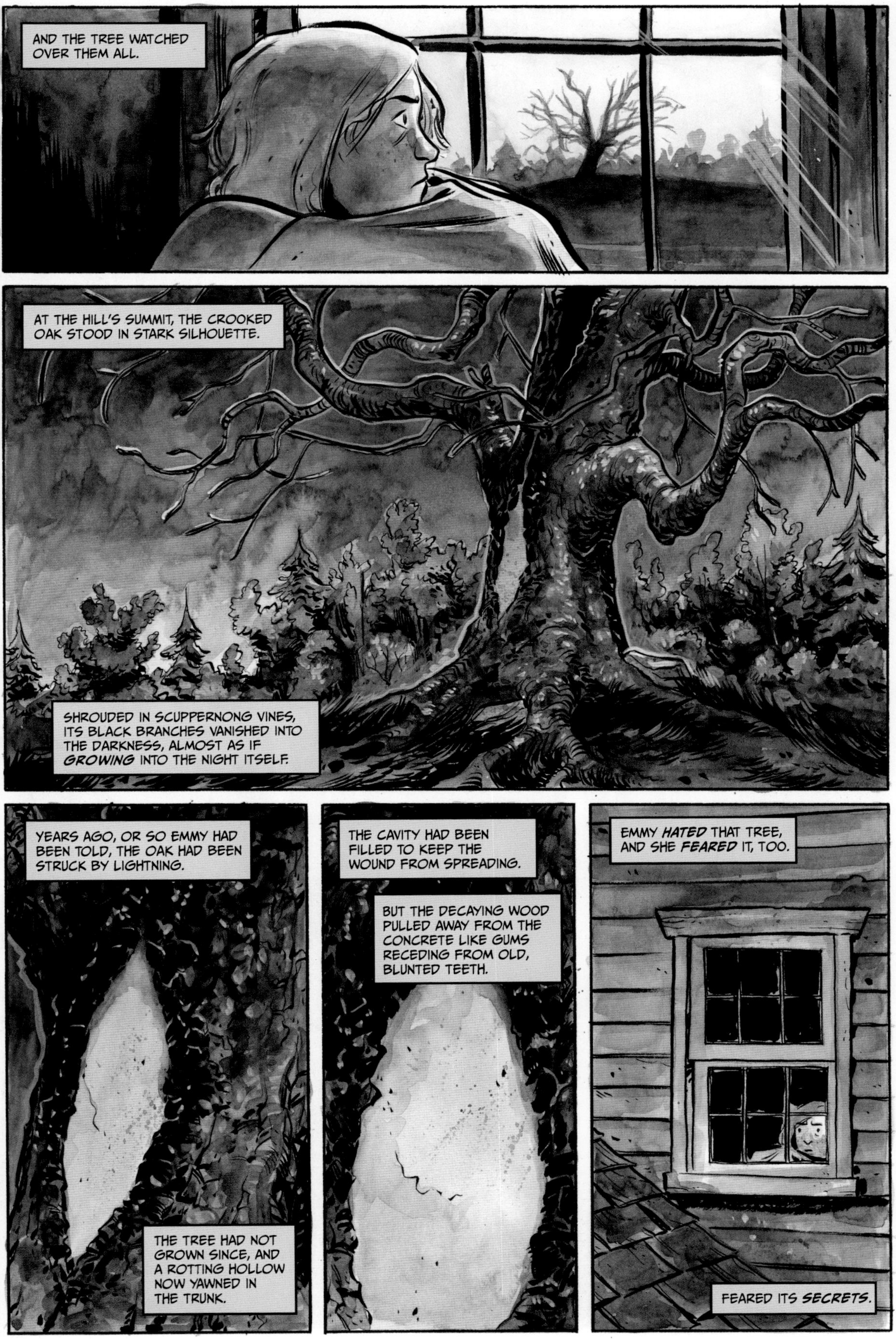
AND THE TREE WATCHED OVER THEM ALL.
AT THE HILL'S SUMMIT, THE CROOKED OAK STOOD IN STARK SILHOUETTE.
SHROUDED IN SCUPPERNONG VINES, ITS BLACK BRANCHES VANISHED INTO THE DARKNESS, ALMOST AS IF *GROWING* INTO THE NIGHT ITSELF.
YEARS AGO, OR SO EMMY HAD BEEN TOLD, THE OAK HAD BEEN STRUCK BY LIGHTNING.
THE TREE HAD NOT GROWN SINCE, AND A ROTTING HOLLOW NOW YAWNED IN THE TRUNK.
THE CAVITY HAD BEEN FILLED TO KEEP THE WOUND FROM SPREADING.
BUT THE DECAYING WOOD PULLED AWAY FROM THE CONCRETE LIKE GUMS RECEDING FROM OLD, BLUNTED TEETH.
EMMY *HATED* THAT TREE, AND SHE *FEARED* IT, TOO.
FEARED ITS *SECRETS*.

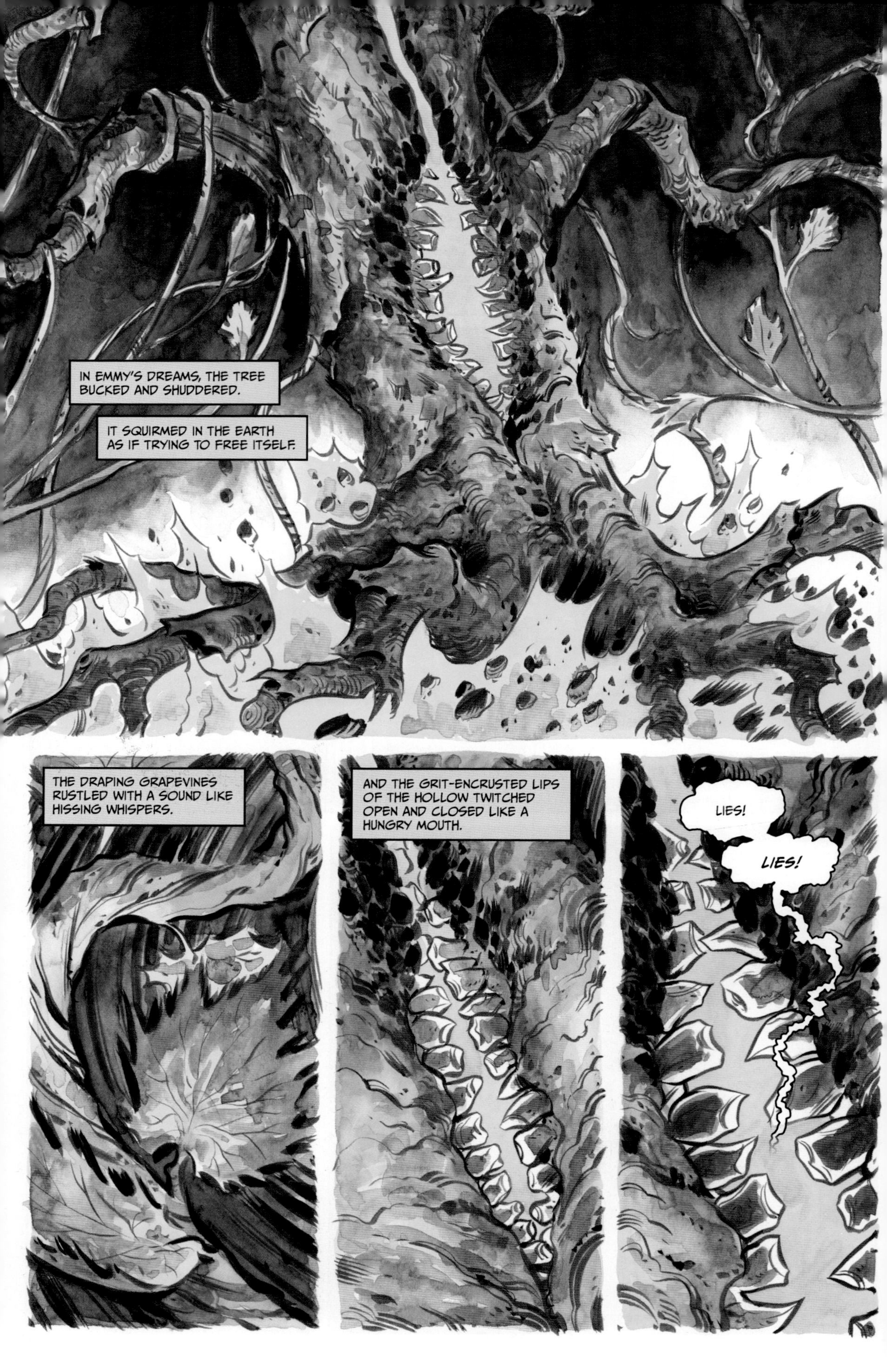
IN EMMY'S DREAMS, THE TREE BUCKED AND SHUDDERED.
IT SQUIRMED IN THE EARTH AS IF TRYING TO FREE ITSELF.
THE DRAPING GRAPEVINES RUSTLED WITH A SOUND LIKE HISSING WHISPERS.
AND THE GRIT-ENCRUSTED LIPS OF THE HOLLOW TWITCHED OPEN AND CLOSED LIKE A HUNGRY MOUTH.
LIES!
LIES!

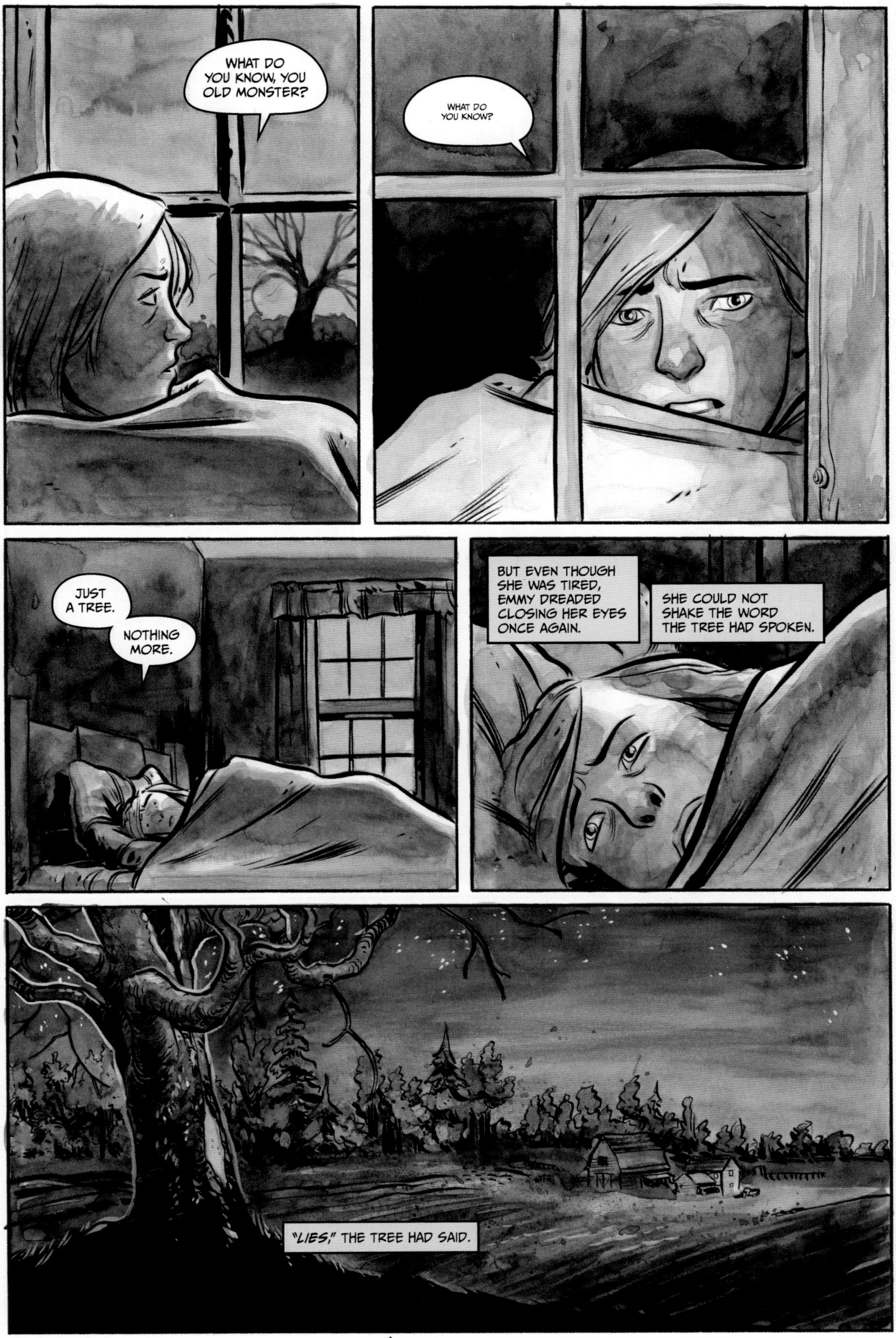
WHAT DO YOU KNOW, YOU OLD MONSTER?
WHAT DO YOU KNOW?
JUST A TREE.
NOTHING MORE.
BUT EVEN THOUGH SHE WAS TIRED, EMMY DREADED CLOSING HER EYES ONCE AGAIN.
SHE COULD NOT SHAKE THE WORD THE TREE HAD SPOKEN.
"LIES," THE TREE HAD SAID.

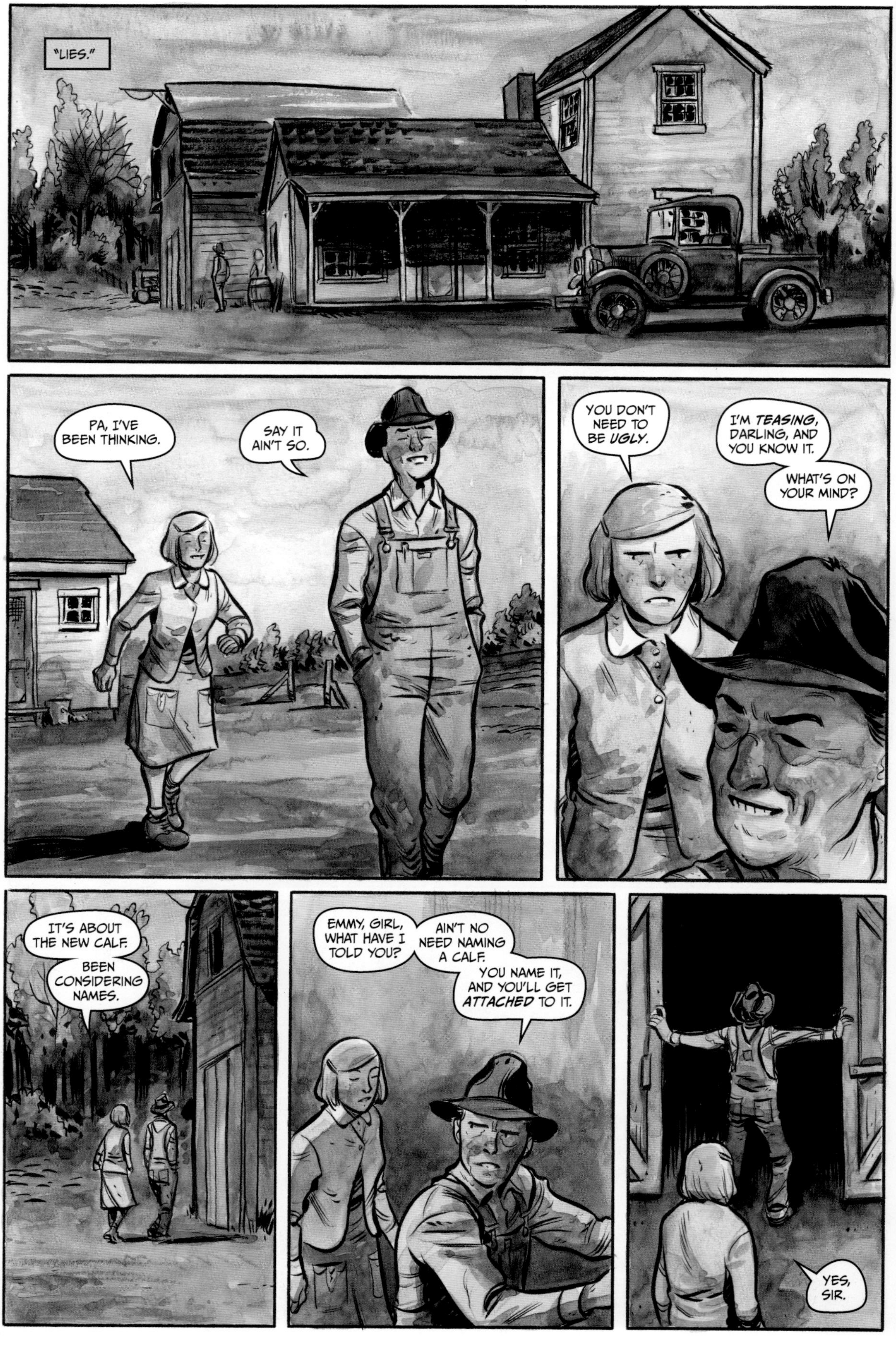
"LIES."
PA, I'VE BEEN THINKING.
SAY IT AIN'T SO.
YOU DON'T NEED TO BE *UGLY*.
I'M *TEASING*, DARLING, AND YOU KNOW IT.
WHAT'S ON YOUR MIND?
IT'S ABOUT THE NEW CALF.
BEEN CONSIDERING NAMES.
EMMY, GIRL, WHAT HAVE I TOLD YOU?
AIN'T NO NEED NAMING A CALF.
YOU NAME IT, AND YOU'LL GET *ATTACHED* TO IT.
YES, SIR.

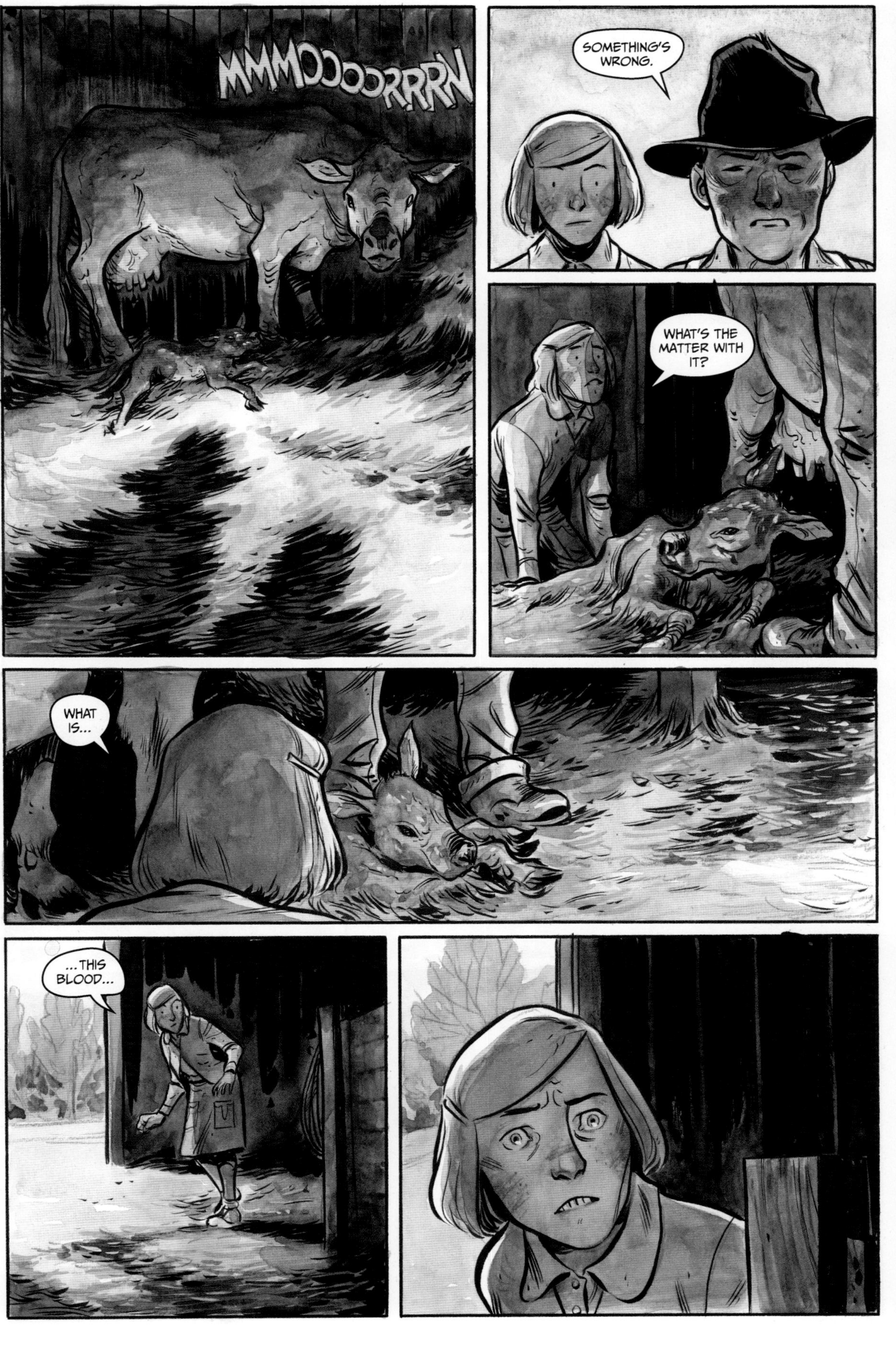
MMMOOOORRRRN
SOMETHING'S WRONG.
WHAT'S THE MATTER WITH IT?
WHAT IS...
...THIS BLOOD...

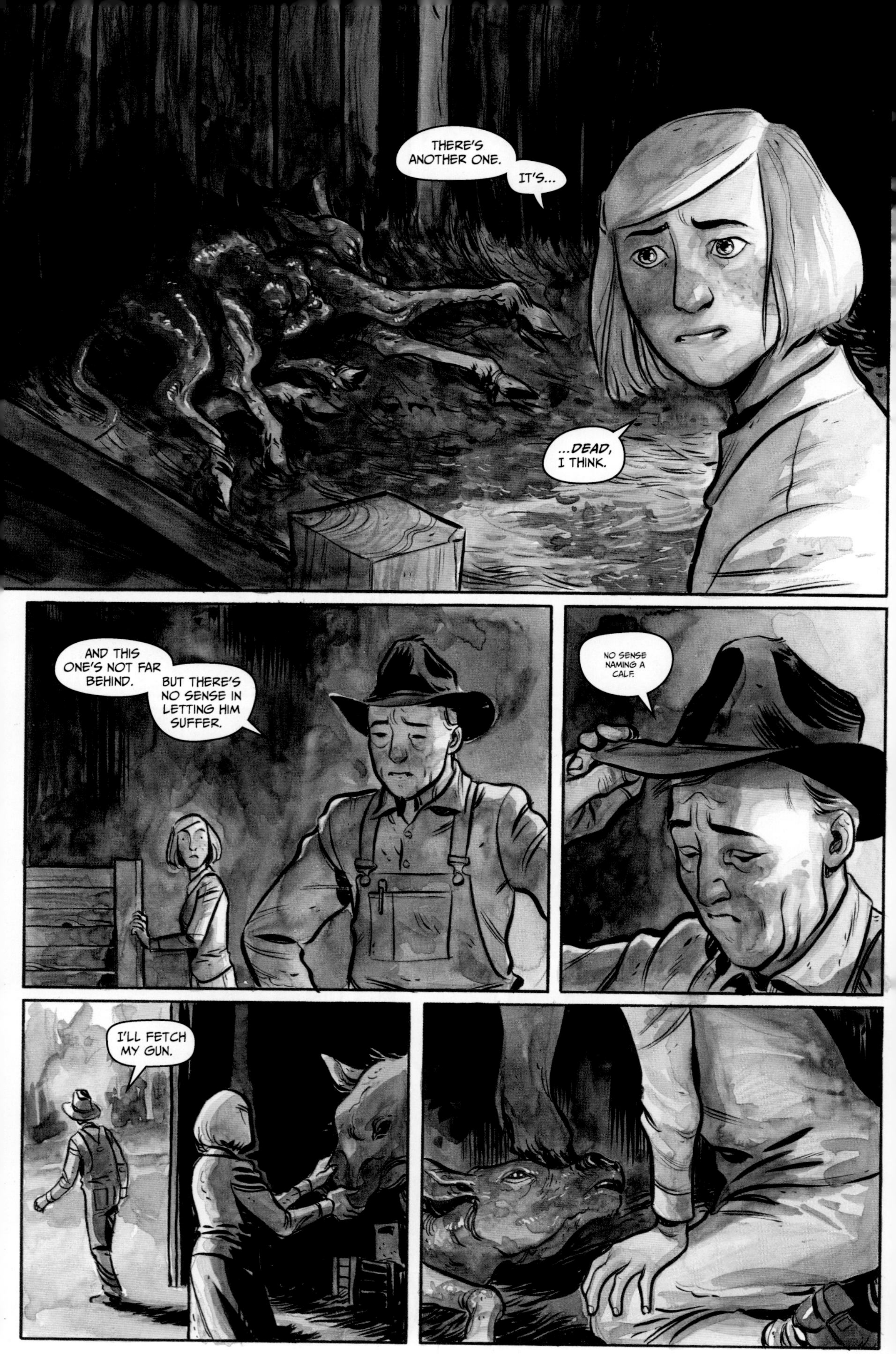
THERE'S ANOTHER ONE.
IT'S...
...DEAD, I THINK.
AND THIS ONE'S NOT FAR BEHIND.
BUT THERE'S NO SENSE IN LETTING HIM SUFFER.
NO SENSE NAMING A CALF.
I'LL FETCH MY GUN.

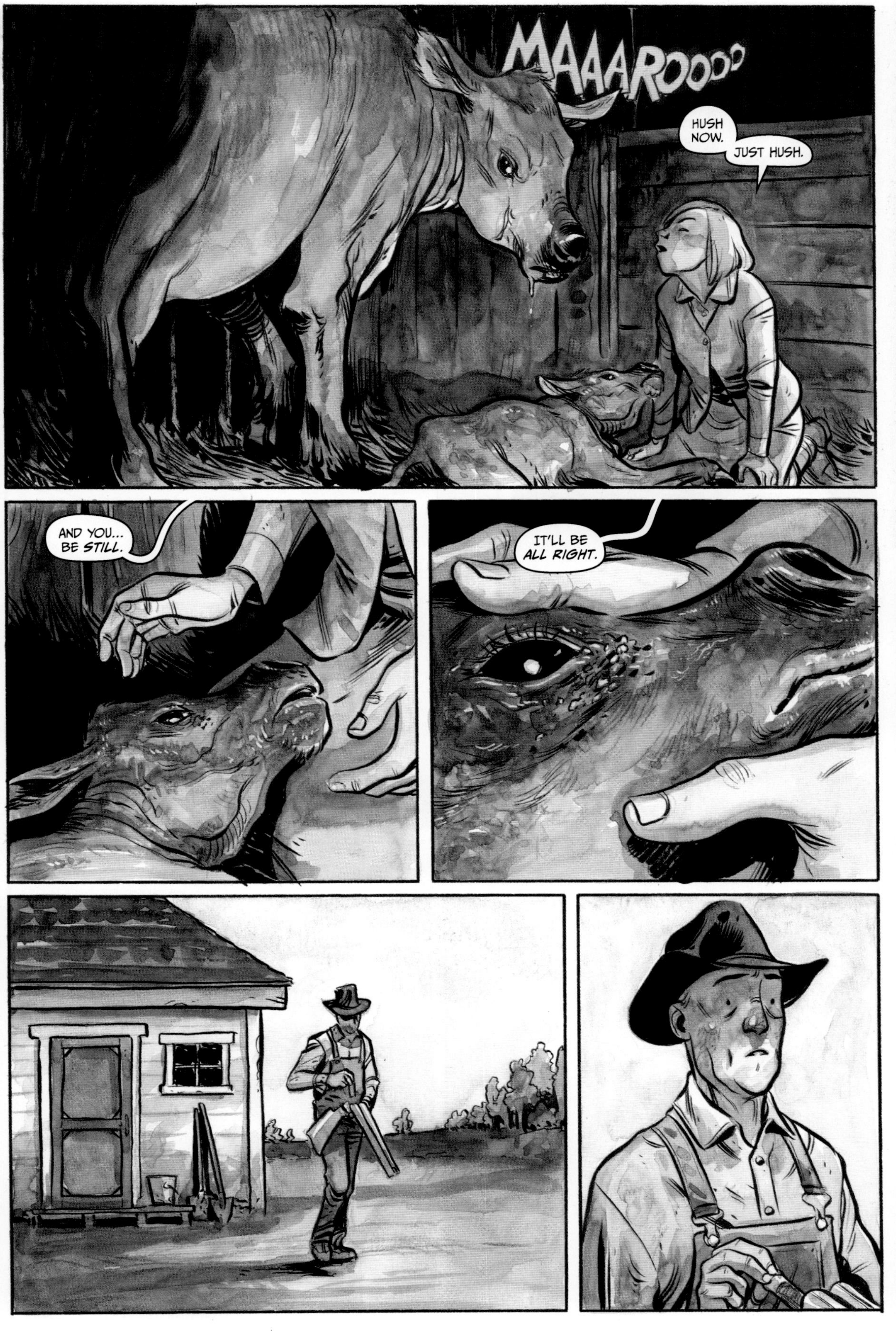
MAAAROOOO
HUSH NOW.
JUST HUSH.
AND YOU... BE STILL.
IT'LL BE ALL RIGHT.

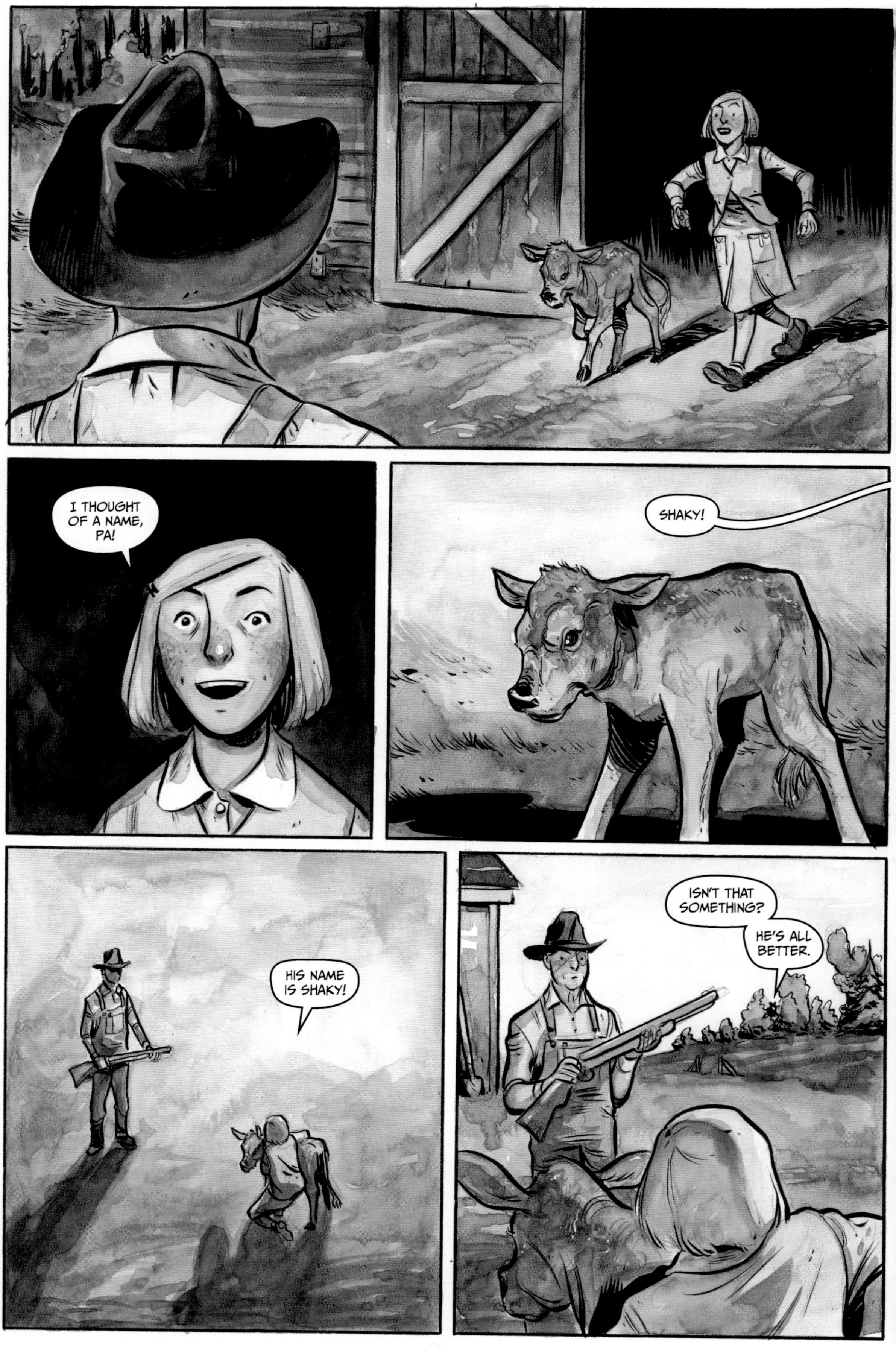
I THOUGHT OF A NAME, PA!
SHAKY!
HIS NAME IS SHAKY!
ISN'T THAT SOMETHING?
HE'S ALL BETTER.

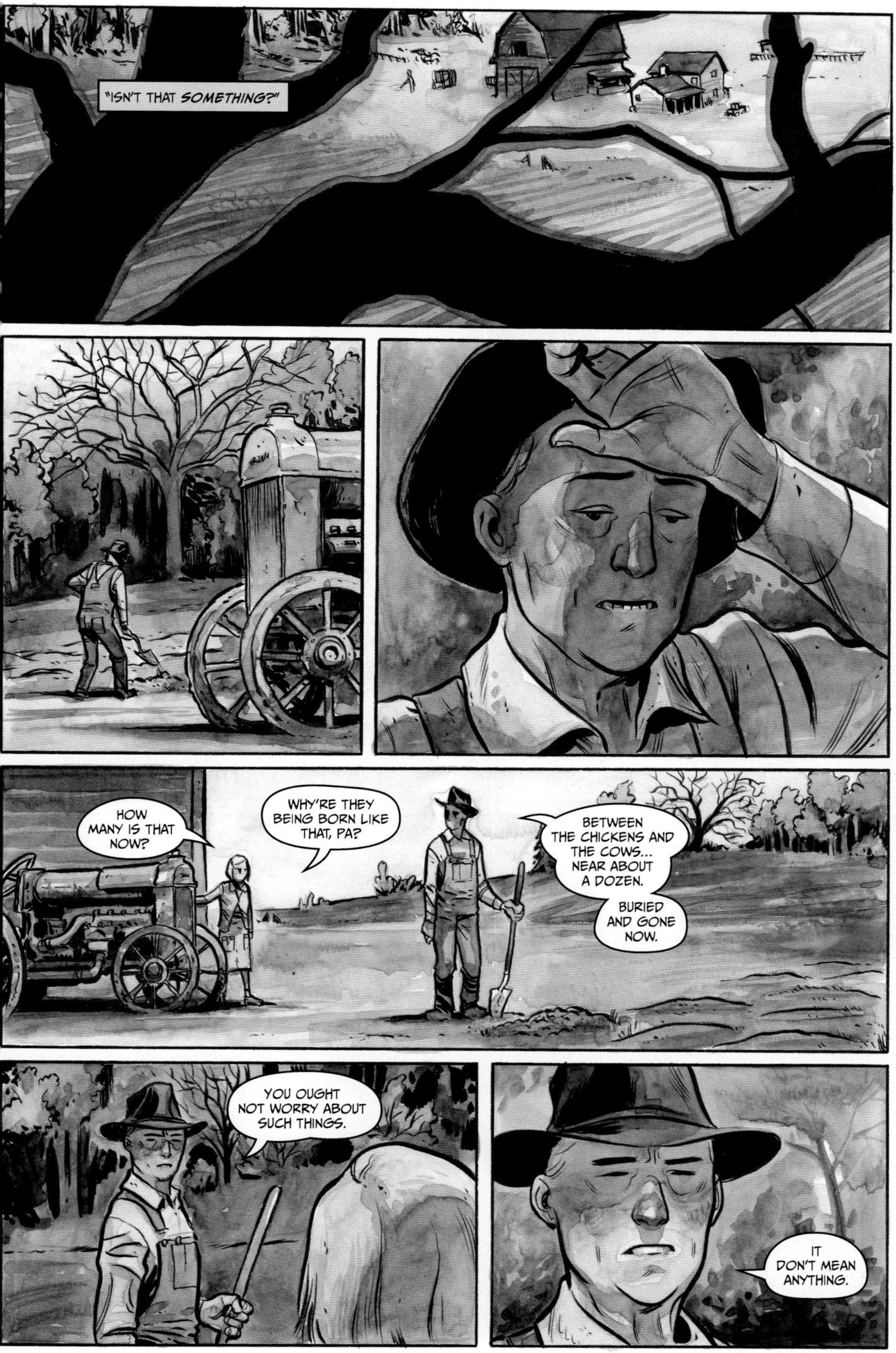
"ISN'T THAT SOMETHING?"
HOW MANY IS THAT NOW?
WHY'RE THEY BEING BORN LIKE THAT, PA?
BETWEEN THE CHICKENS AND THE COWS... NEAR ABOUT A DOZEN.
BURIED AND GONE NOW.
YOU OUGHT NOT WORRY ABOUT SUCH THINGS.
IT DON'T MEAN ANYTHING.

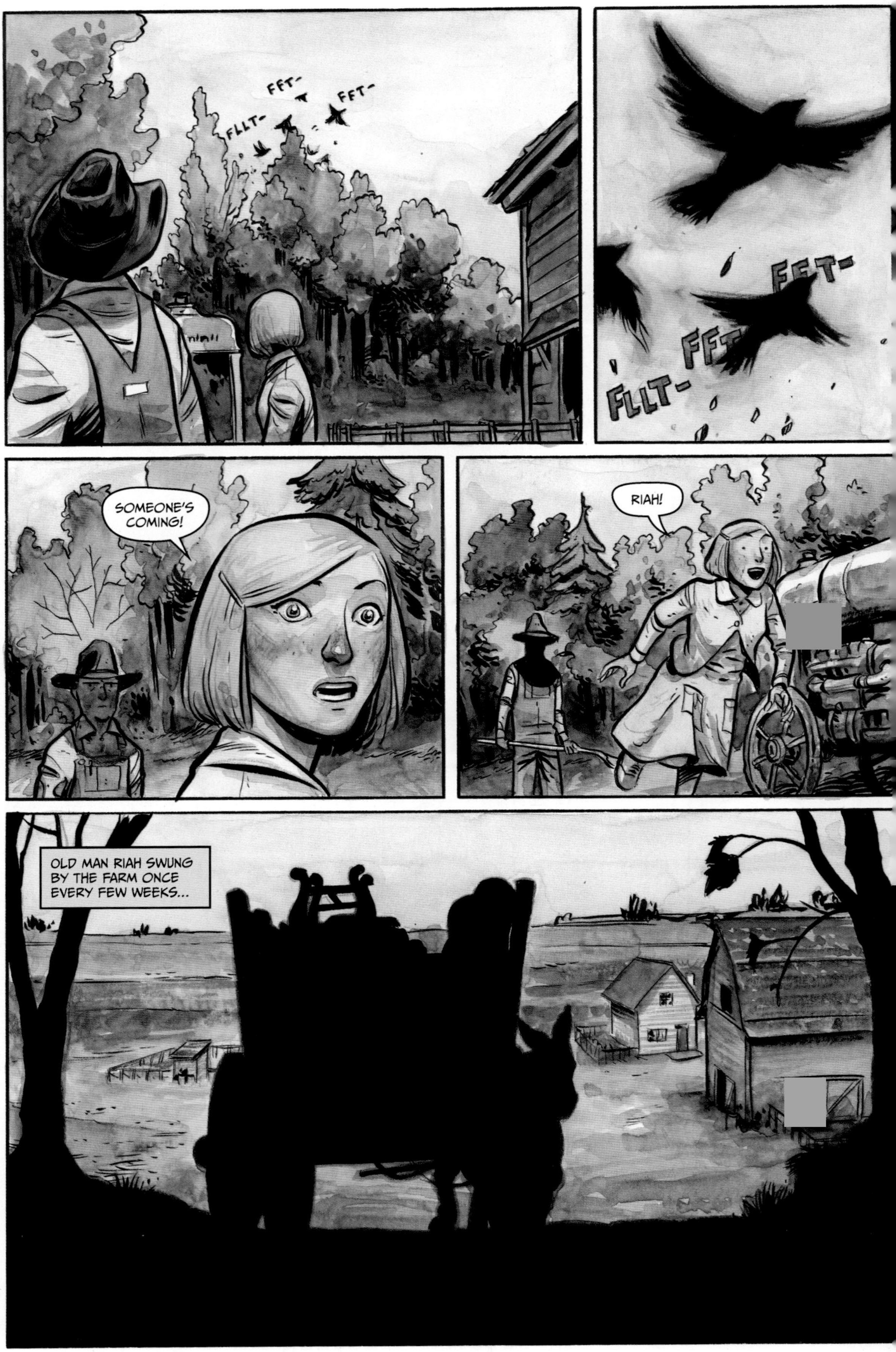
FFT-
FFT-
FLLT-
FFT-
FFT-
FLLT-
SOMEONE'S COMING!
RIAH!
OLD MAN RIAH SWUNG BY THE FARM ONCE EVERY FEW WEEKS...

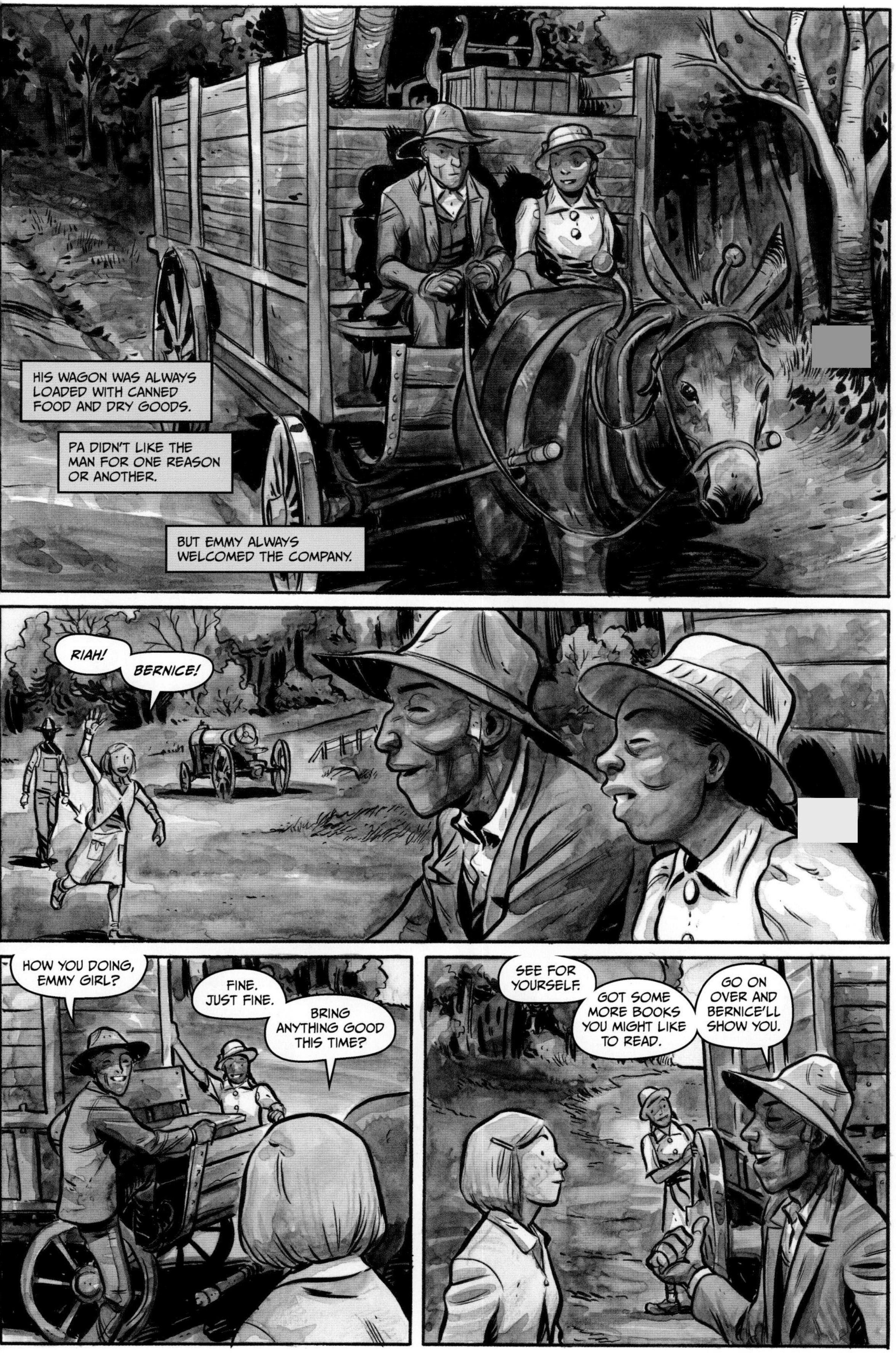
HIS WAGON WAS ALWAYS LOADED WITH CANNED FOOD AND DRY GOODS.
PA DIDN'T LIKE THE MAN FOR ONE REASON OR ANOTHER.
BUT EMMY ALWAYS WELCOMED THE COMPANY.
RIAH!
BERNICE!
HOW YOU DOING, EMMY GIRL?
FINE. JUST FINE.
BRING ANYTHING GOOD THIS TIME?
SEE FOR YOURSELF.
GOT SOME MORE BOOKS YOU MIGHT LIKE TO READ.
GO ON OVER AND BERNICE'LL SHOW YOU.

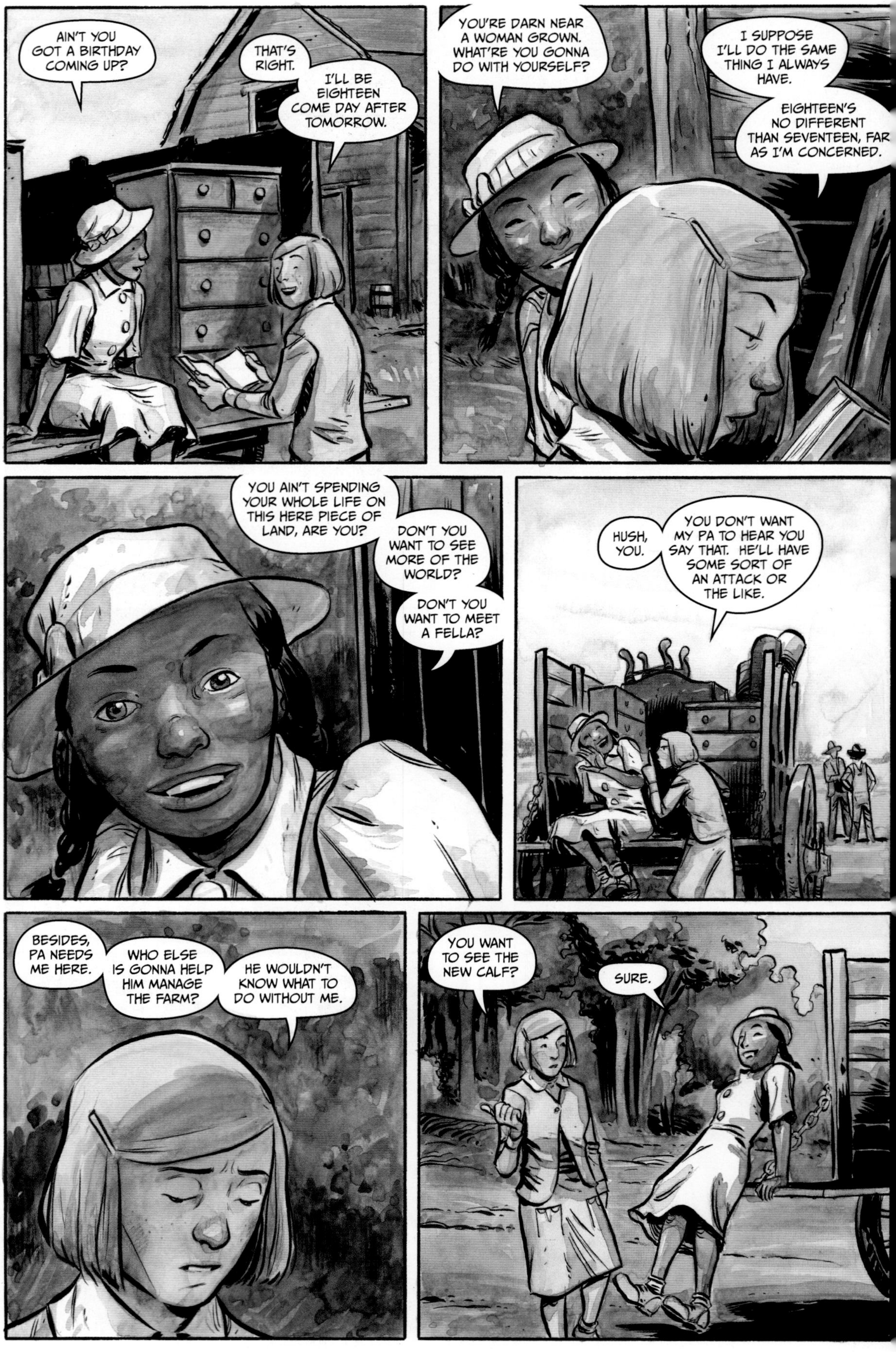
AIN'T YOU GOT A BIRTHDAY COMING UP?
THAT'S RIGHT.
I'LL BE EIGHTEEN COME DAY AFTER TOMORROW.
YOU'RE DARN NEAR A WOMAN GROWN. WHAT'RE YOU GONNA DO WITH YOURSELF?
I SUPPOSE I'LL DO THE SAME THING I ALWAYS HAVE.
EIGHTEEN'S NO DIFFERENT THAN SEVENTEEN, FAR AS I'M CONCERNED.
YOU AIN'T SPENDING YOUR WHOLE LIFE ON THIS HERE PIECE OF LAND, ARE YOU?
DON'T YOU WANT TO SEE MORE OF THE WORLD?
DON'T YOU WANT TO MEET A FELLA?
HUSH, YOU.
YOU DON'T WANT MY PA TO HEAR YOU SAY THAT. HE'LL HAVE SOME SORT OF AN ATTACK OR THE LIKE.
BESIDES, PA NEEDS ME HERE.
WHO ELSE IS GONNA HELP HIM MANAGE THE FARM?
HE WOULDN'T KNOW WHAT TO DO WITHOUT ME.
YOU WANT TO SEE THE NEW CALF?
SURE.

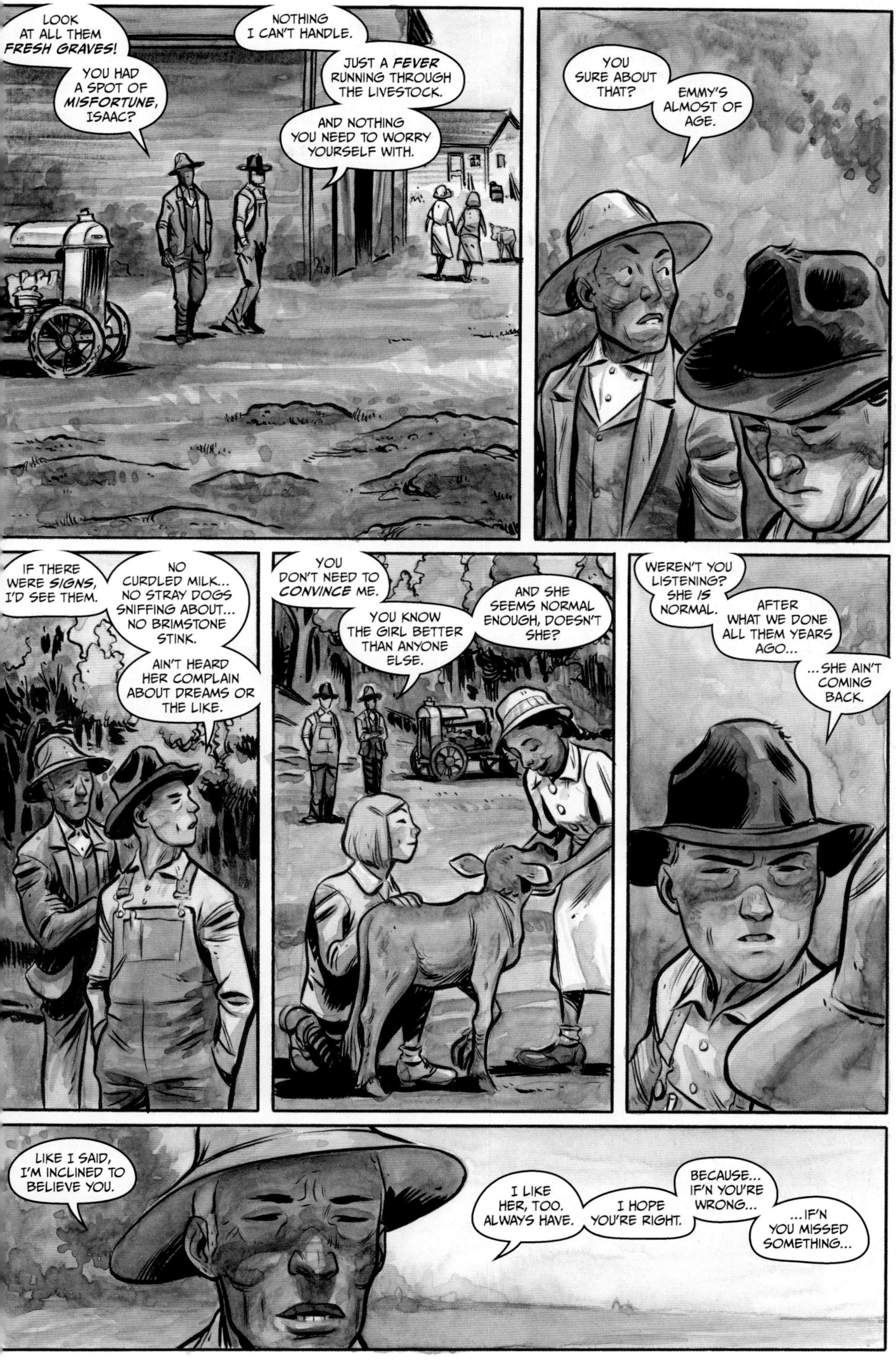

LOOK AT ALL THEM FRESH GRAVES!
YOU HAD A SPOT OF MISFORTUNE, ISAAC?
NOTHING I CAN'T HANDLE.
JUST A FEVER RUNNING THROUGH THE LIVESTOCK.
AND NOTHING YOU NEED TO WORRY YOURSELF WITH.
YOU SURE ABOUT THAT?
EMMY'S ALMOST OF AGE.
IF THERE WERE SIGNS, I'D SEE THEM.
NO CURDLED MILK... NO STRAY DOGS SNIFFING ABOUT... NO BRIMSTONE STINK.
AIN'T HEARD HER COMPLAIN ABOUT DREAMS OR THE LIKE.
YOU DON'T NEED TO CONVINCE ME.
YOU KNOW THE GIRL BETTER THAN ANYONE ELSE.
AND SHE SEEMS NORMAL ENOUGH, DOESN'T SHE?
WEREN'T YOU LISTENING? SHE IS NORMAL.
AFTER WHAT WE DONE ALL THEM YEARS AGO...
...SHE AIN'T COMING BACK.
LIKE I SAID, I'M INCLINED TO BELIEVE YOU.
I LIKE HER, TOO. ALWAYS HAVE.
I HOPE YOU'RE RIGHT.
BECAUSE... IF'N YOU'RE WRONG...
...IF'N YOU MISSED SOMETHING...

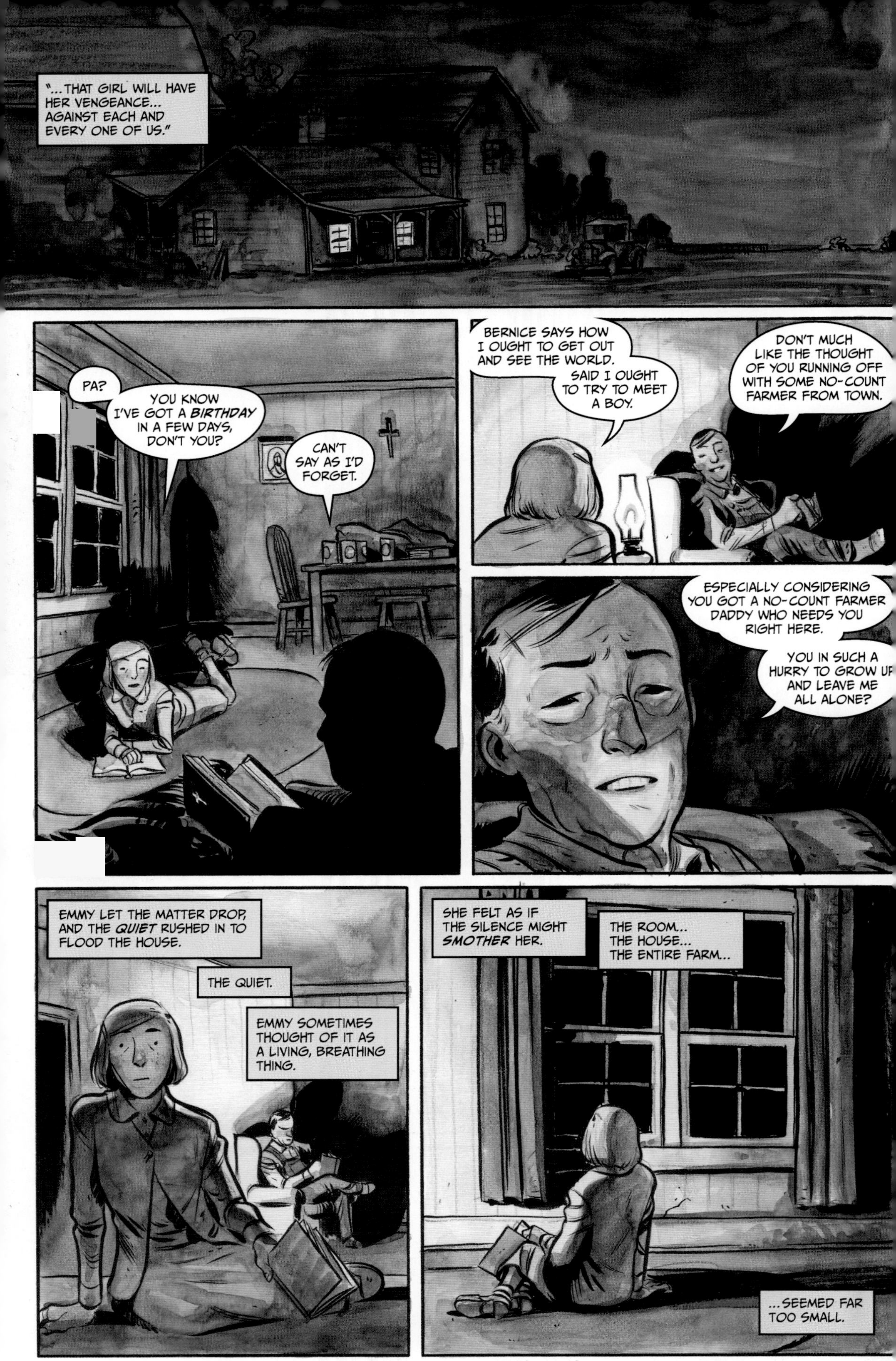
"...THAT GIRL WILL HAVE HER VENGEANCE... AGAINST EACH AND EVERY ONE OF US."
PA?
YOU KNOW I'VE GOT A *BIRTHDAY* IN A FEW DAYS, DON'T YOU?
CAN'T SAY AS I'D FORGET.
BERNICE SAYS HOW I OUGHT TO GET OUT AND SEE THE WORLD.
SAID I OUGHT TO TRY TO MEET A BOY.
DON'T MUCH LIKE THE THOUGHT OF YOU RUNNING OFF WITH SOME NO-COUNT FARMER FROM TOWN.
ESPECIALLY CONSIDERING YOU GOT A NO-COUNT FARMER DADDY WHO NEEDS YOU RIGHT HERE.
YOU IN SUCH A HURRY TO GROW UP AND LEAVE ME ALL ALONE?
EMMY LET THE MATTER DROP, AND THE *QUIET* RUSHED IN TO FLOOD THE HOUSE.
THE QUIET.
EMMY SOMETIMES THOUGHT OF IT AS A LIVING, BREATHING THING.
SHE FELT AS IF THE SILENCE MIGHT *SMOTHER* HER.
THE ROOM... THE HOUSE... THE ENTIRE FARM...
...SEEMED FAR TOO SMALL.

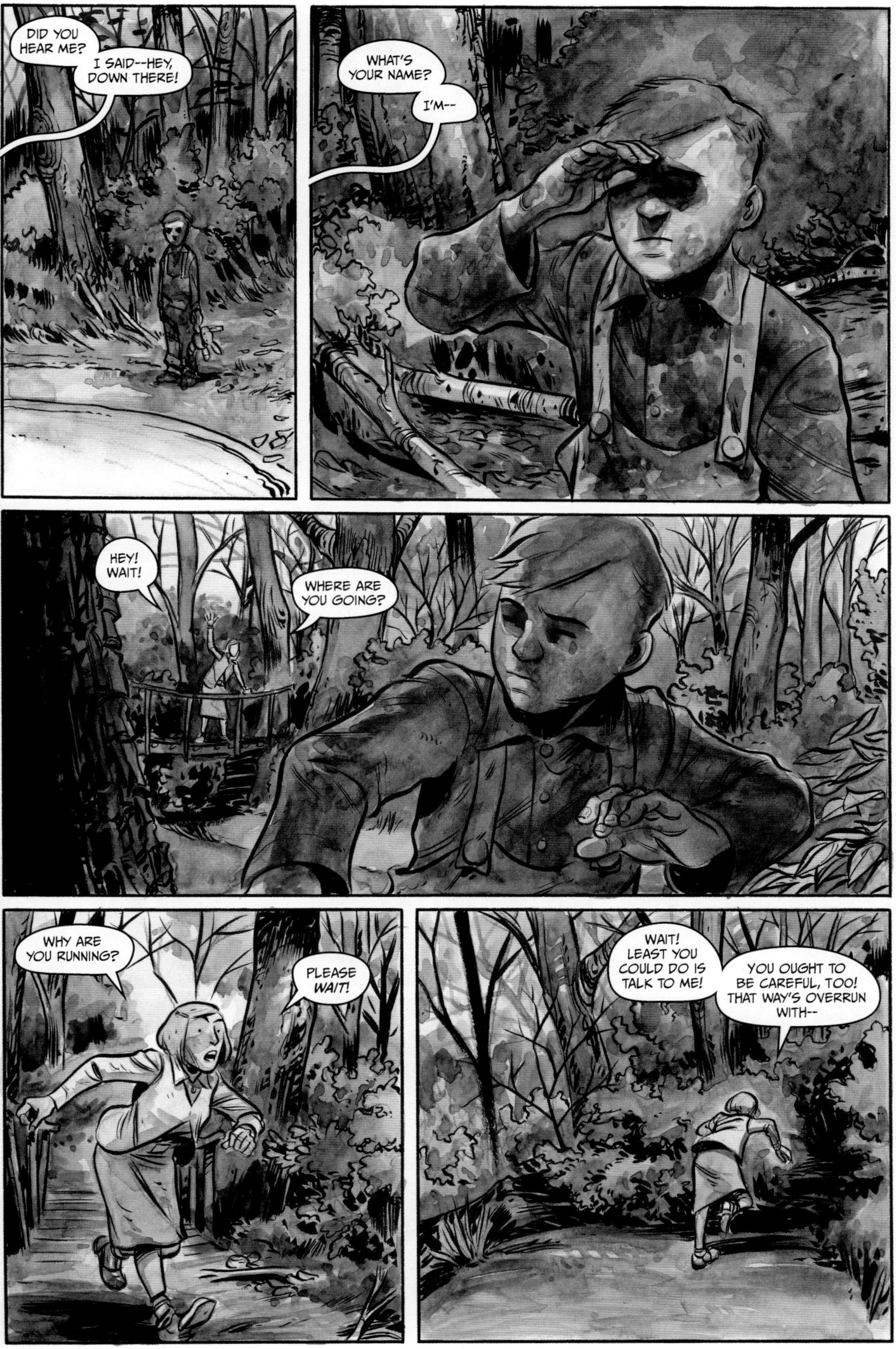
DID YOU HEAR ME?
I SAID--HEY, DOWN THERE!
WHAT'S YOUR NAME?
I'M--
HEY! WAIT!
WHERE ARE YOU GOING?
WHY ARE YOU RUNNING?
PLEASE WAIT!
WAIT! LEAST YOU COULD DO IS TALK TO ME!
YOU OUGHT TO BE CAREFUL, TOO! THAT WAY'S OVERRUN WITH--

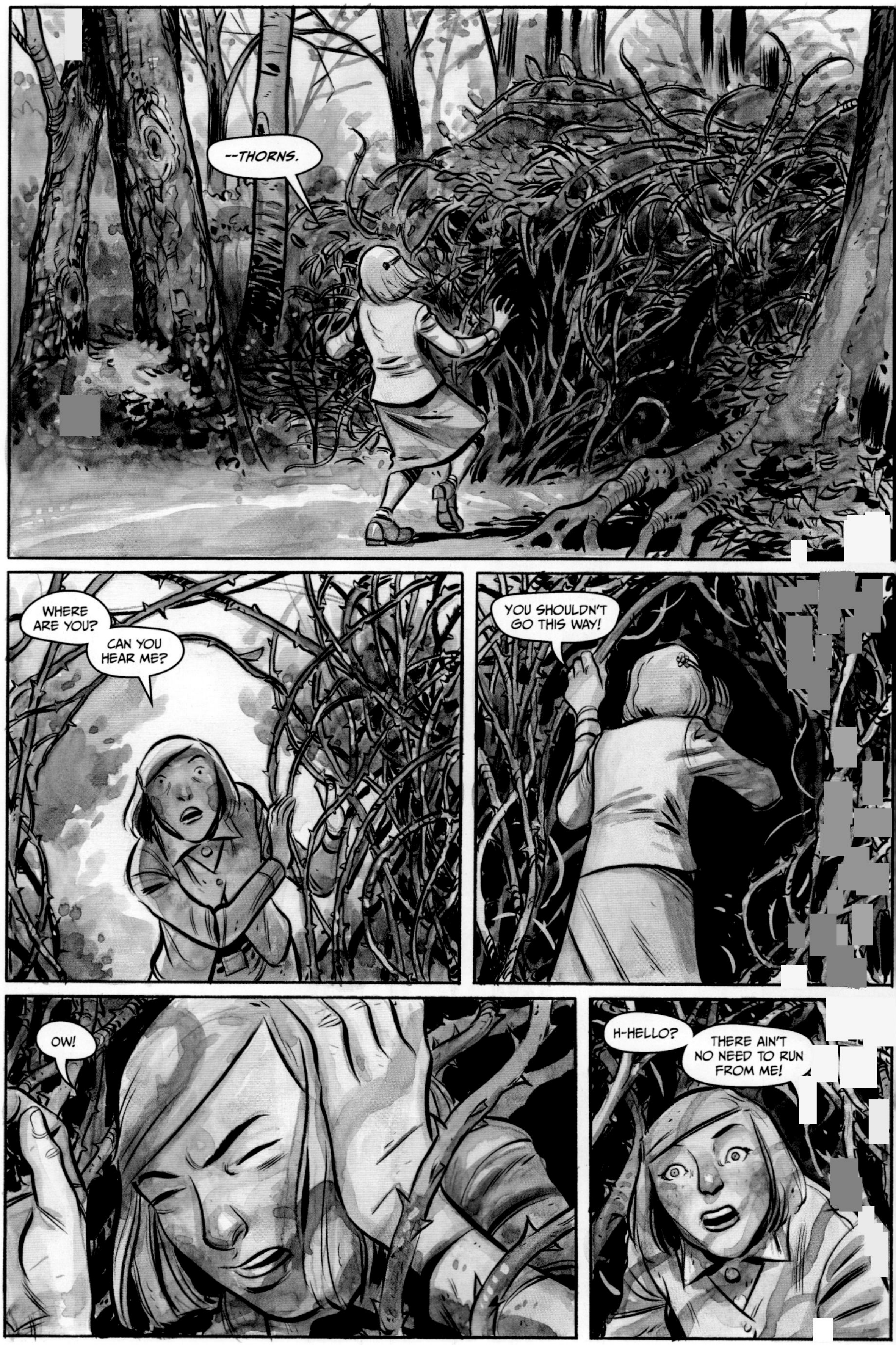
--THORNS.
WHERE ARE YOU?
CAN YOU HEAR ME?
YOU SHOULDN'T GO THIS WAY!
OW!
H-HELLO?
THERE AIN'T NO NEED TO RUN FROM ME!

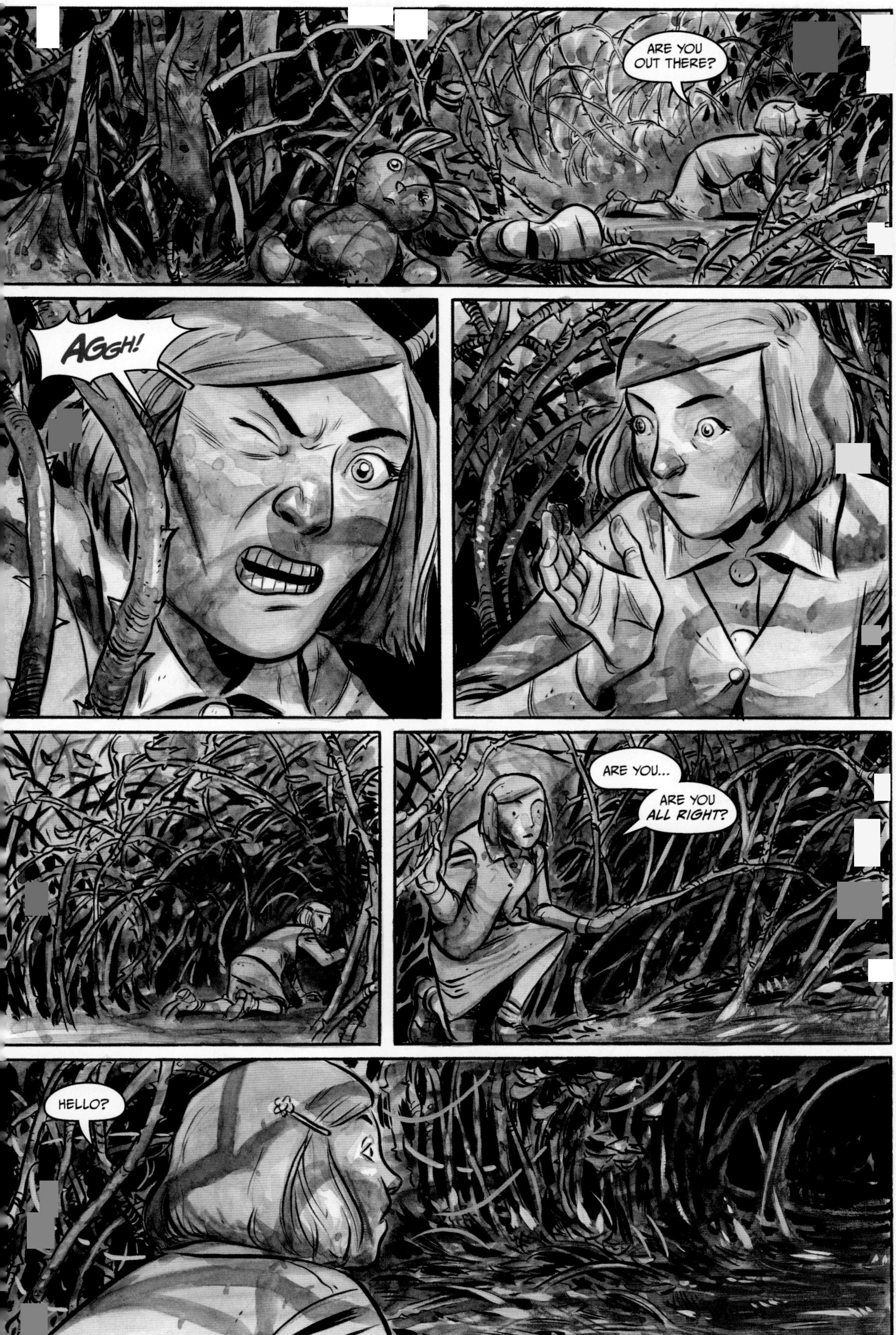
ARE YOU OUT THERE?
AGGH!
ARE YOU...
ARE YOU ALL RIGHT?
HELLO?

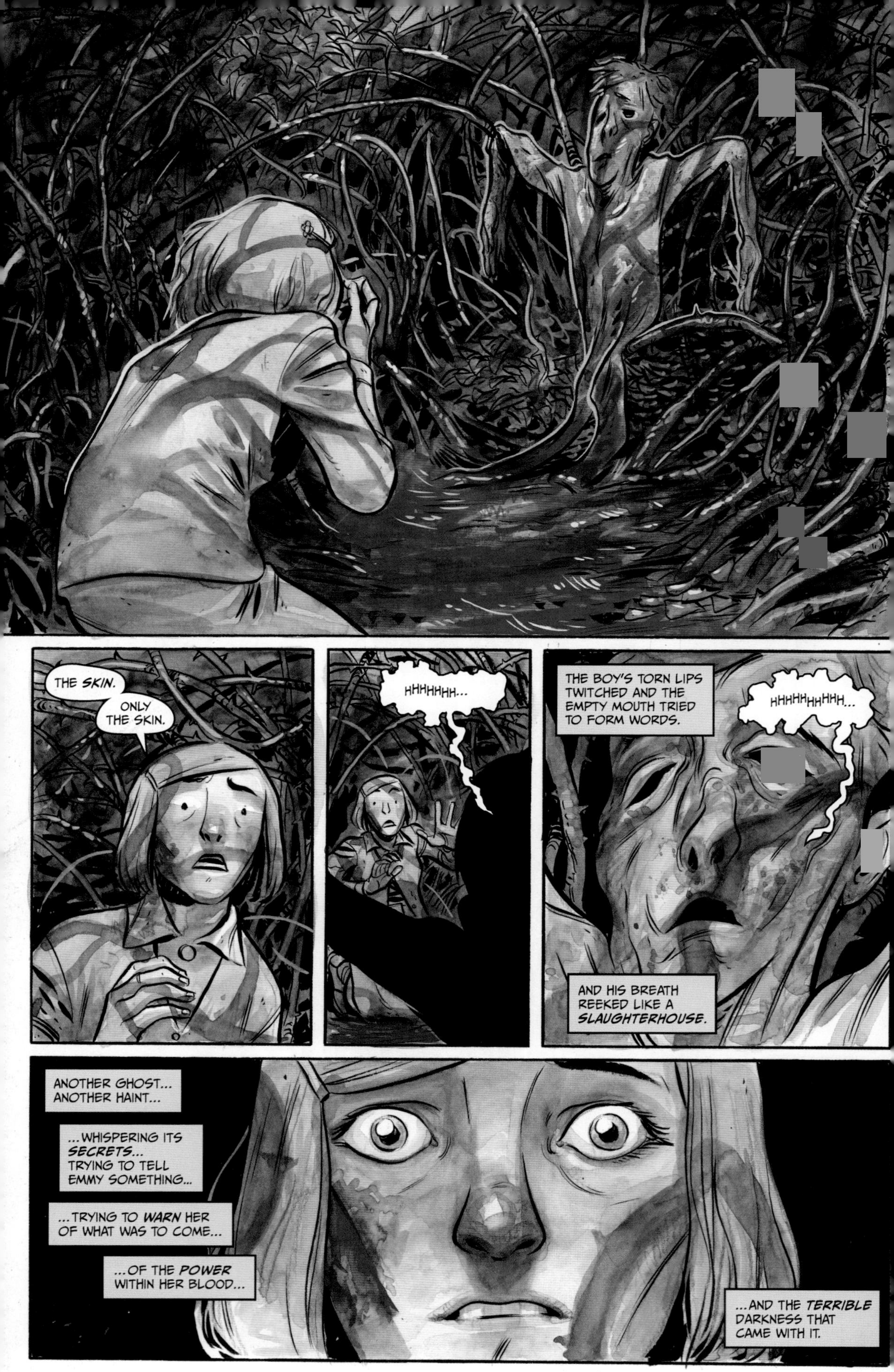
THE *SKIN.*
ONLY THE SKIN.
HHHHHHH...
THE BOY'S TORN LIPS TWITCHED AND THE EMPTY MOUTH TRIED TO FORM WORDS.
HHHHHHHHHH...
AND HIS BREATH REEKED LIKE A *SLAUGHTERHOUSE.*
ANOTHER GHOST... ANOTHER HAINT...
...WHISPERING ITS *SECRETS...* TRYING TO TELL EMMY SOMETHING...
...TRYING TO *WARN* HER OF WHAT WAS TO COME...
...OF THE *POWER* WITHIN HER BLOOD...
...AND THE *TERRIBLE* DARKNESS THAT CAME WITH IT.

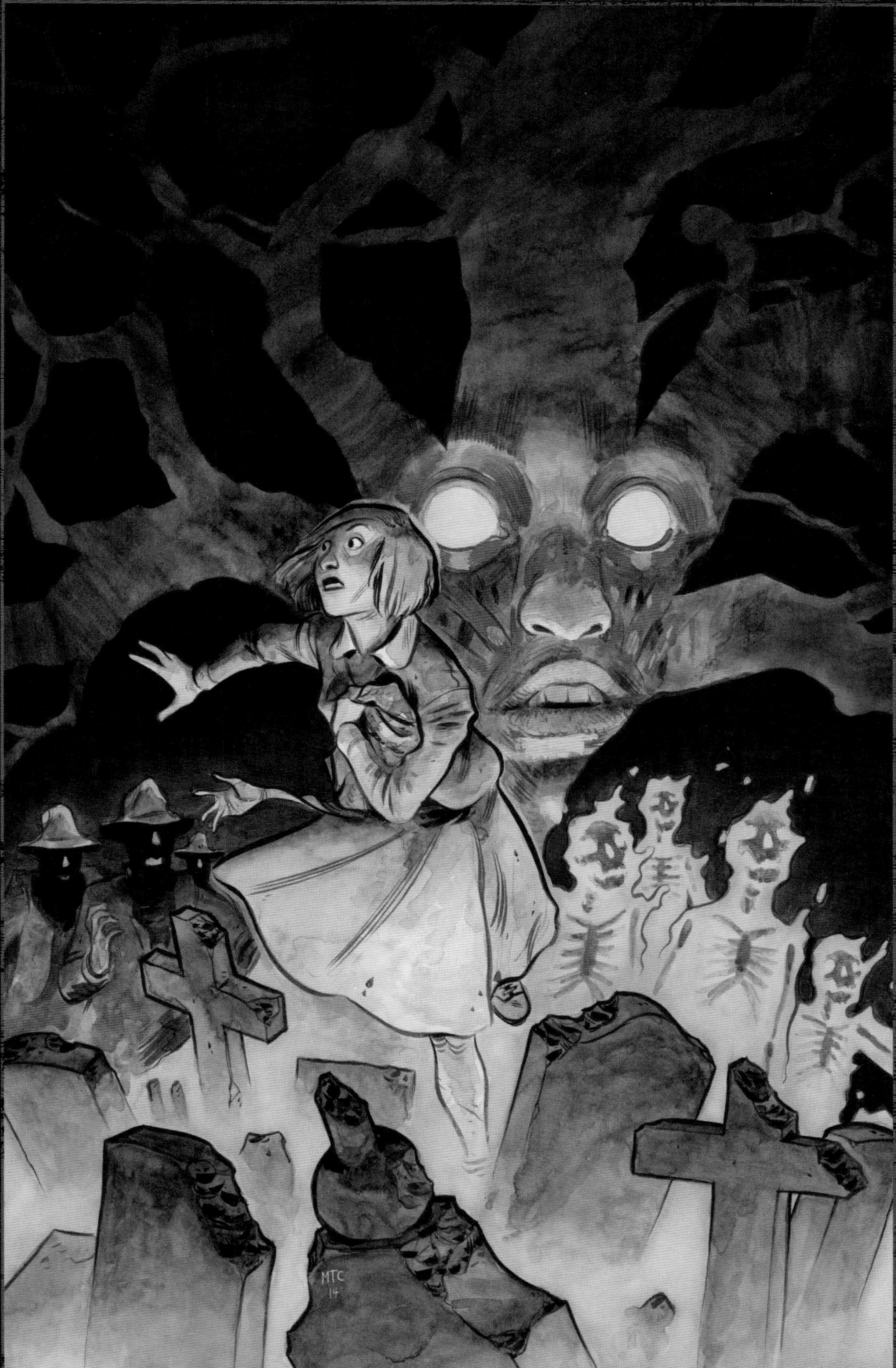
MTC
14

TWO

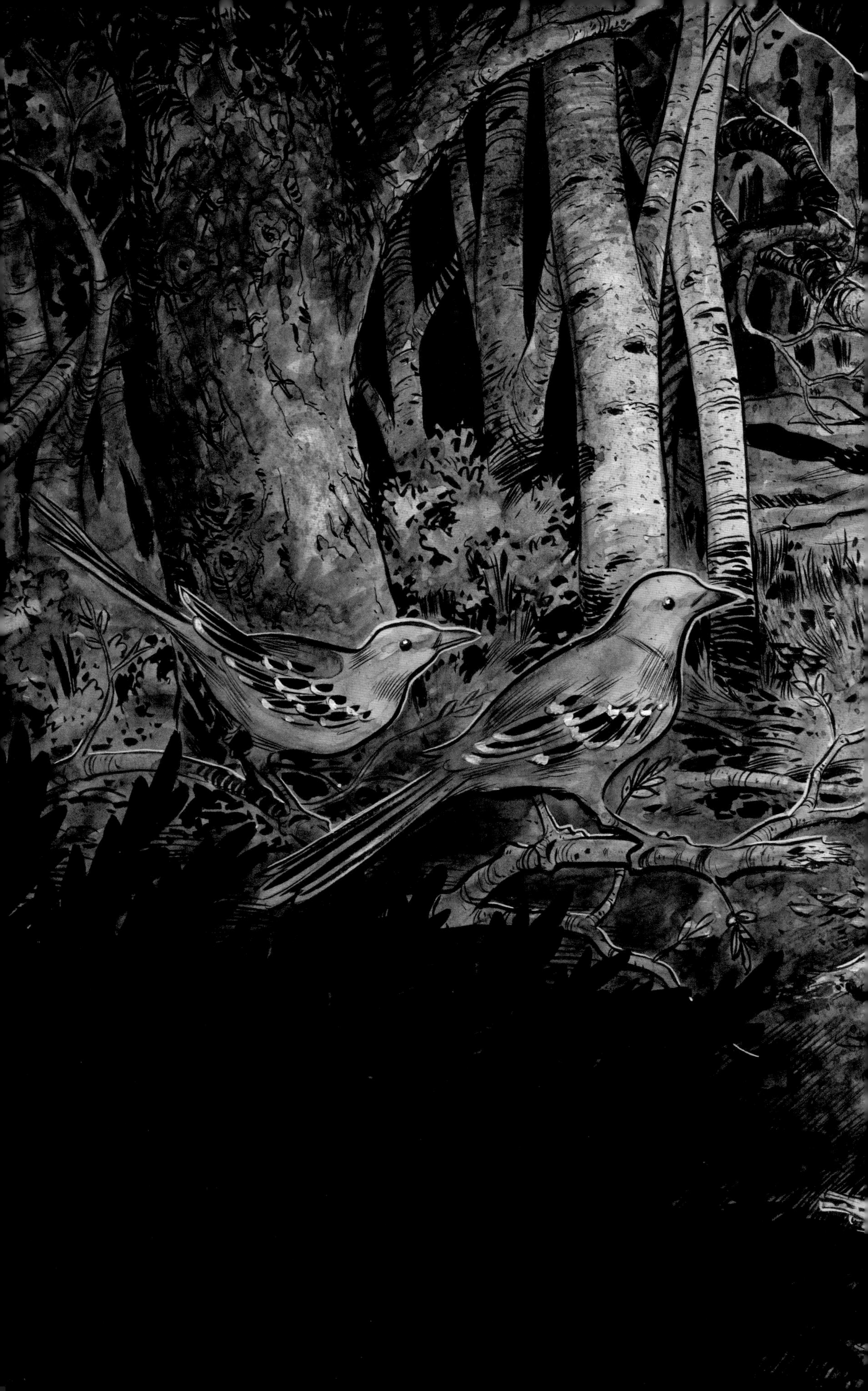

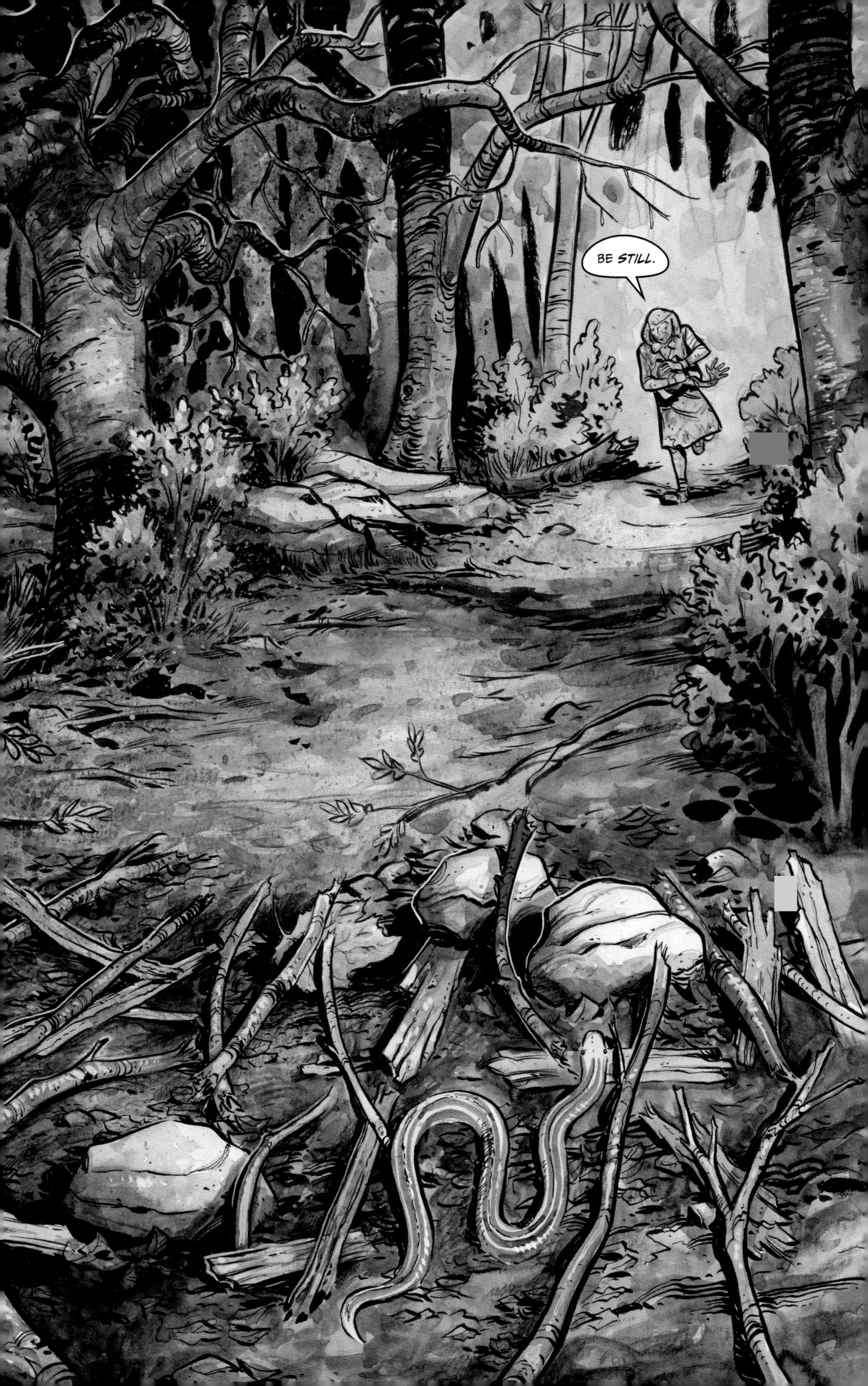
BE STILL.

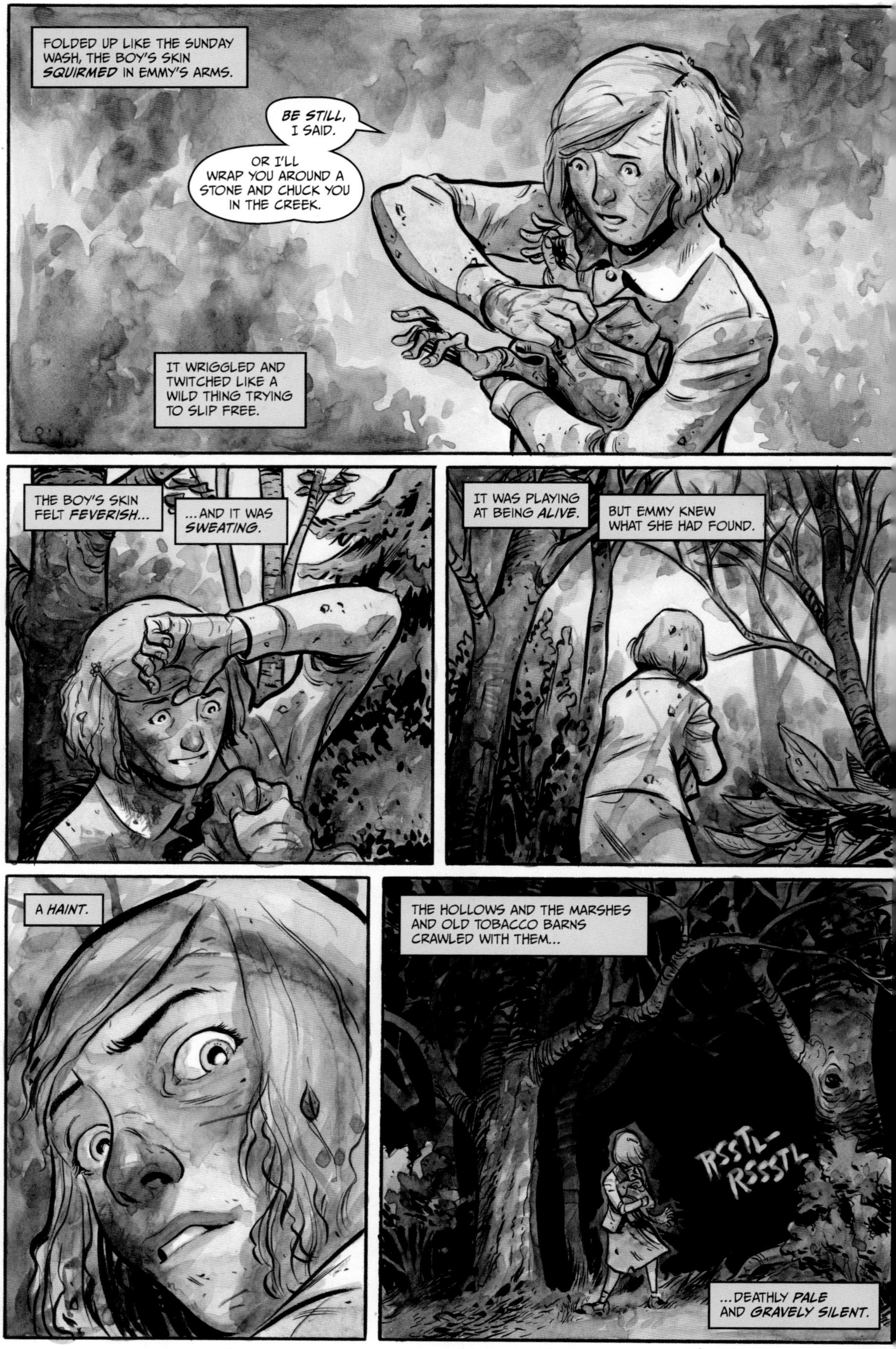
FOLDED UP LIKE THE SUNDAY WASH, THE BOY'S SKIN SQUIRMED IN EMMY'S ARMS.
BE STILL, I SAID.
OR I'LL WRAP YOU AROUND A STONE AND CHUCK YOU IN THE CREEK.
IT WRIGGLED AND TWITCHED LIKE A WILD THING TRYING TO SLIP FREE.
THE BOY'S SKIN FELT FEVERISH...
...AND IT WAS SWEATING.
IT WAS PLAYING AT BEING ALIVE.
BUT EMMY KNEW WHAT SHE HAD FOUND.
A HAINT.
THE HOLLOWS AND THE MARSHES AND OLD TOBACCO BARNS CRAWLED WITH THEM...
RSSTL-RSSSTL
...DEATHLY PALE AND GRAVELY SILENT.

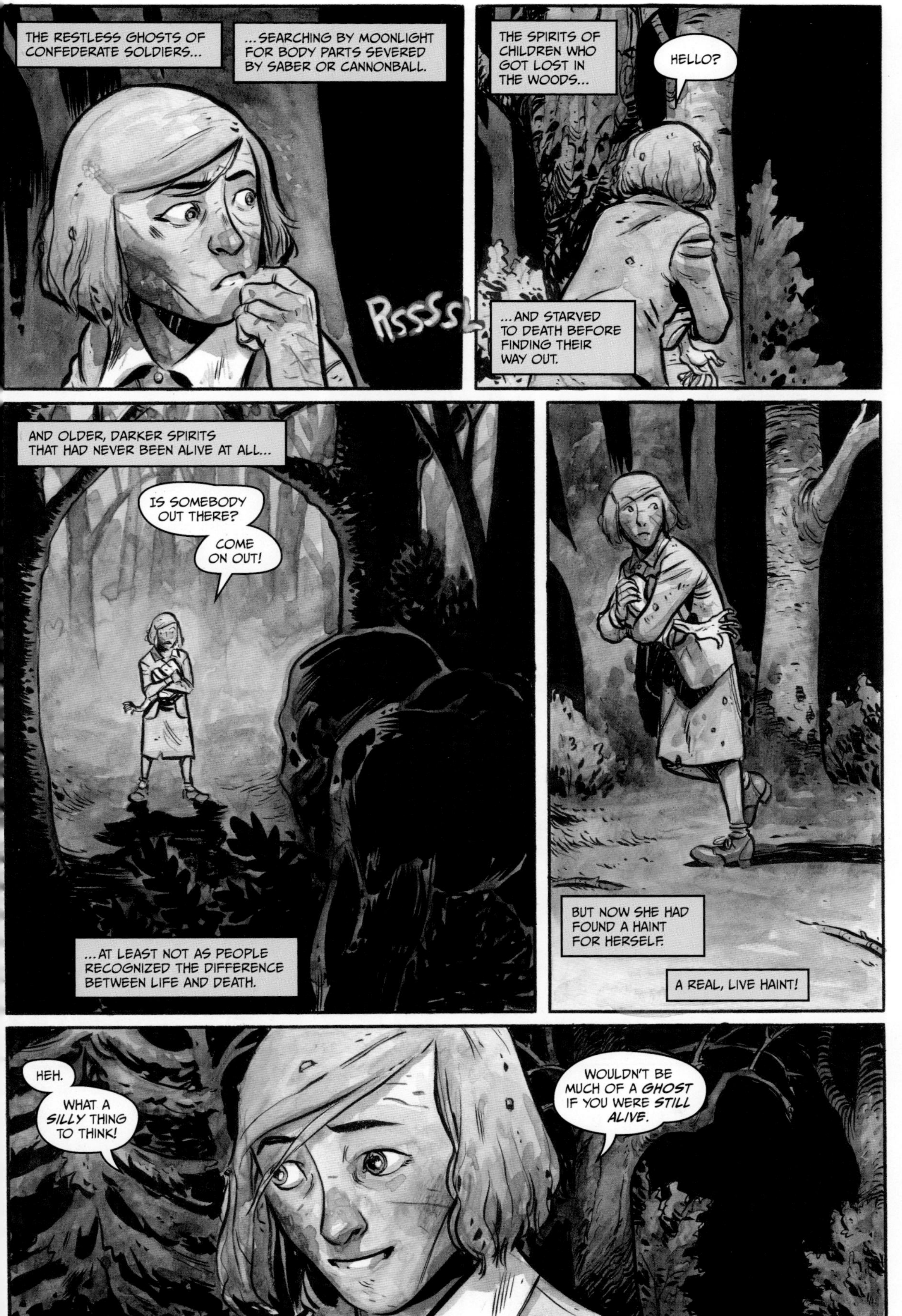
THE RESTLESS GHOSTS OF CONFEDERATE SOLDIERS...
...SEARCHING BY MOONLIGHT FOR BODY PARTS SEVERED BY SABER OR CANNONBALL.
RSSSSL
THE SPIRITS OF CHILDREN WHO GOT LOST IN THE WOODS...
HELLO?
...AND STARVED TO DEATH BEFORE FINDING THEIR WAY OUT.
AND OLDER, DARKER SPIRITS THAT HAD NEVER BEEN ALIVE AT ALL...
IS SOMEBODY OUT THERE?
COME ON OUT!
...AT LEAST NOT AS PEOPLE RECOGNIZED THE DIFFERENCE BETWEEN LIFE AND DEATH.
BUT NOW SHE HAD FOUND A HAINT FOR HERSELF.
A REAL, LIVE HAINT!
HEH.
WHAT A SILLY THING TO THINK!
WOULDN'T BE MUCH OF A GHOST IF YOU WERE STILL ALIVE.

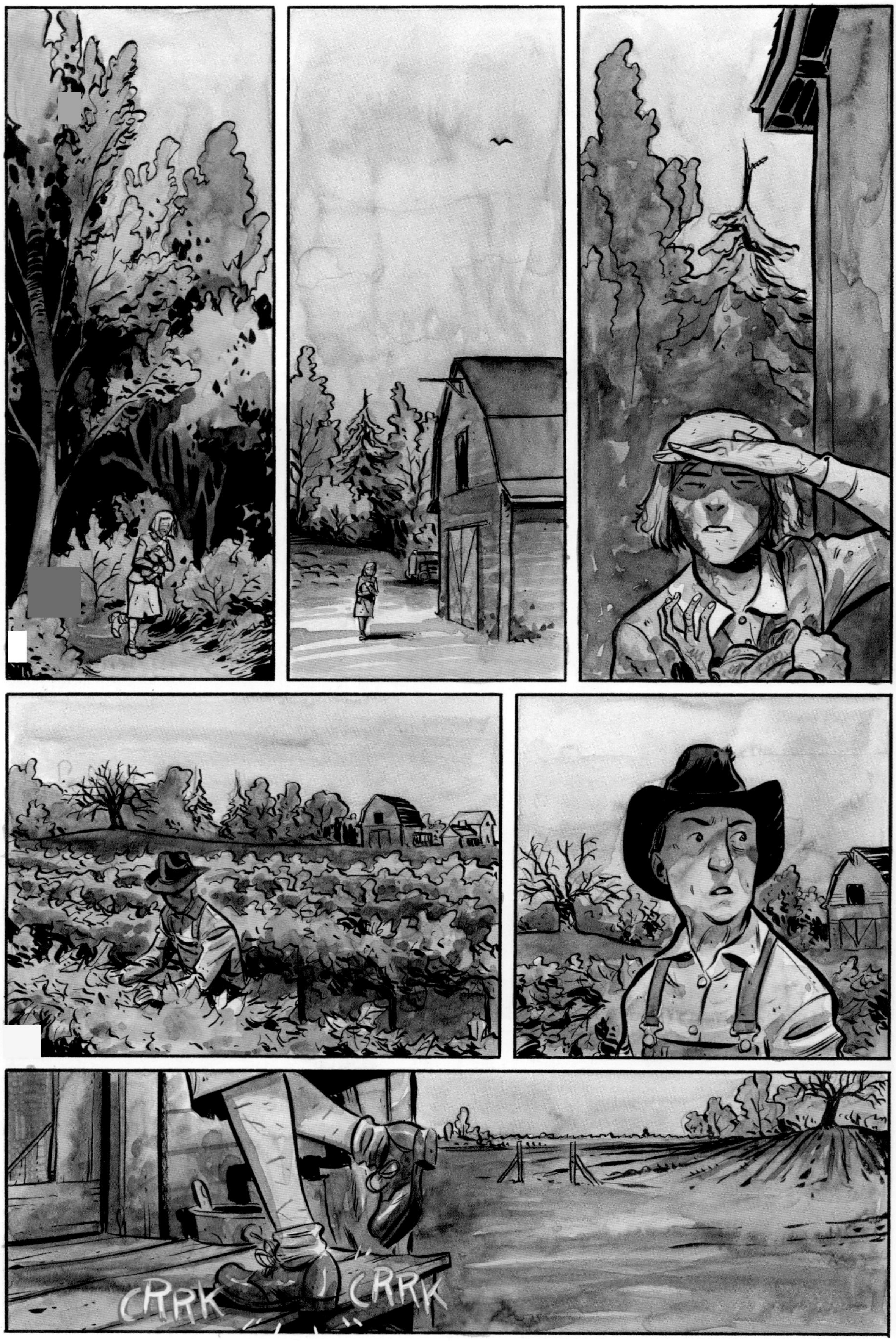
CRRK
CRRK

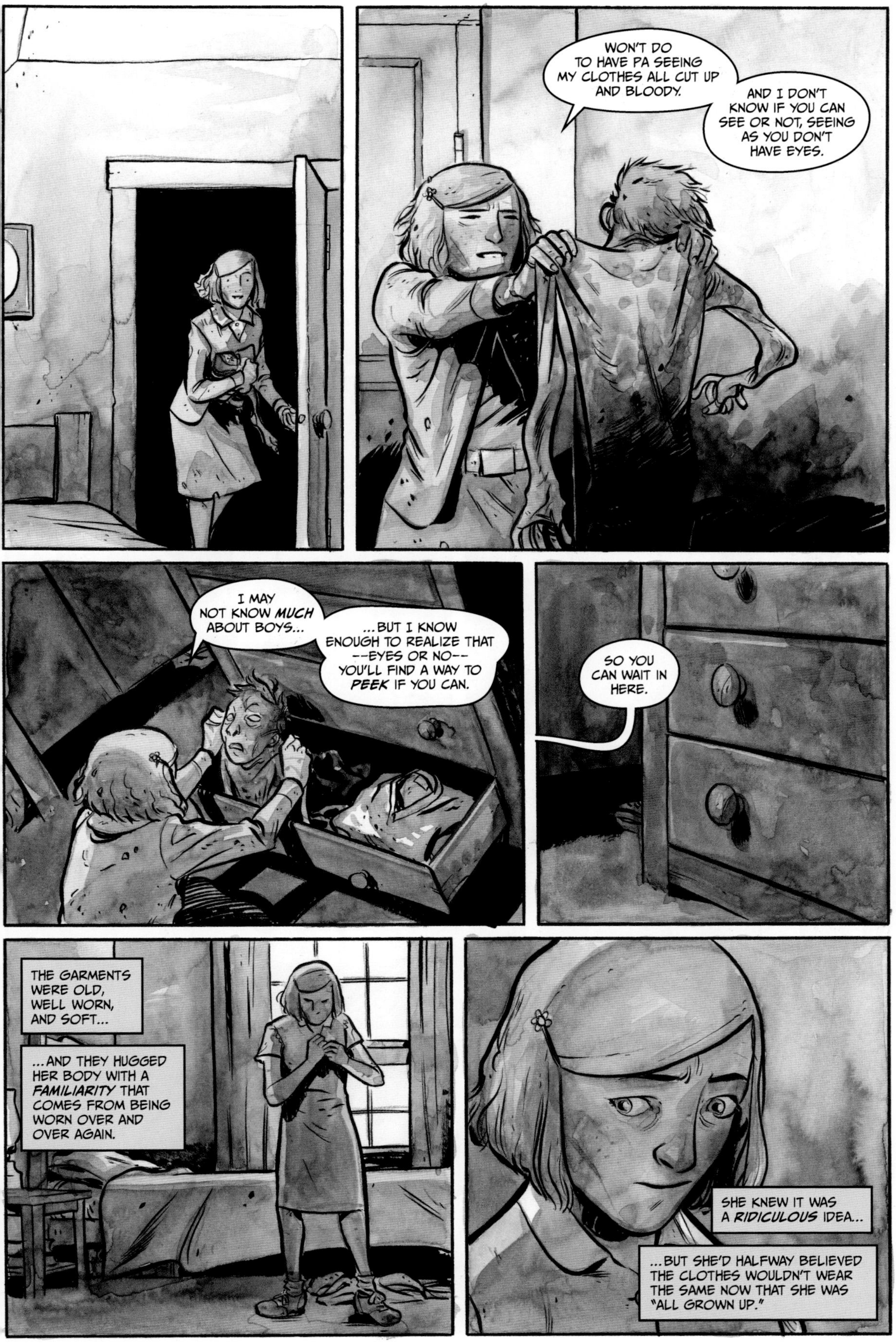
WON'T DO TO HAVE PA SEEING MY CLOTHES ALL CUT UP AND BLOODY.
AND I DON'T KNOW IF YOU CAN SEE OR NOT, SEEING AS YOU DON'T HAVE EYES.
I MAY NOT KNOW *MUCH* ABOUT BOYS...
...BUT I KNOW ENOUGH TO REALIZE THAT --EYES OR NO-- YOU'LL FIND A WAY TO *PEEK* IF YOU CAN.
SO YOU CAN WAIT IN HERE.
THE GARMENTS WERE OLD, WELL WORN, AND SOFT...
...AND THEY HUGGED HER BODY WITH A *FAMILIARITY* THAT COMES FROM BEING WORN OVER AND OVER AGAIN.
SHE KNEW IT WAS A *RIDICULOUS* IDEA...
...BUT SHE'D HALFWAY BELIEVED THE CLOTHES WOULDN'T WEAR THE SAME NOW THAT SHE WAS "ALL GROWN UP."

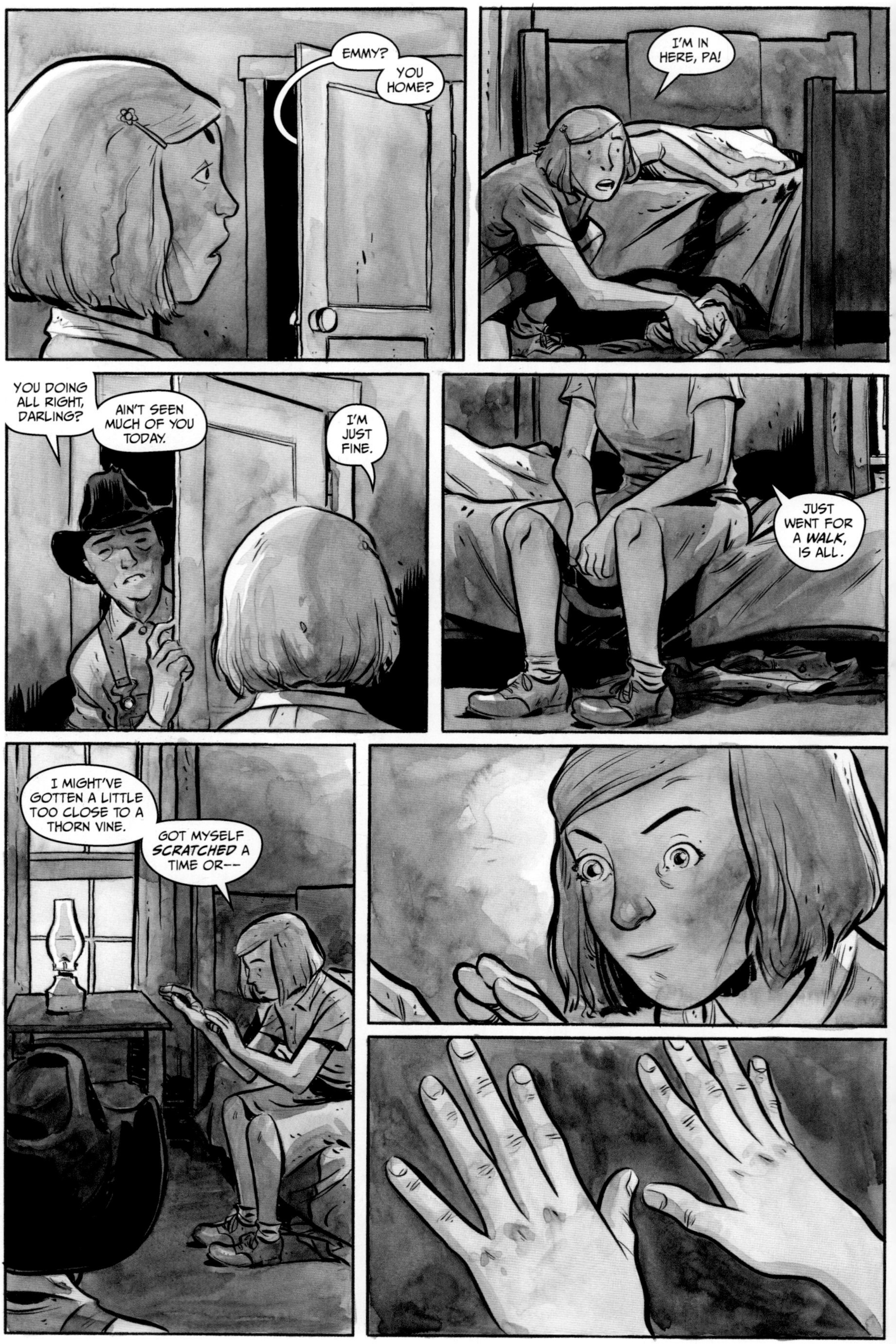
EMMY?
YOU HOME?
I'M IN HERE, PA!
YOU DOING ALL RIGHT, DARLING?
AIN'T SEEN MUCH OF YOU TODAY.
I'M JUST FINE.
JUST WENT FOR A *WALK*, IS ALL.
I MIGHT'VE GOTTEN A LITTLE TOO CLOSE TO A THORN VINE.
GOT MYSELF *SCRATCHED* A TIME OR--

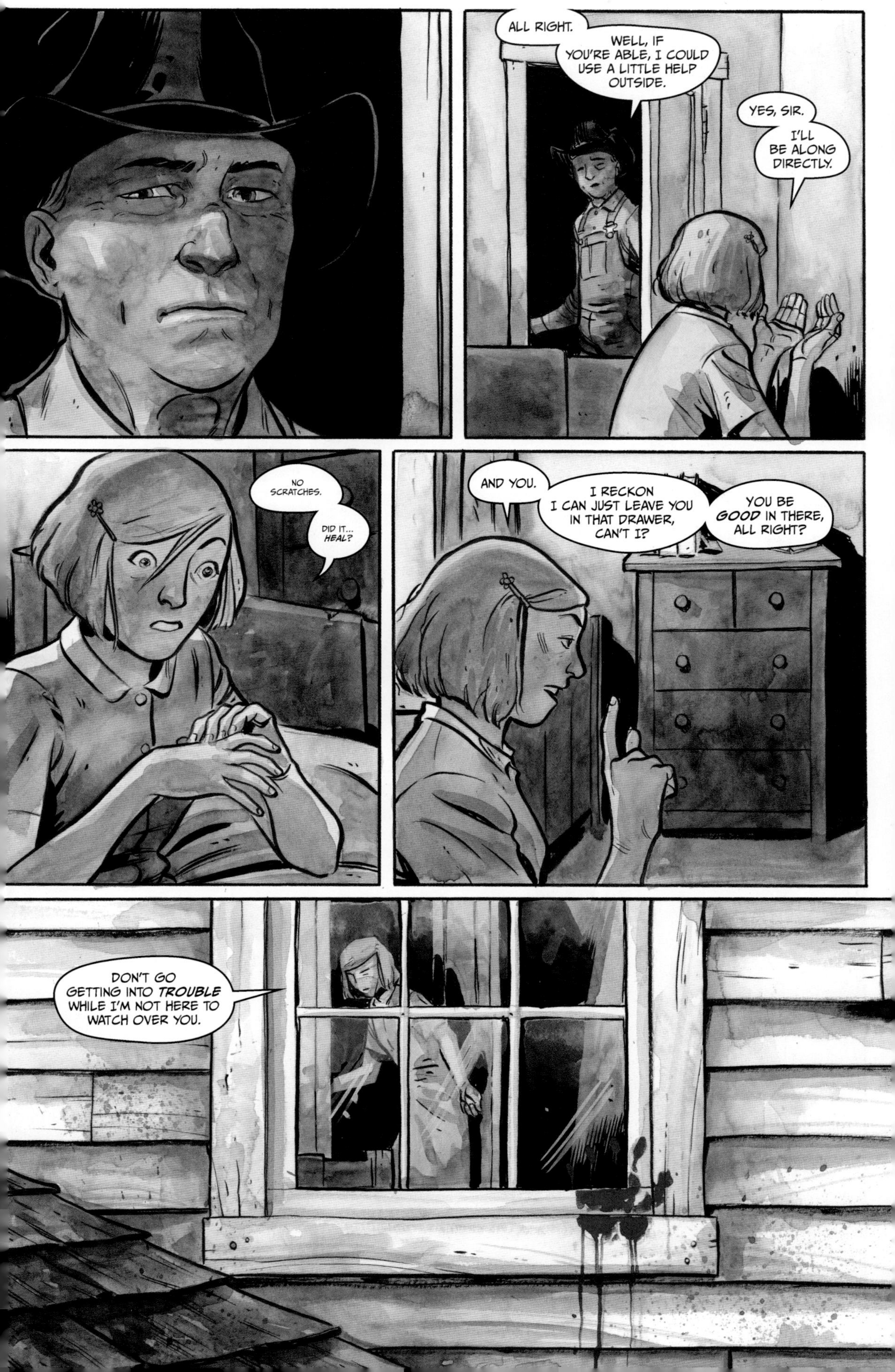
ALL RIGHT.
WELL, IF YOU'RE ABLE, I COULD USE A LITTLE HELP OUTSIDE.
YES, SIR.
I'LL BE ALONG DIRECTLY.
NO SCRATCHES.
DID IT... *HEAL?*
AND YOU.
I RECKON I CAN JUST LEAVE YOU IN THAT DRAWER, CAN'T I?
YOU BE *GOOD* IN THERE, ALL RIGHT?
DON'T GO GETTING INTO *TROUBLE* WHILE I'M NOT HERE TO WATCH OVER YOU.

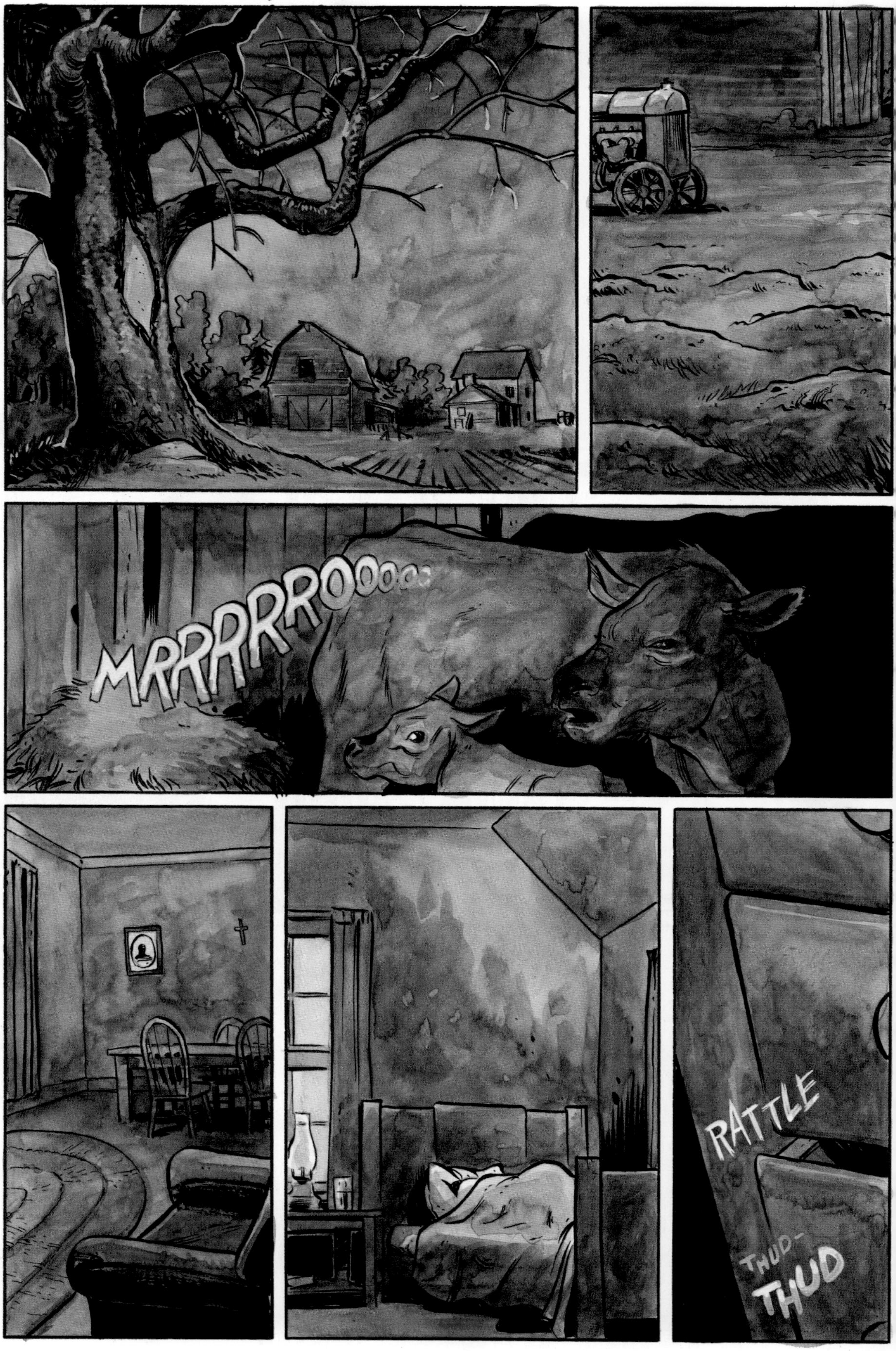
MRRRRRROooo
RATTLE
THUD-
THUD

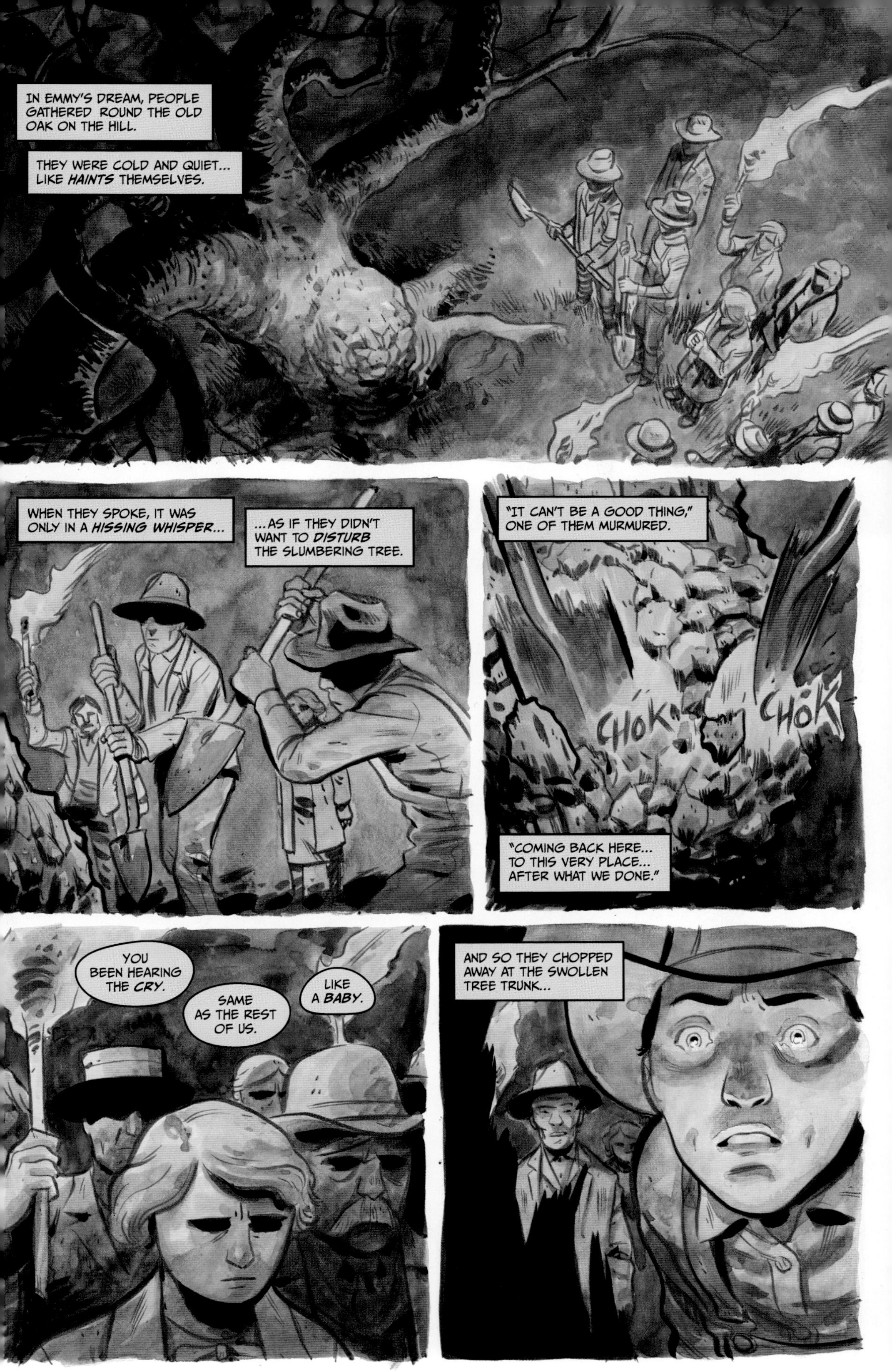
IN EMMY'S DREAM, PEOPLE GATHERED ROUND THE OLD OAK ON THE HILL.
THEY WERE COLD AND QUIET... LIKE *HAINTS* THEMSELVES.
WHEN THEY SPOKE, IT WAS ONLY IN A *HISSING WHISPER*...
...AS IF THEY DIDN'T WANT TO *DISTURB* THE SLUMBERING TREE.
"IT CAN'T BE A GOOD THING," ONE OF THEM MURMURED.
CHOK
CHOK
"COMING BACK HERE... TO THIS VERY PLACE... AFTER WHAT WE DONE."
YOU BEEN HEARING THE *CRY*.
SAME AS THE REST OF US.
LIKE A *BABY*.
AND SO THEY CHOPPED AWAY AT THE SWOLLEN TREE TRUNK...

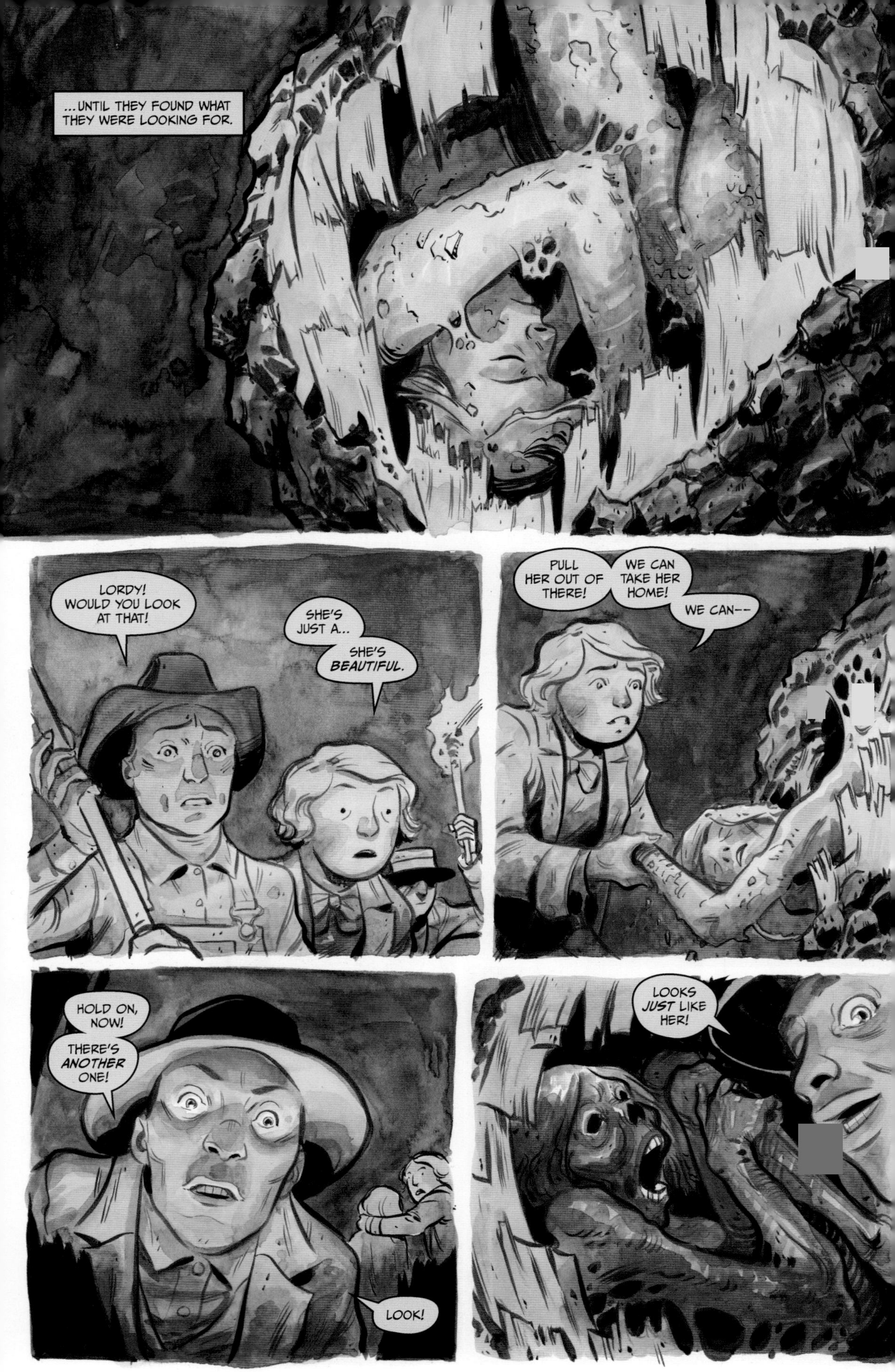
...UNTIL THEY FOUND WHAT THEY WERE LOOKING FOR.
LORDY! WOULD YOU LOOK AT THAT!
SHE'S JUST A...
SHE'S *BEAUTIFUL.*
PULL HER OUT OF THERE!
WE CAN TAKE HER HOME!
WE CAN--
HOLD ON, NOW!
THERE'S *ANOTHER* ONE!
LOOK!
LOOKS *JUST* LIKE HER!

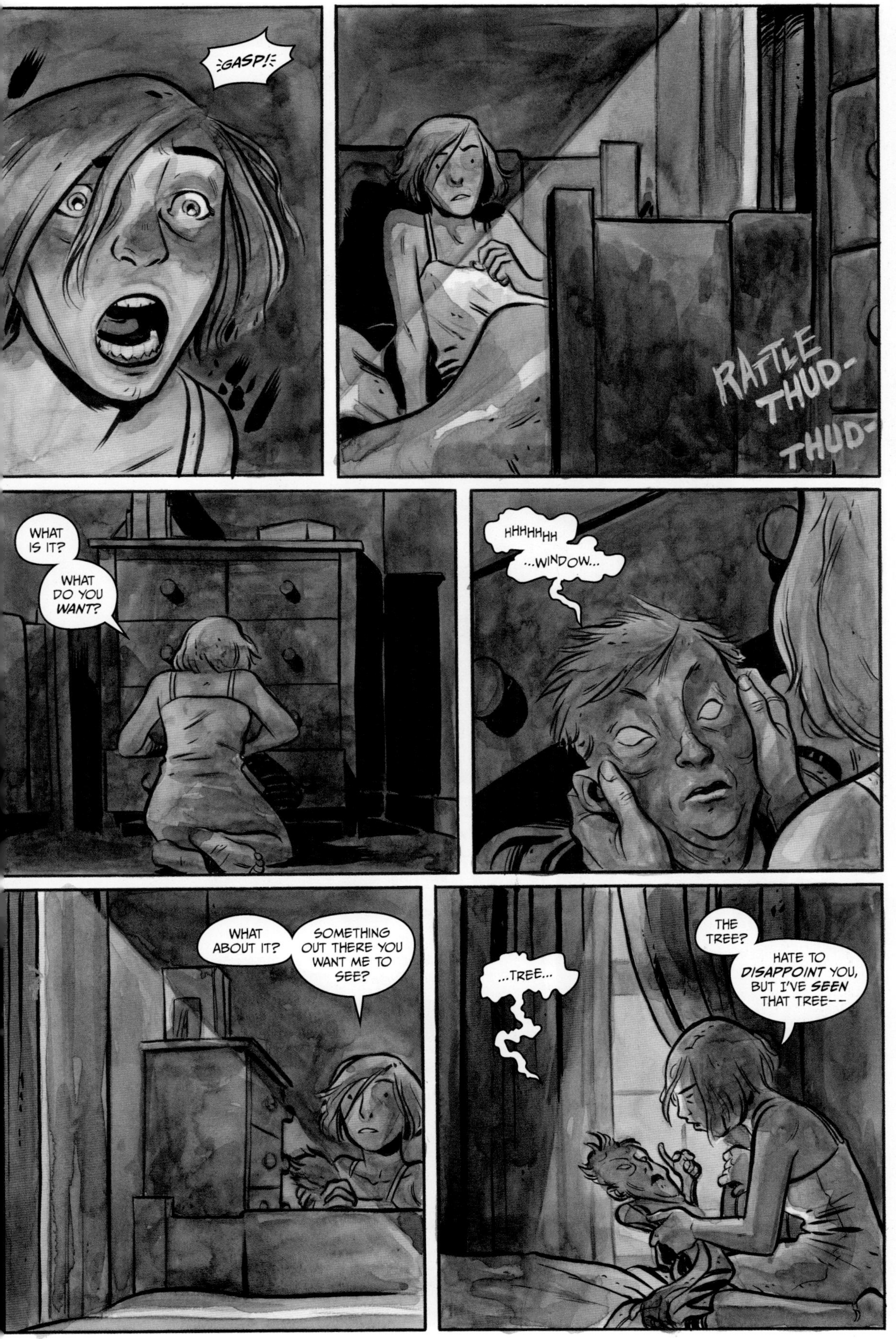
GASP!
RATTLE
THUD-
THUD-
WHAT IS IT?
WHAT DO YOU *WANT*?
HHHHHHH
...WINDOW...
WHAT ABOUT IT?
SOMETHING OUT THERE YOU WANT ME TO SEE?
...TREE...
THE TREE?
HATE TO *DISAPPOINT* YOU, BUT I'VE *SEEN* THAT TREE--

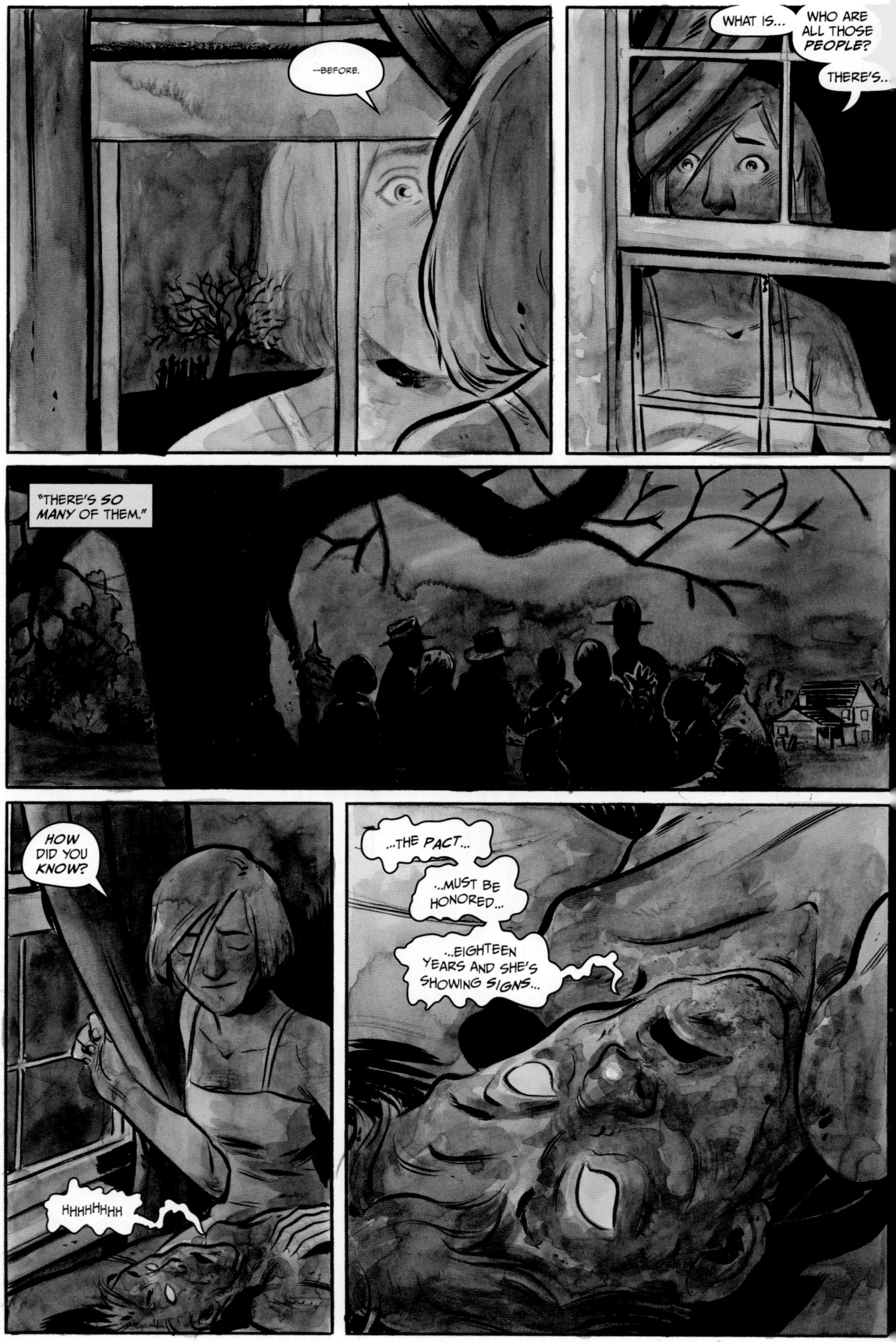
--BEFORE.
WHAT IS...
WHO ARE ALL THOSE PEOPLE?
THERE'S...
"THERE'S SO MANY OF THEM."
HOW DID YOU KNOW?
HHHHHHHH
...THE PACT...
...MUST BE HONORED...
...EIGHTEEN YEARS AND SHE'S SHOWING SIGNS...

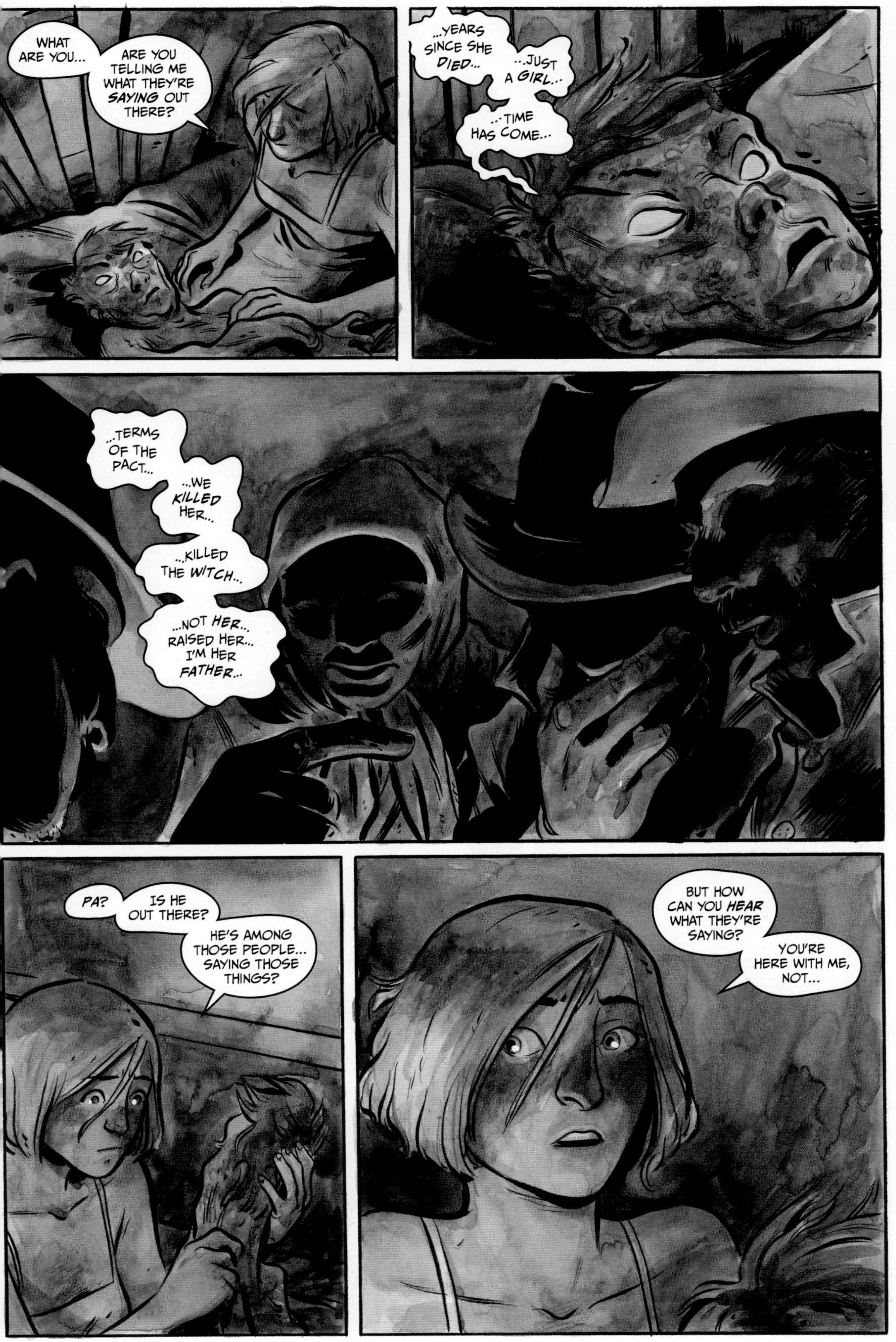
WHAT ARE YOU...
ARE YOU TELLING ME WHAT THEY'RE SAYING OUT THERE?
...YEARS SINCE SHE DIED...
...JUST A GIRL...
...TIME HAS COME...
...TERMS OF THE PACT...
...WE KILLED HER...
...KILLED THE WITCH...
...NOT HER... RAISED HER... I'M HER FATHER...
PA?
IS HE OUT THERE?
HE'S AMONG THOSE PEOPLE... SAYING THOSE THINGS?
BUT HOW CAN YOU HEAR WHAT THEY'RE SAYING?
YOU'RE HERE WITH ME, NOT...

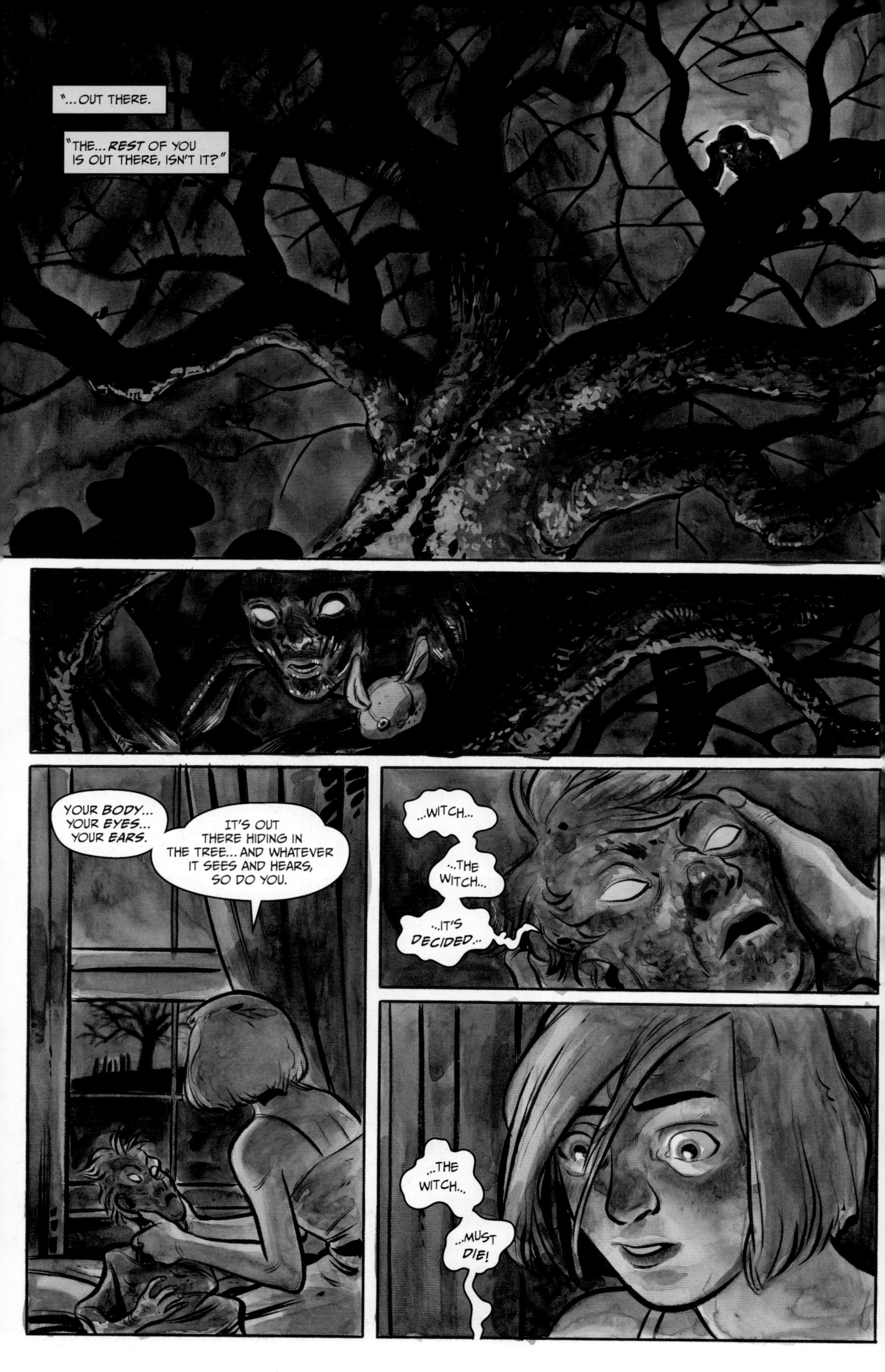
"...OUT THERE.
"THE... REST OF YOU IS OUT THERE, ISN'T IT?"
YOUR BODY... YOUR EYES... YOUR EARS.
IT'S OUT THERE HIDING IN THE TREE... AND WHATEVER IT SEES AND HEARS, SO DO YOU.
...WITCH...
...THE WITCH...
...IT'S DECIDED...
...THE WITCH...
...MUST DIE!

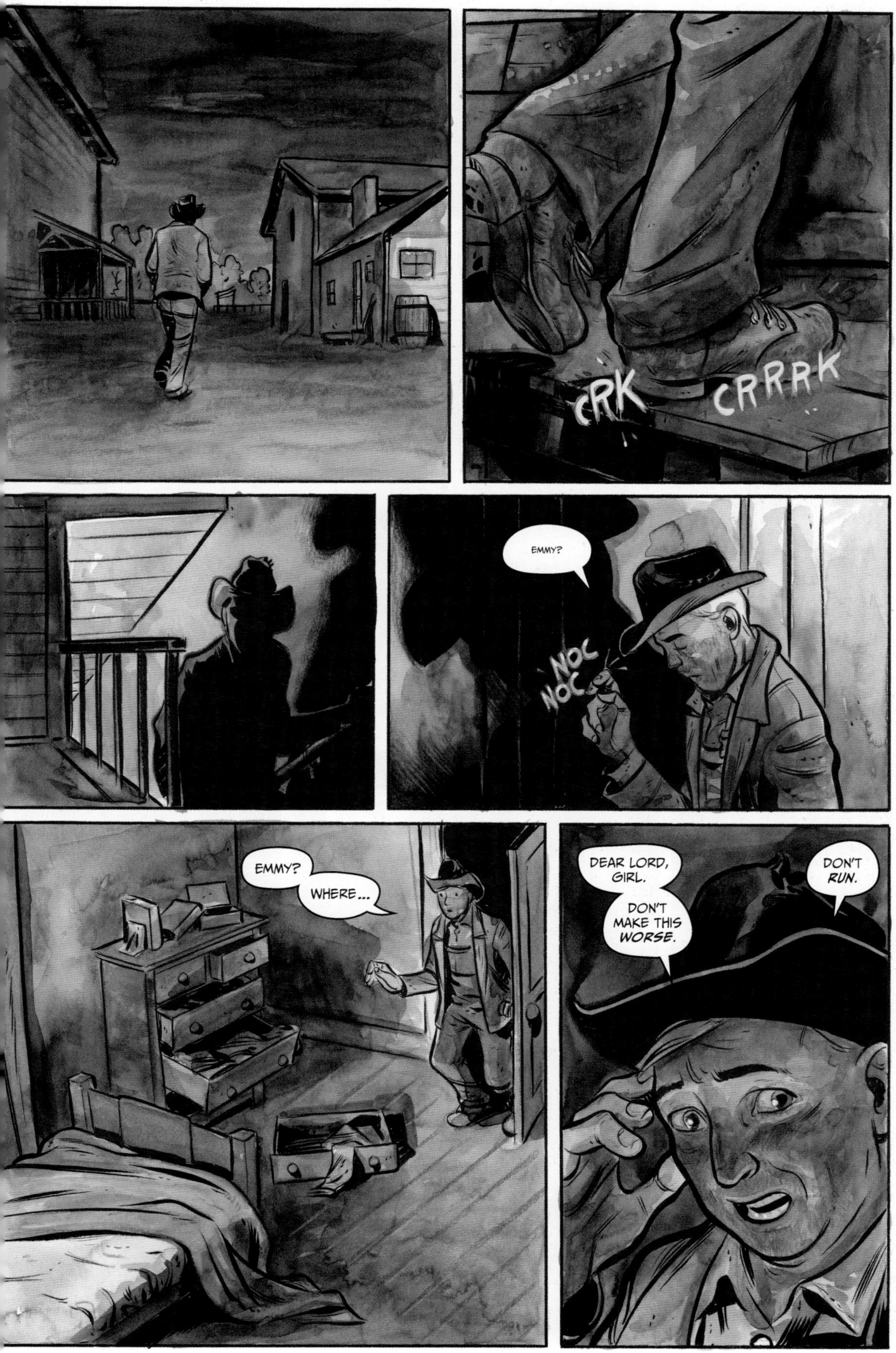
CRK
CRRRK
EMMY?
NOC NOC
EMMY?
WHERE...
DEAR LORD, GIRL.
DON'T MAKE THIS *WORSE*.
DON'T *RUN*.

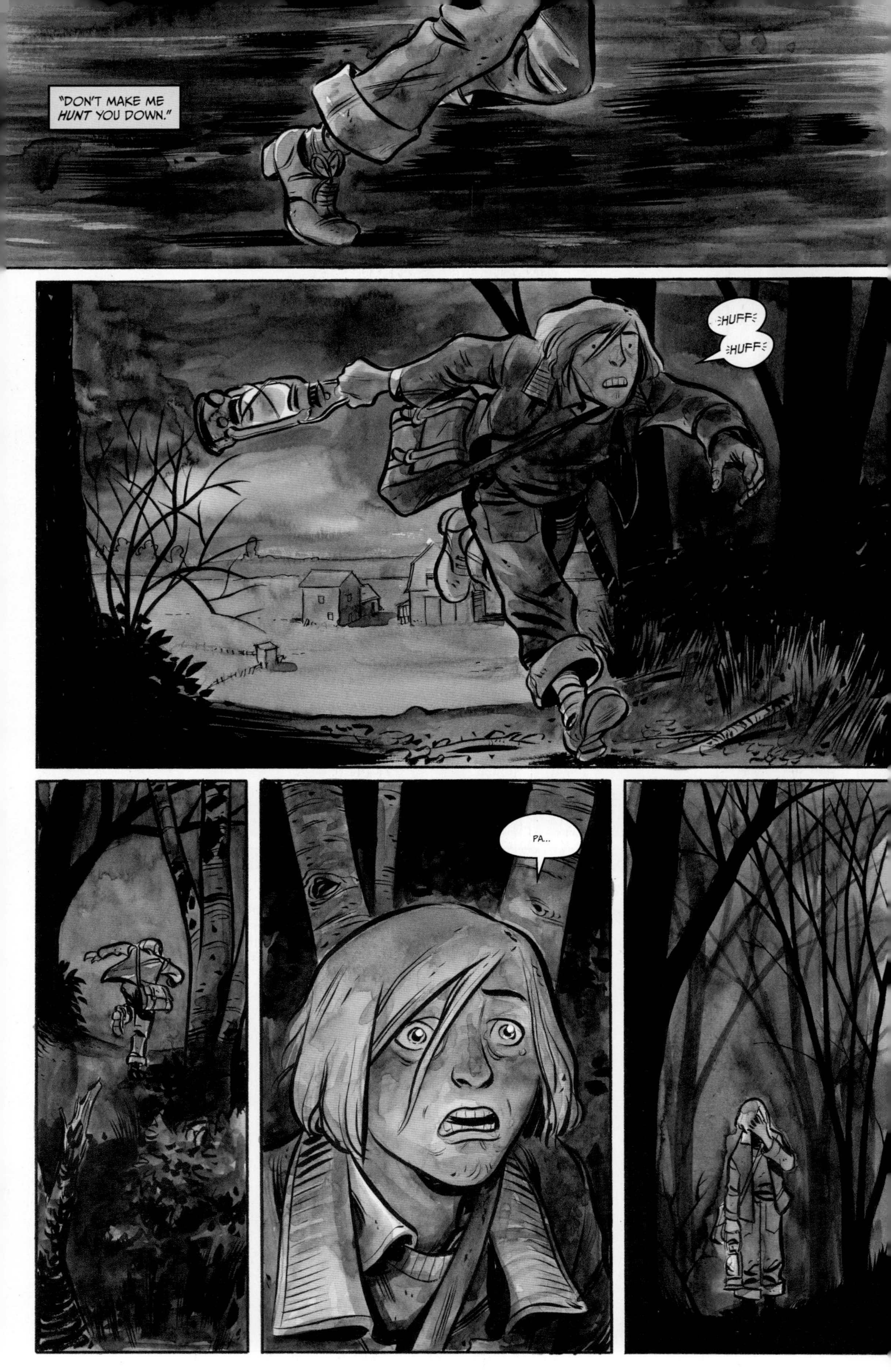
"DON'T MAKE ME
HUNT YOU DOWN."
HUFF
HUFF
PA...

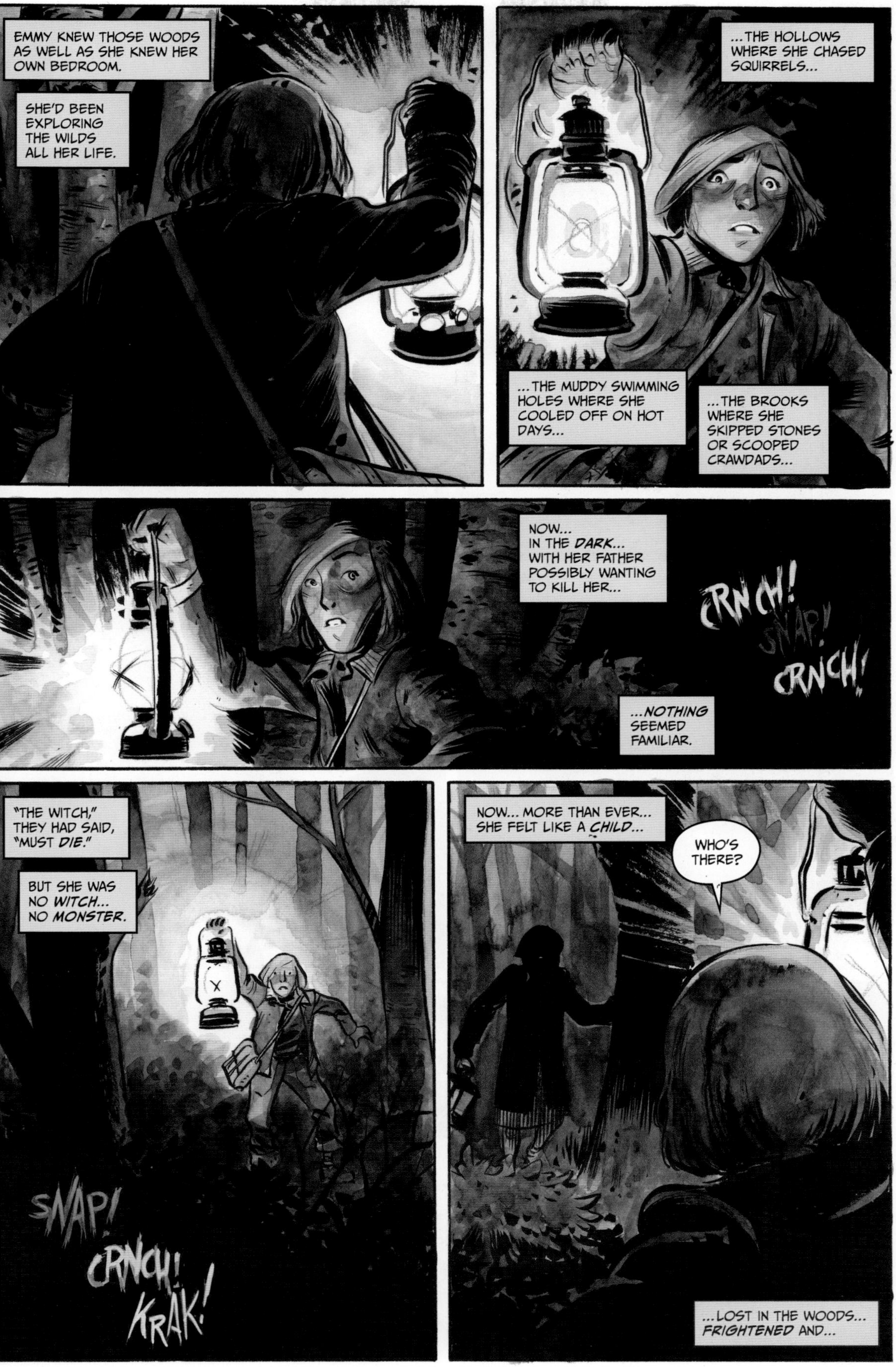
EMMY KNEW THOSE WOODS AS WELL AS SHE KNEW HER OWN BEDROOM.
SHE'D BEEN EXPLORING THE WILDS ALL HER LIFE.
...THE HOLLOWS WHERE SHE CHASED SQUIRRELS...
...THE MUDDY SWIMMING HOLES WHERE SHE COOLED OFF ON HOT DAYS...
...THE BROOKS WHERE SHE SKIPPED STONES OR SCOOPED CRAWDADS...
NOW... IN THE DARK... WITH HER FATHER POSSIBLY WANTING TO KILL HER...
CRNCH! SNAP! CRNCH!
...NOTHING SEEMED FAMILIAR.
"THE WITCH," THEY HAD SAID, "MUST DIE."
BUT SHE WAS NO WITCH... NO MONSTER.
SNAP! CRNCH! KRAK!
NOW... MORE THAN EVER... SHE FELT LIKE A CHILD...
WHO'S THERE?
...LOST IN THE WOODS... FRIGHTENED AND...

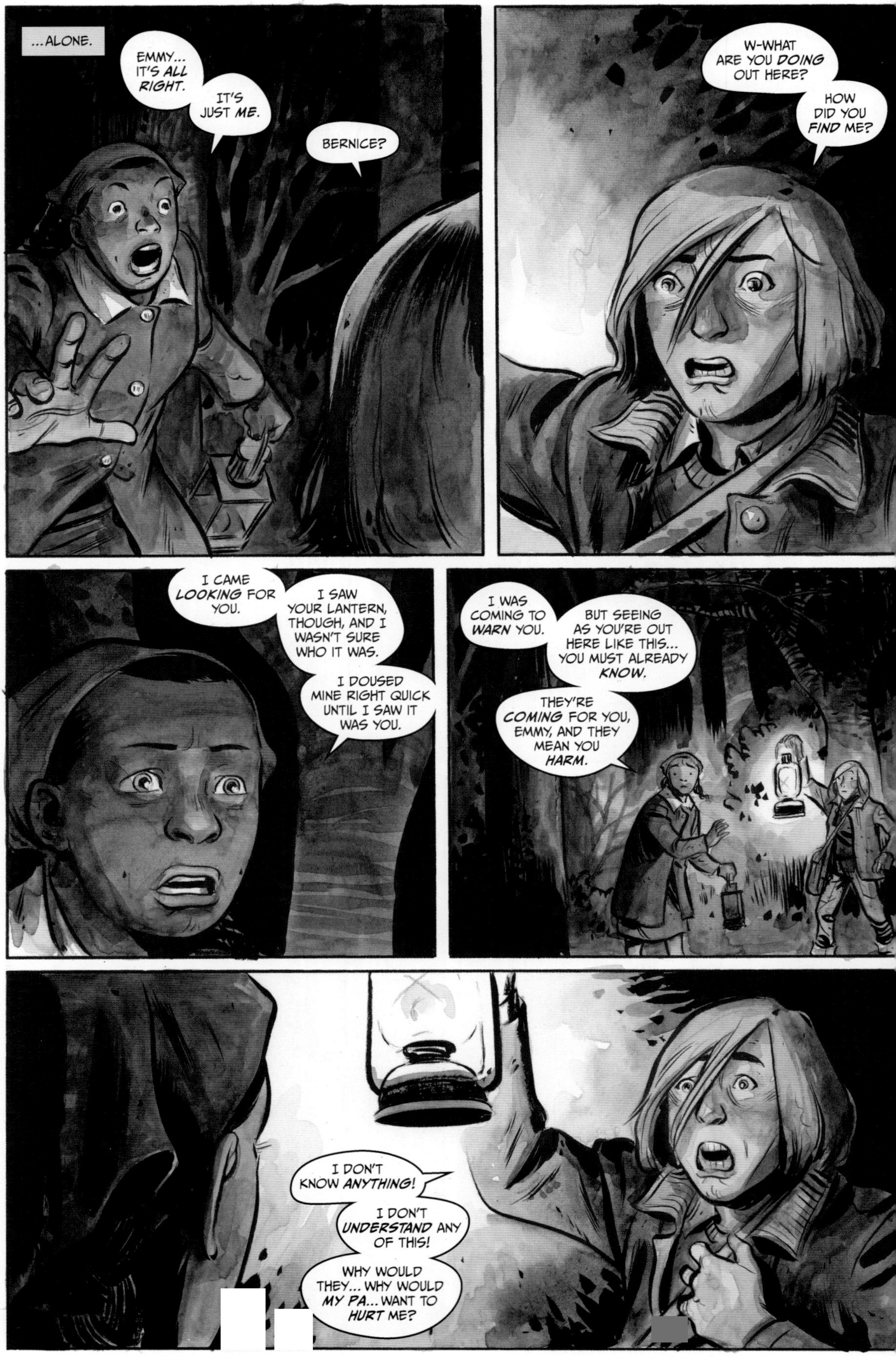

...ALONE.
EMMY... IT'S ALL RIGHT.
IT'S JUST ME.
BERNICE?
W-WHAT ARE YOU DOING OUT HERE?
HOW DID YOU FIND ME?
I CAME LOOKING FOR YOU.
I SAW YOUR LANTERN, THOUGH, AND I WASN'T SURE WHO IT WAS.
I DOUSED MINE RIGHT QUICK UNTIL I SAW IT WAS YOU.
I WAS COMING TO WARN YOU.
BUT SEEING AS YOU'RE OUT HERE LIKE THIS... YOU MUST ALREADY KNOW.
THEY'RE COMING FOR YOU, EMMY, AND THEY MEAN YOU HARM.
I DON'T KNOW ANYTHING!
I DON'T UNDERSTAND ANY OF THIS!
WHY WOULD THEY... WHY WOULD MY PA... WANT TO HURT ME?

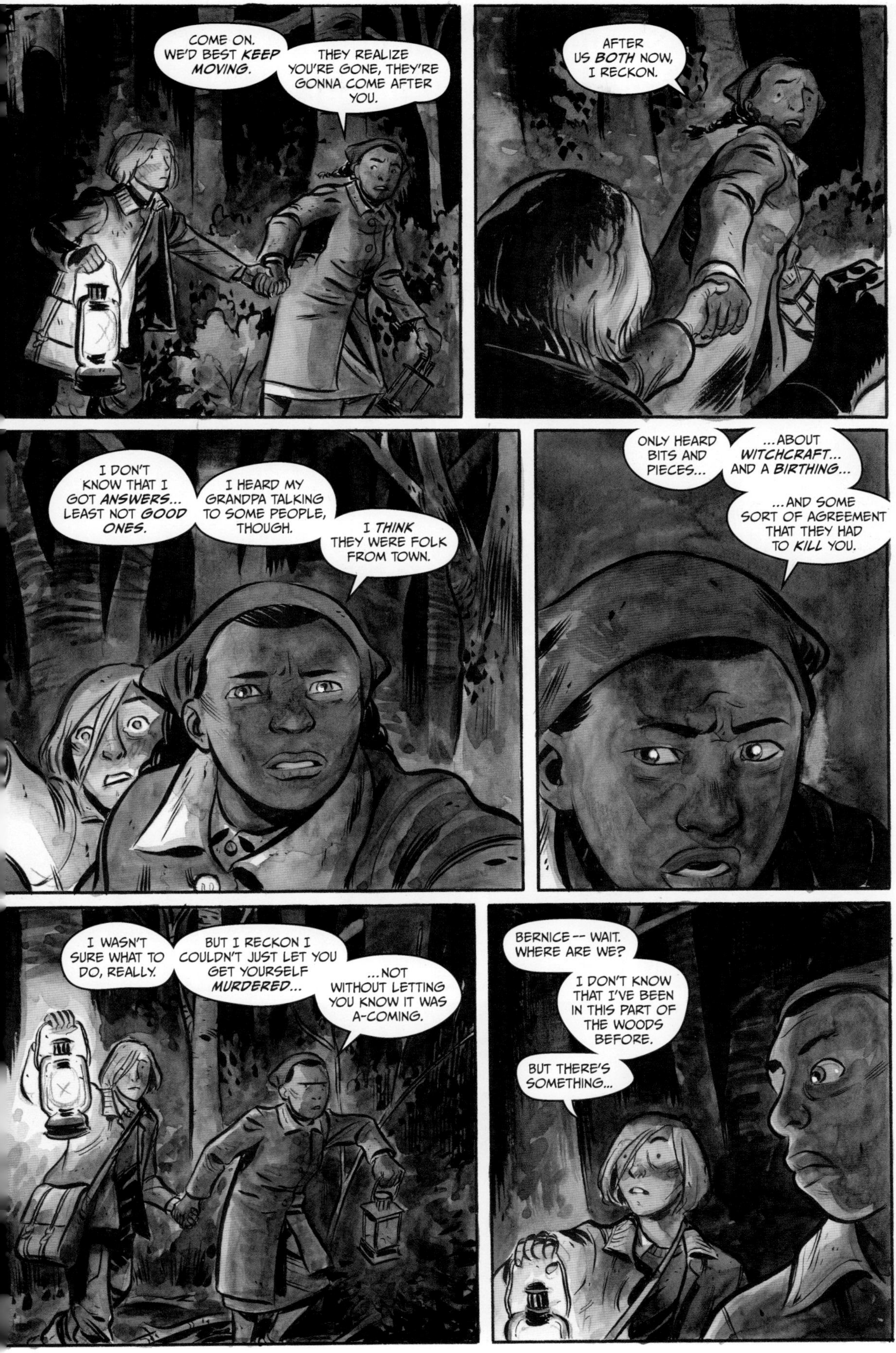
COME ON. WE'D BEST KEEP MOVING.
THEY REALIZE YOU'RE GONE, THEY'RE GONNA COME AFTER YOU.
AFTER US BOTH NOW, I RECKON.
I DON'T KNOW THAT I GOT ANSWERS... LEAST NOT GOOD ONES.
I HEARD MY GRANDPA TALKING TO SOME PEOPLE, THOUGH.
I THINK THEY WERE FOLK FROM TOWN.
ONLY HEARD BITS AND PIECES...
...ABOUT WITCHCRAFT... AND A BIRTHING...
...AND SOME SORT OF AGREEMENT THAT THEY HAD TO KILL YOU.
I WASN'T SURE WHAT TO DO, REALLY.
BUT I RECKON I COULDN'T JUST LET YOU GET YOURSELF MURDERED...
...NOT WITHOUT LETTING YOU KNOW IT WAS A-COMING.
BERNICE -- WAIT. WHERE ARE WE?
I DON'T KNOW THAT I'VE BEEN IN THIS PART OF THE WOODS BEFORE.
BUT THERE'S SOMETHING...

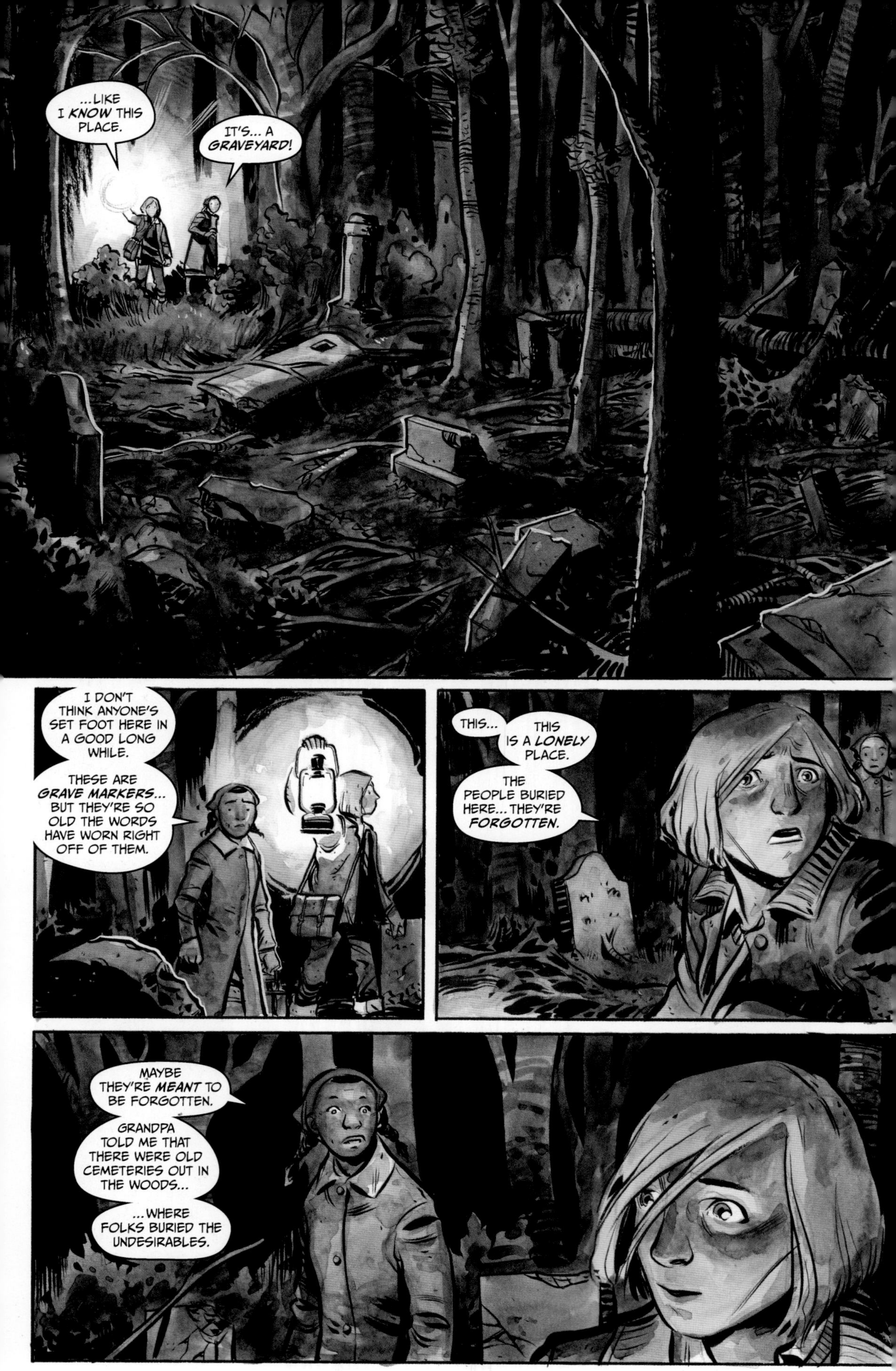
...LIKE I KNOW THIS PLACE.
IT'S... A GRAVEYARD!
I DON'T THINK ANYONE'S SET FOOT HERE IN A GOOD LONG WHILE.
THESE ARE GRAVE MARKERS... BUT THEY'RE SO OLD THE WORDS HAVE WORN RIGHT OFF OF THEM.
THIS...
THIS IS A LONELY PLACE.
THE PEOPLE BURIED HERE... THEY'RE FORGOTTEN.
MAYBE THEY'RE MEANT TO BE FORGOTTEN.
GRANDPA TOLD ME THAT THERE WERE OLD CEMETERIES OUT IN THE WOODS...
...WHERE FOLKS BURIED THE UNDESIRABLES.

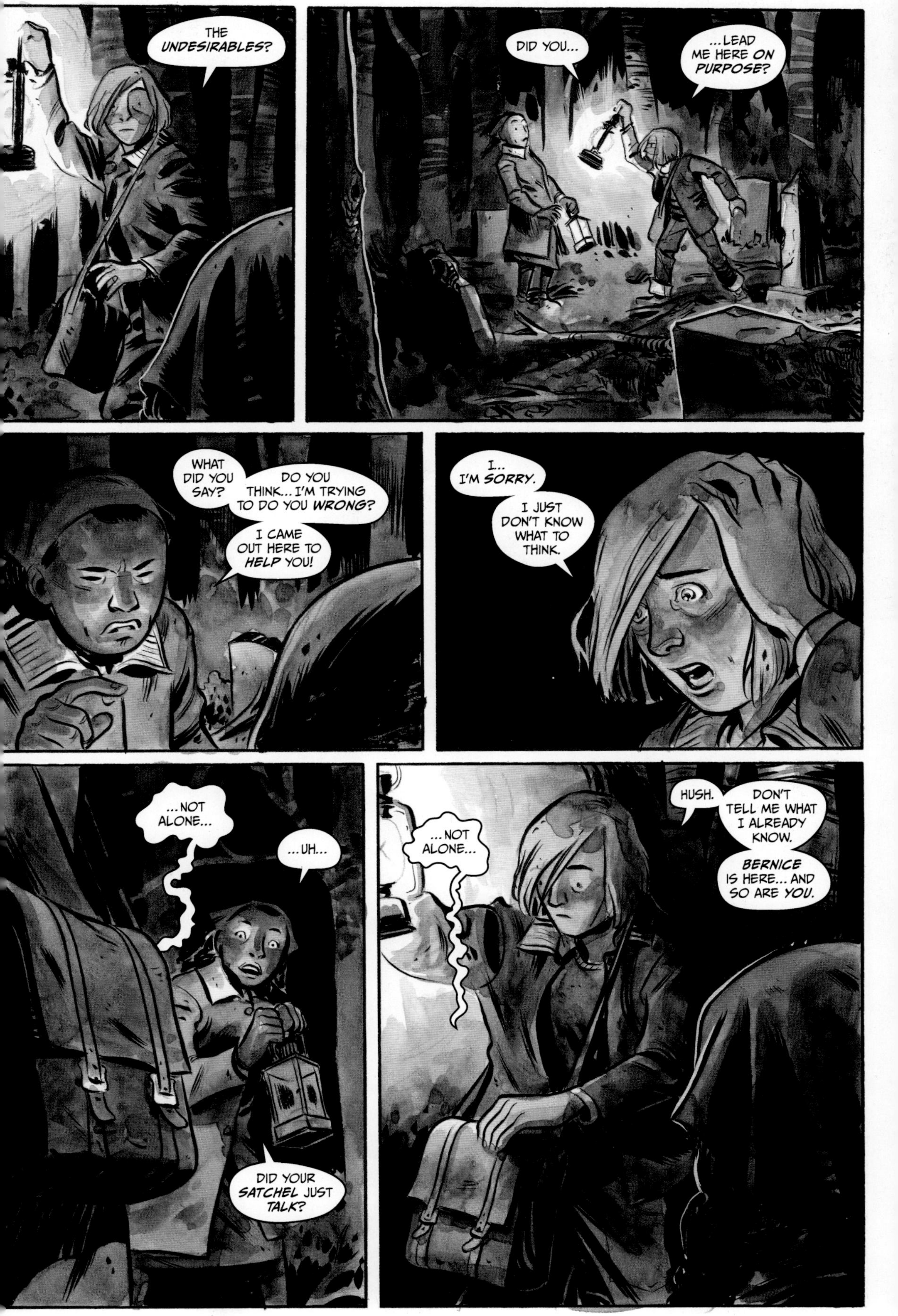
THE UNDESIRABLES?
DID YOU...
...LEAD ME HERE ON PURPOSE?
WHAT DID YOU SAY?
DO YOU THINK... I'M TRYING TO DO YOU WRONG?
I CAME OUT HERE TO HELP YOU!
I... I'M SORRY.
I JUST DON'T KNOW WHAT TO THINK.
...NOT ALONE...
...UH...
DID YOUR SATCHEL JUST TALK?
...NOT ALONE...
HUSH.
DON'T TELL ME WHAT I ALREADY KNOW.
BERNICE IS HERE... AND SO ARE YOU.

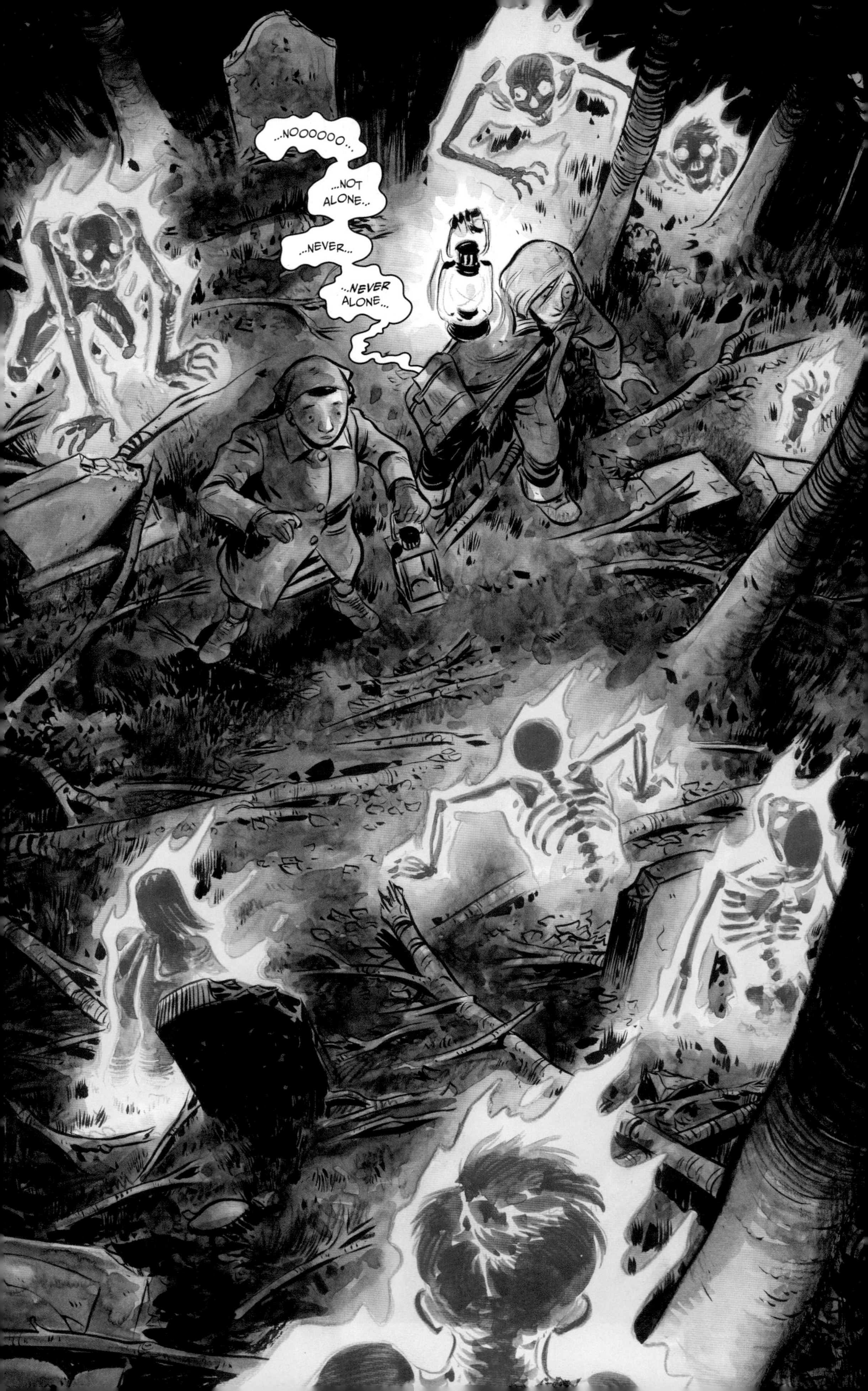
...NOOOOOO...
...NOT ALONE...
...NEVER...
...NEVER ALONE...

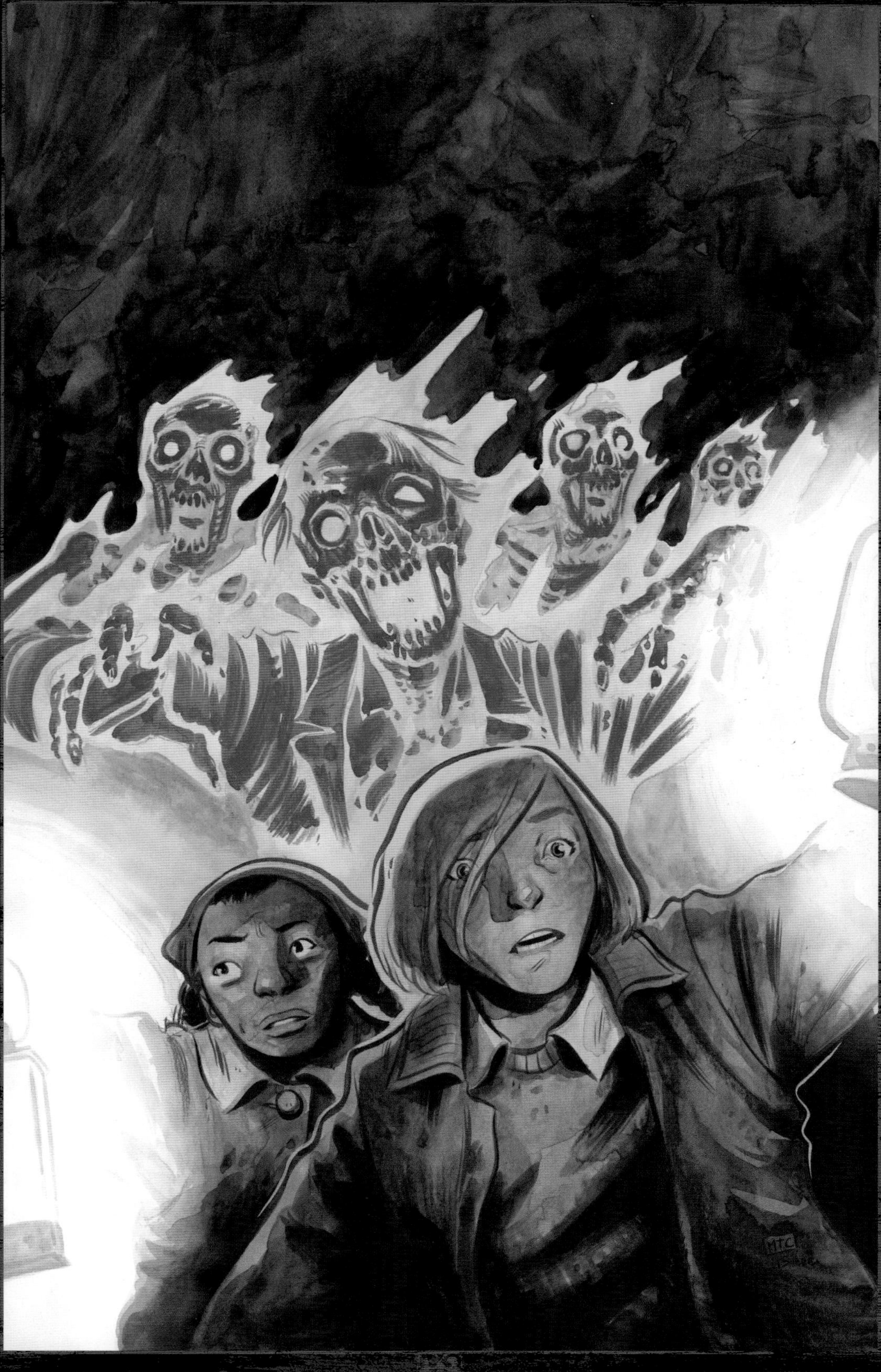

THREE

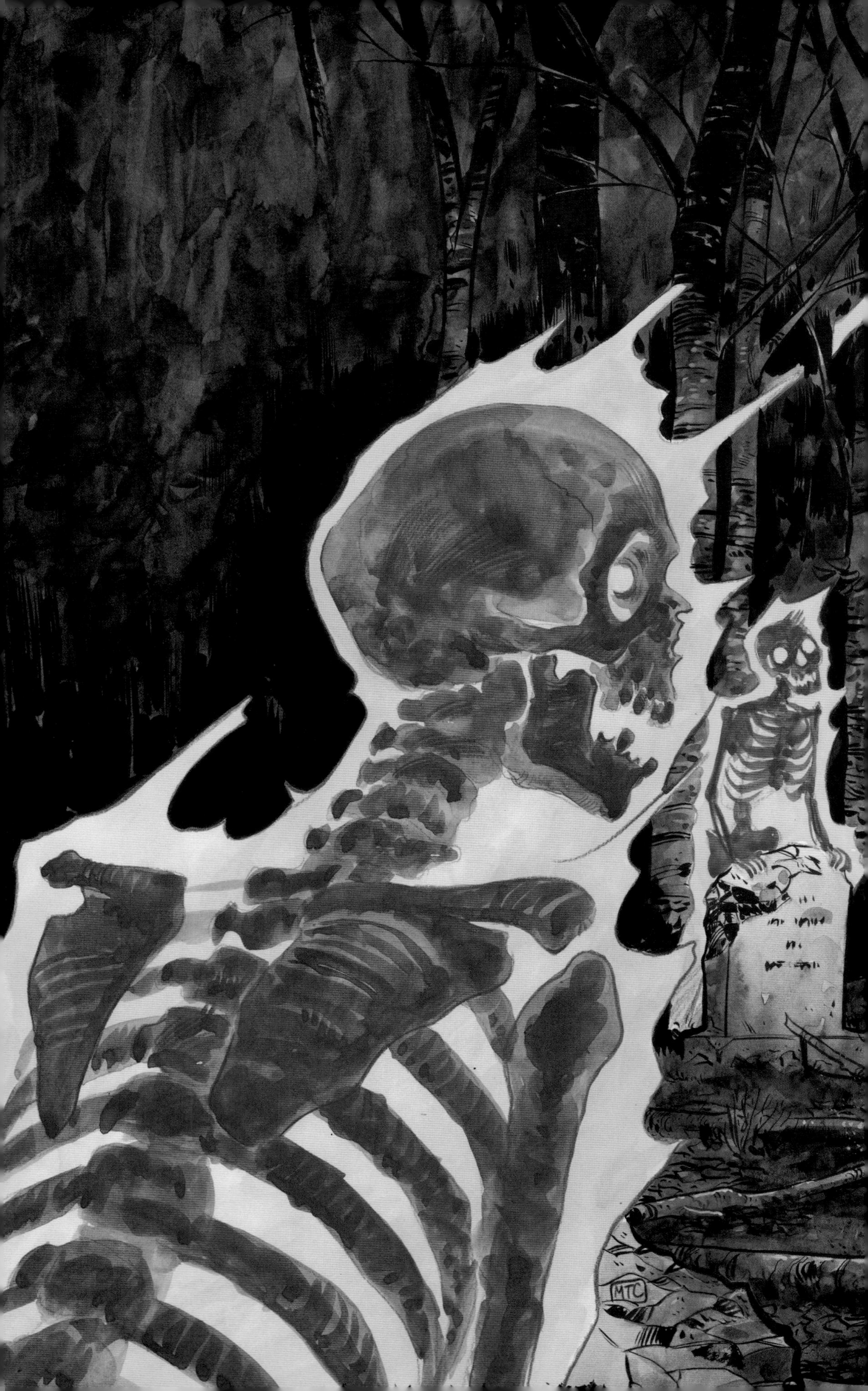
MTC

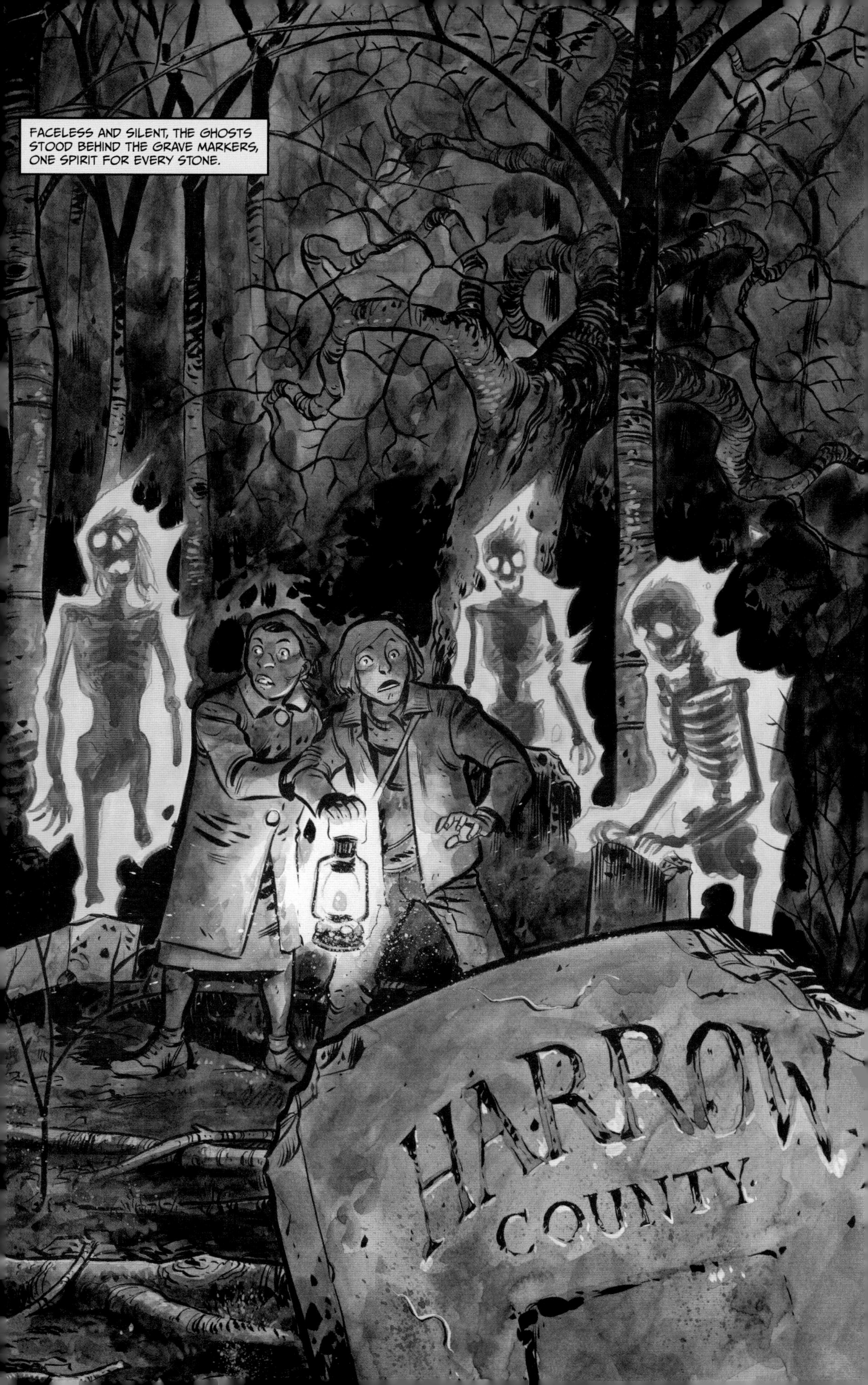
FACELESS AND SILENT, THE GHOSTS STOOD BEHIND THE GRAVE MARKERS, ONE SPIRIT FOR EVERY STONE.
HARROW
COUNTY

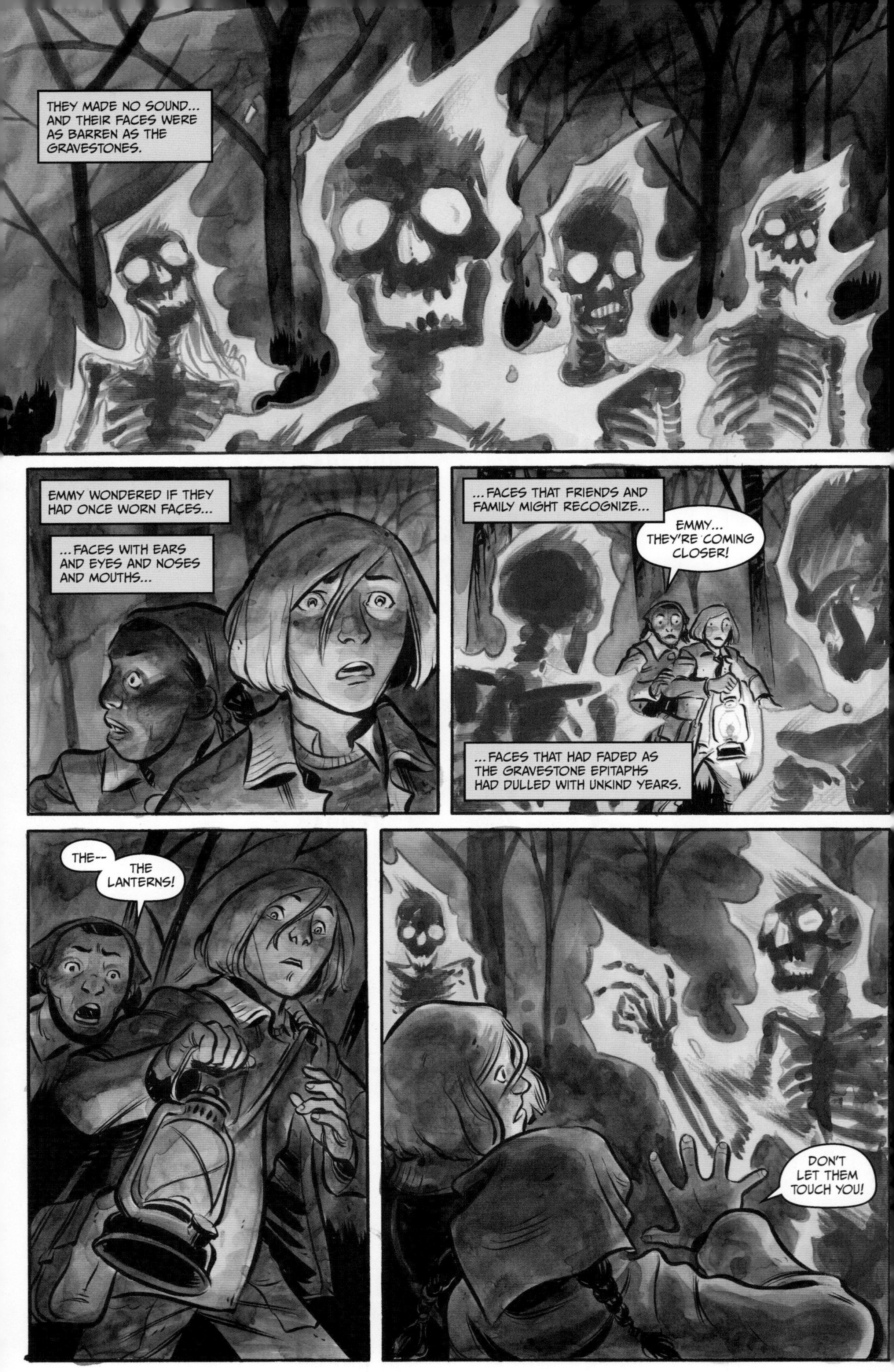
THEY MADE NO SOUND... AND THEIR FACES WERE AS BARREN AS THE GRAVESTONES.
EMMY WONDERED IF THEY HAD ONCE WORN FACES...
...FACES WITH EARS AND EYES AND NOSES AND MOUTHS...
...FACES THAT FRIENDS AND FAMILY MIGHT RECOGNIZE...
EMMY... THEY'RE COMING CLOSER!
...FACES THAT HAD FADED AS THE GRAVESTONE EPITAPHS HAD DULLED WITH UNKIND YEARS.
THE-- THE LANTERNS!
DON'T LET THEM TOUCH YOU!

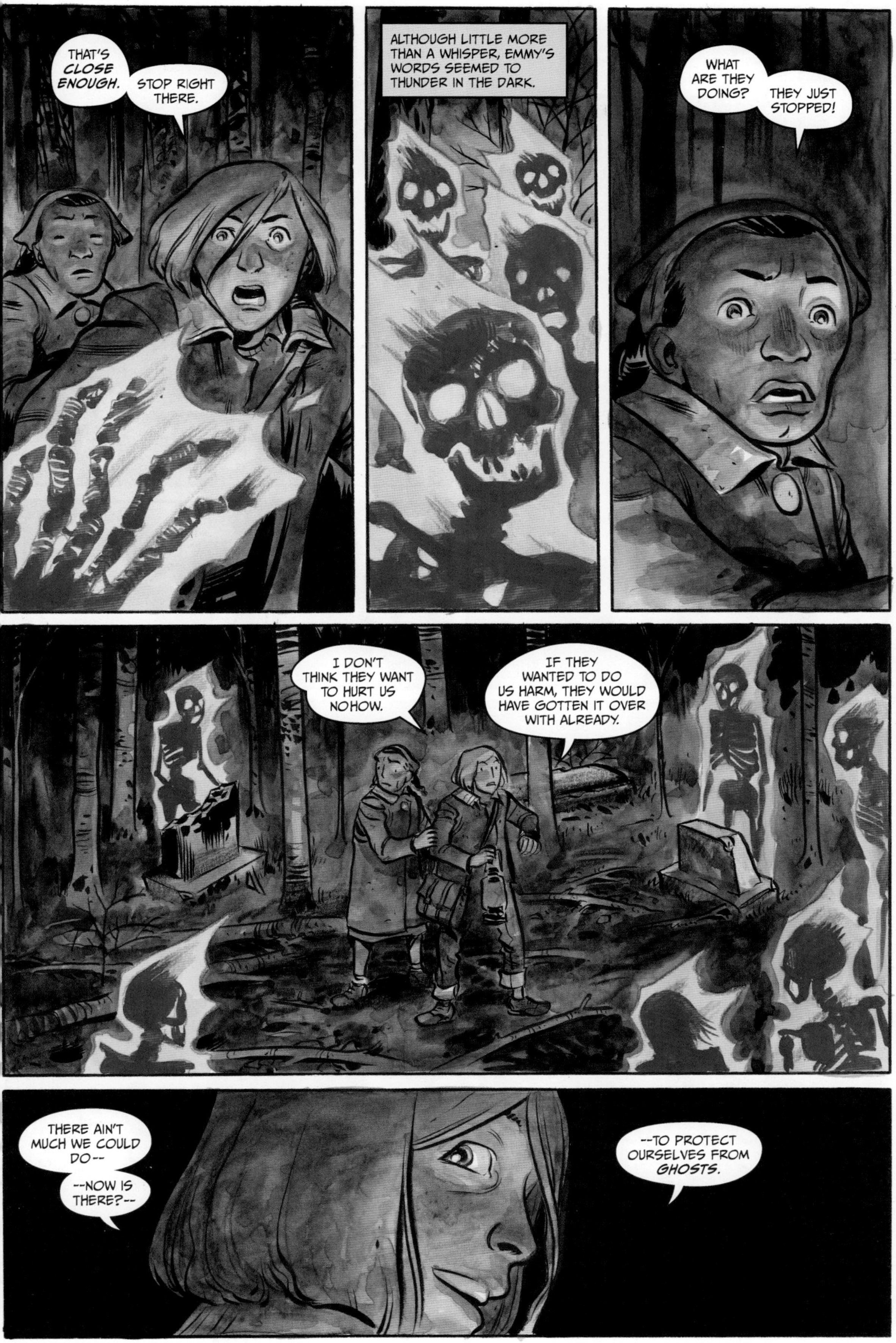
THAT'S *CLOSE ENOUGH.*
STOP RIGHT THERE.
ALTHOUGH LITTLE MORE THAN A WHISPER, EMMY'S WORDS SEEMED TO THUNDER IN THE DARK.
WHAT ARE THEY DOING?
THEY JUST STOPPED!
I DON'T THINK THEY WANT TO HURT US NOHOW.
IF THEY WANTED TO DO US HARM, THEY WOULD HAVE GOTTEN IT OVER WITH ALREADY.
THERE AIN'T MUCH WE COULD DO--
--NOW IS THERE?--
--TO PROTECT OURSELVES FROM *GHOSTS.*

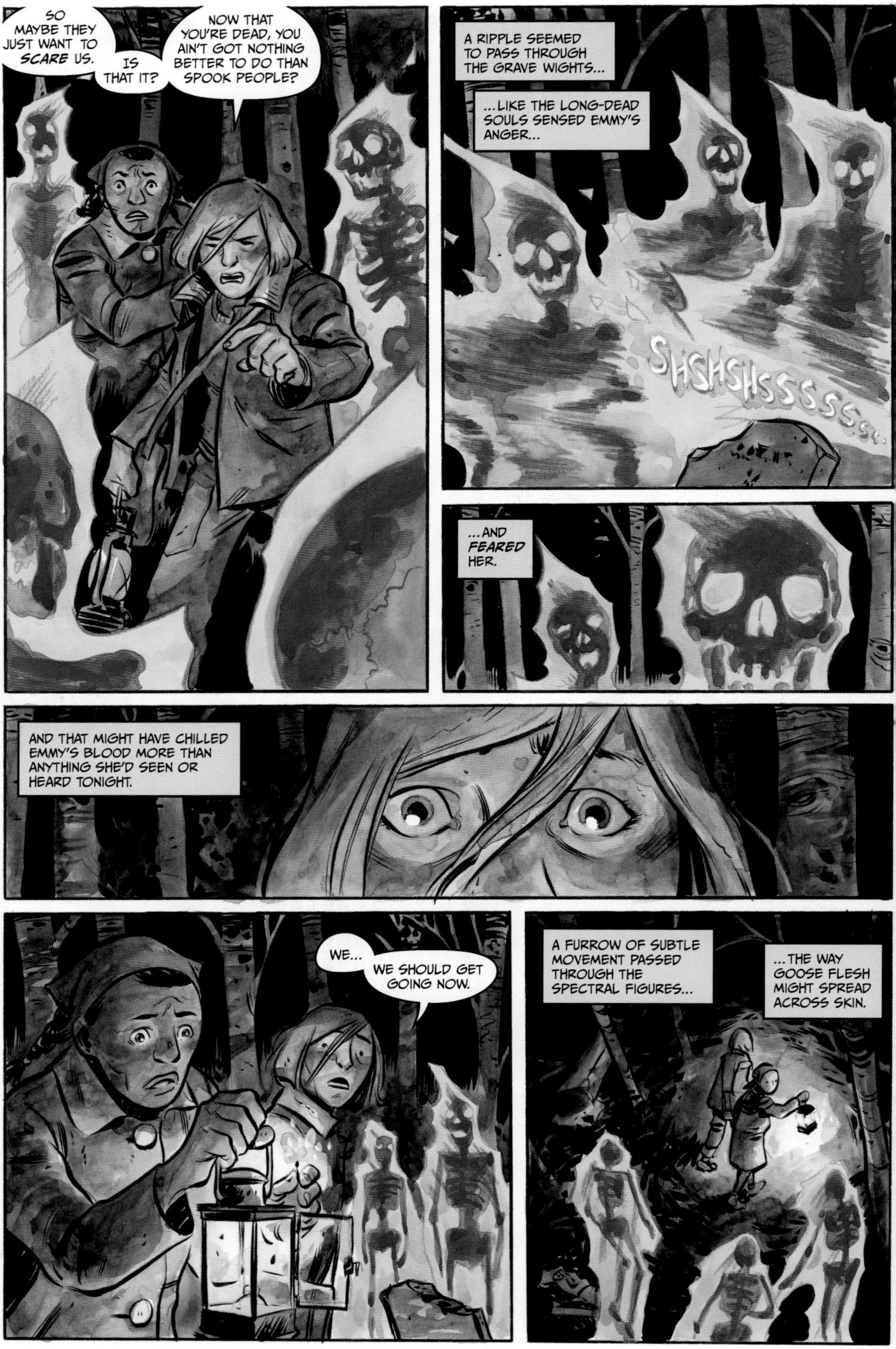
SO MAYBE THEY JUST WANT TO SCARE US.
IS THAT IT?
NOW THAT YOU'RE DEAD, YOU AIN'T GOT NOTHING BETTER TO DO THAN SPOOK PEOPLE?
A RIPPLE SEEMED TO PASS THROUGH THE GRAVE WIGHTS...
...LIKE THE LONG-DEAD SOULS SENSED EMMY'S ANGER...
SHSHSHSSSSSS...
...AND FEARED HER.
AND THAT MIGHT HAVE CHILLED EMMY'S BLOOD MORE THAN ANYTHING SHE'D SEEN OR HEARD TONIGHT.
WE...
WE SHOULD GET GOING NOW.
A FURROW OF SUBTLE MOVEMENT PASSED THROUGH THE SPECTRAL FIGURES...
...THE WAY GOOSE FLESH MIGHT SPREAD ACROSS SKIN.

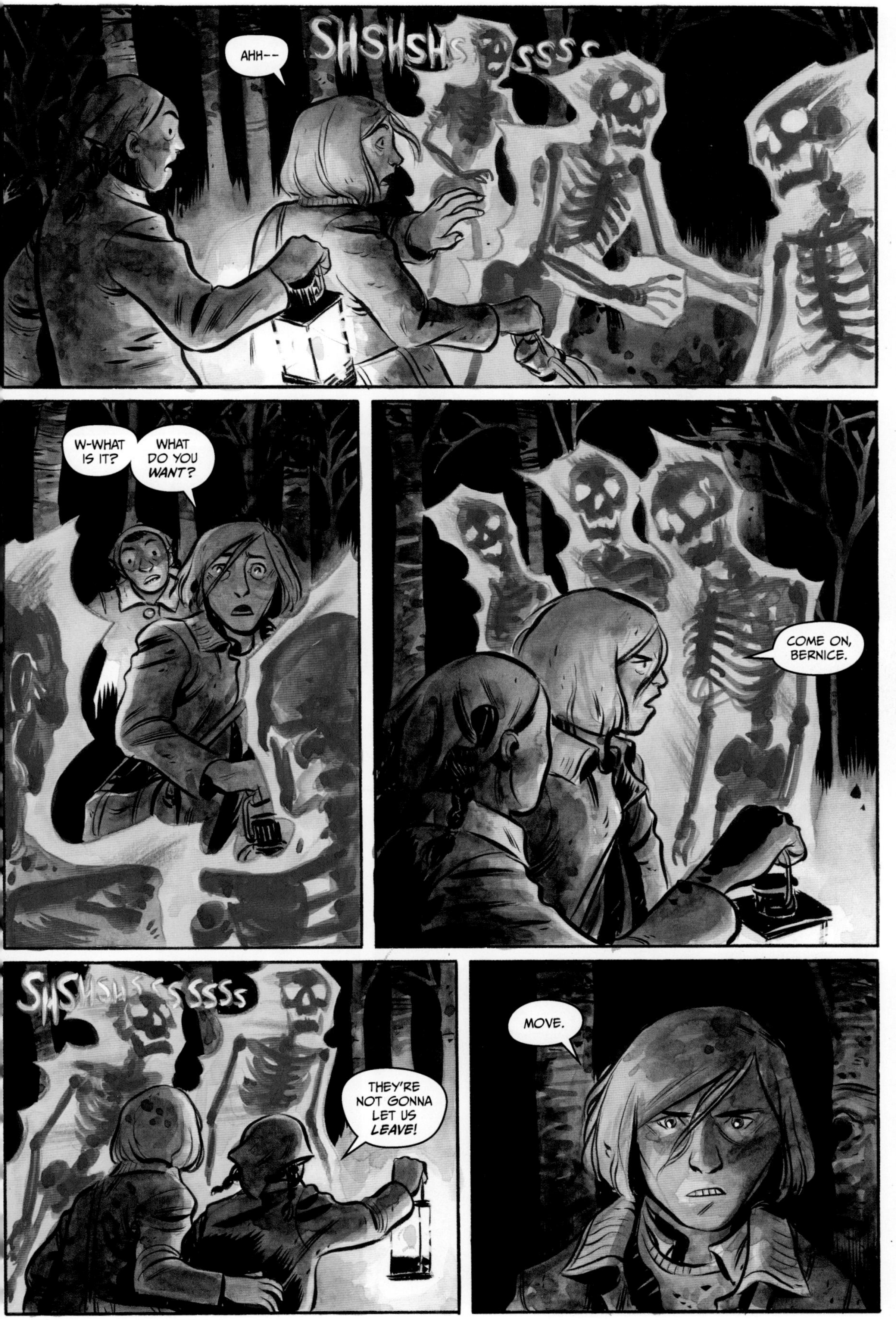
AHH--
SHSHSHSSSSS
W-WHAT IS IT?
WHAT DO YOU *WANT*?
COME ON, BERNICE.
SHSHSHSSSSSSS
THEY'RE NOT GONNA LET US *LEAVE*!
MOVE.

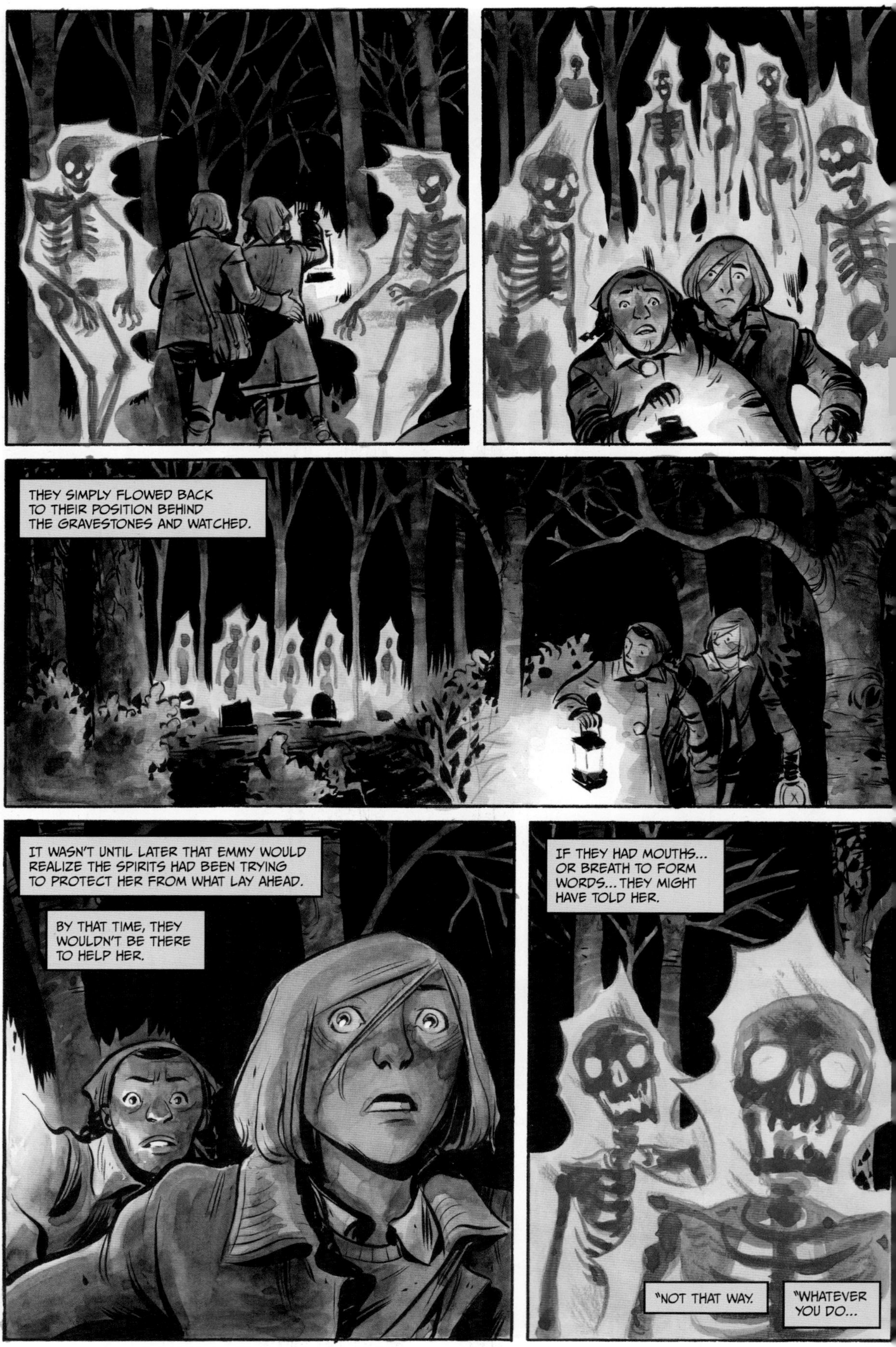
THEY SIMPLY FLOWED BACK TO THEIR POSITION BEHIND THE GRAVESTONES AND WATCHED.
IT WASN'T UNTIL LATER THAT EMMY WOULD REALIZE THE SPIRITS HAD BEEN TRYING TO PROTECT HER FROM WHAT LAY AHEAD.
BY THAT TIME, THEY WOULDN'T BE THERE TO HELP HER.
IF THEY HAD MOUTHS... OR BREATH TO FORM WORDS... THEY MIGHT HAVE TOLD HER.
"NOT THAT WAY.
"WHATEVER YOU DO...

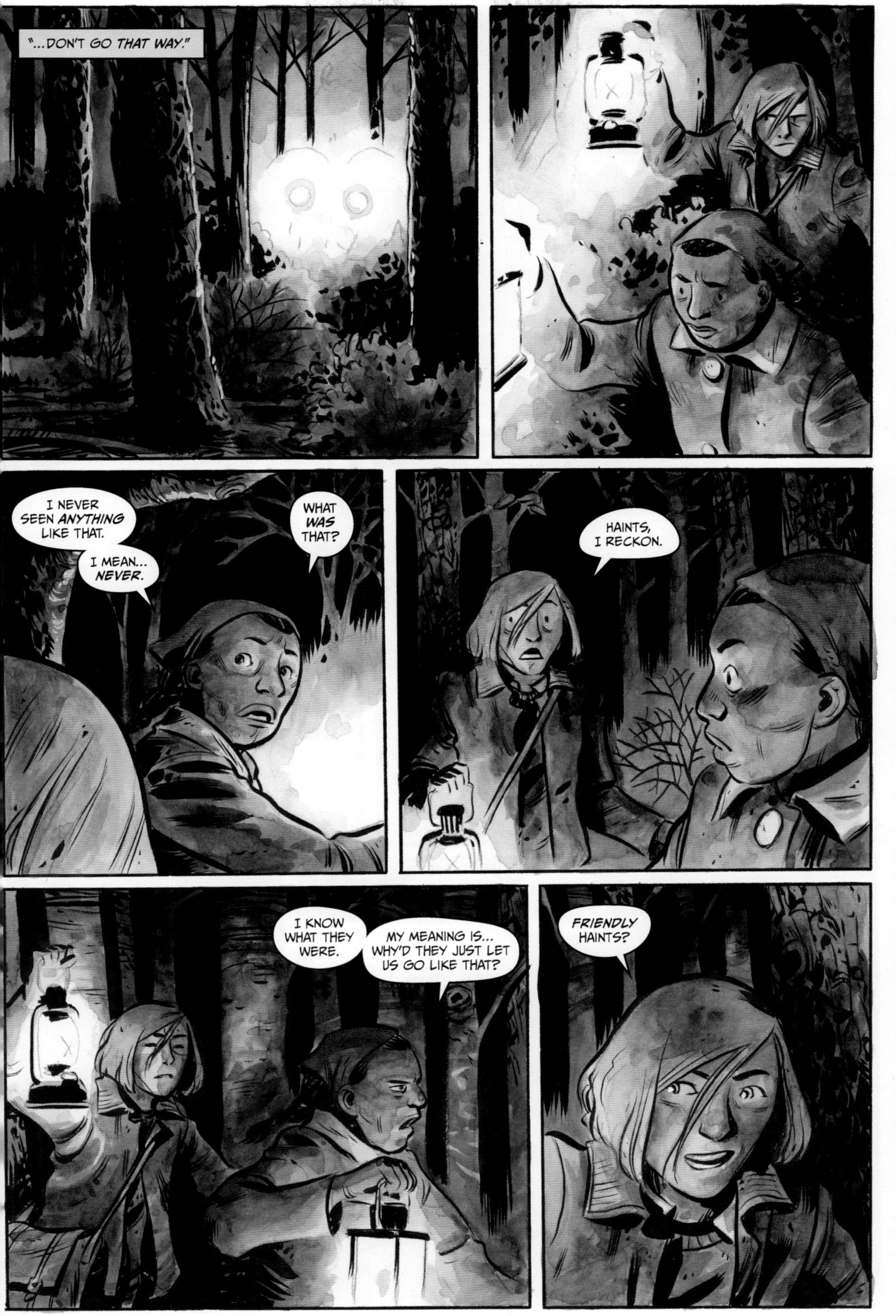
"...DON'T GO THAT WAY."
I NEVER SEEN ANYTHING LIKE THAT.
I MEAN... NEVER.
WHAT WAS THAT?
HAINTS, I RECKON.
I KNOW WHAT THEY WERE.
MY MEANING IS... WHY'D THEY JUST LET US GO LIKE THAT?
FRIENDLY HAINTS?

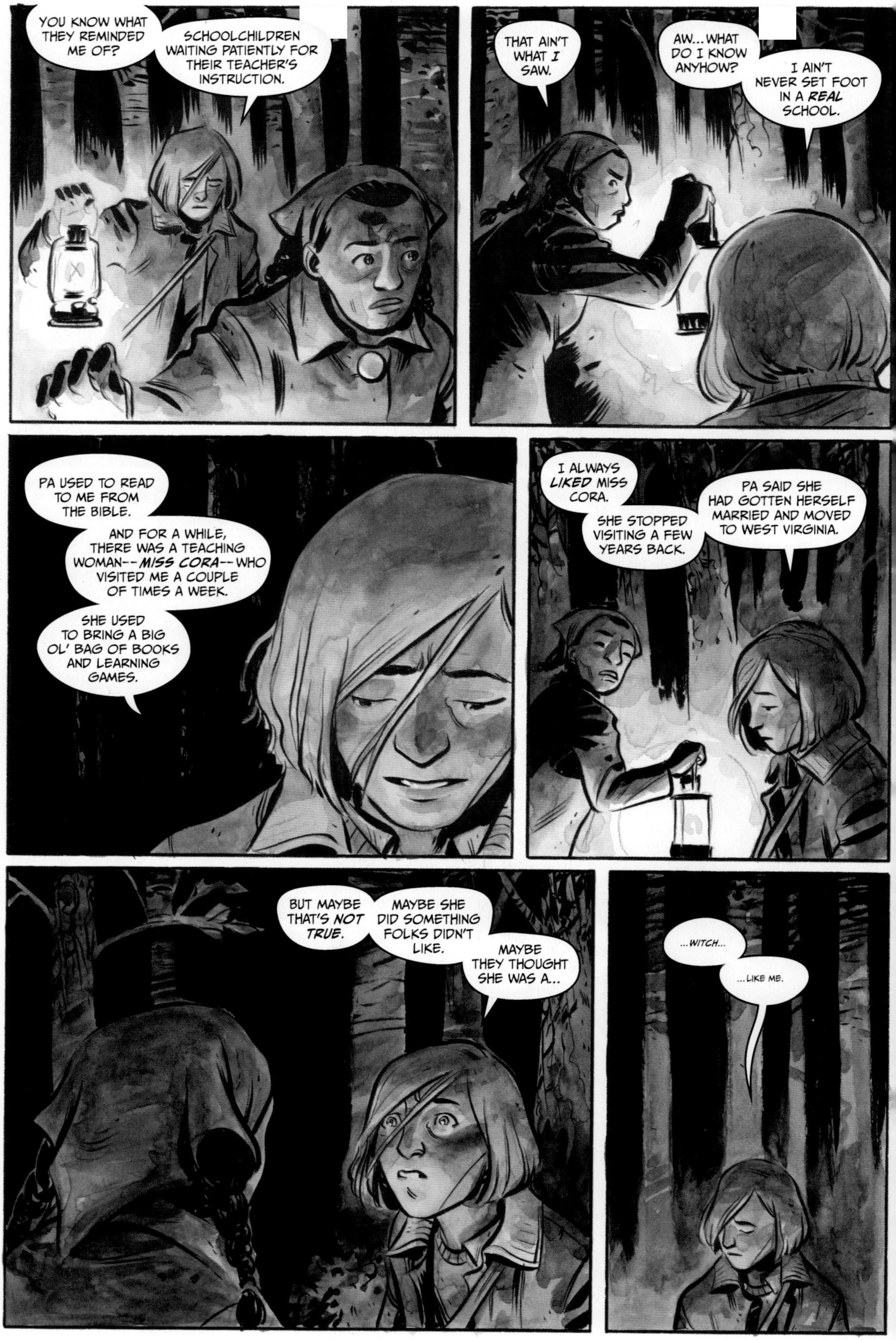
YOU KNOW WHAT THEY REMINDED ME OF?
SCHOOLCHILDREN WAITING PATIENTLY FOR THEIR TEACHER'S INSTRUCTION.
THAT AIN'T WHAT *I* SAW.
AW... WHAT DO I KNOW ANYHOW?
I AIN'T NEVER SET FOOT IN A ***REAL*** SCHOOL.
PA USED TO READ TO ME FROM THE BIBLE.
AND FOR A WHILE, THERE WAS A TEACHING WOMAN-- ***MISS CORA***-- WHO VISITED ME A COUPLE OF TIMES A WEEK.
SHE USED TO BRING A BIG OL' BAG OF BOOKS AND LEARNING GAMES.
I ALWAYS ***LIKED*** MISS CORA.
SHE STOPPED VISITING A FEW YEARS BACK.
PA SAID SHE HAD GOTTEN HERSELF MARRIED AND MOVED TO WEST VIRGINIA.
BUT MAYBE THAT'S ***NOT TRUE.***
MAYBE SHE DID SOMETHING FOLKS DIDN'T LIKE.
MAYBE THEY THOUGHT SHE WAS A...
...WITCH...
...LIKE ME.

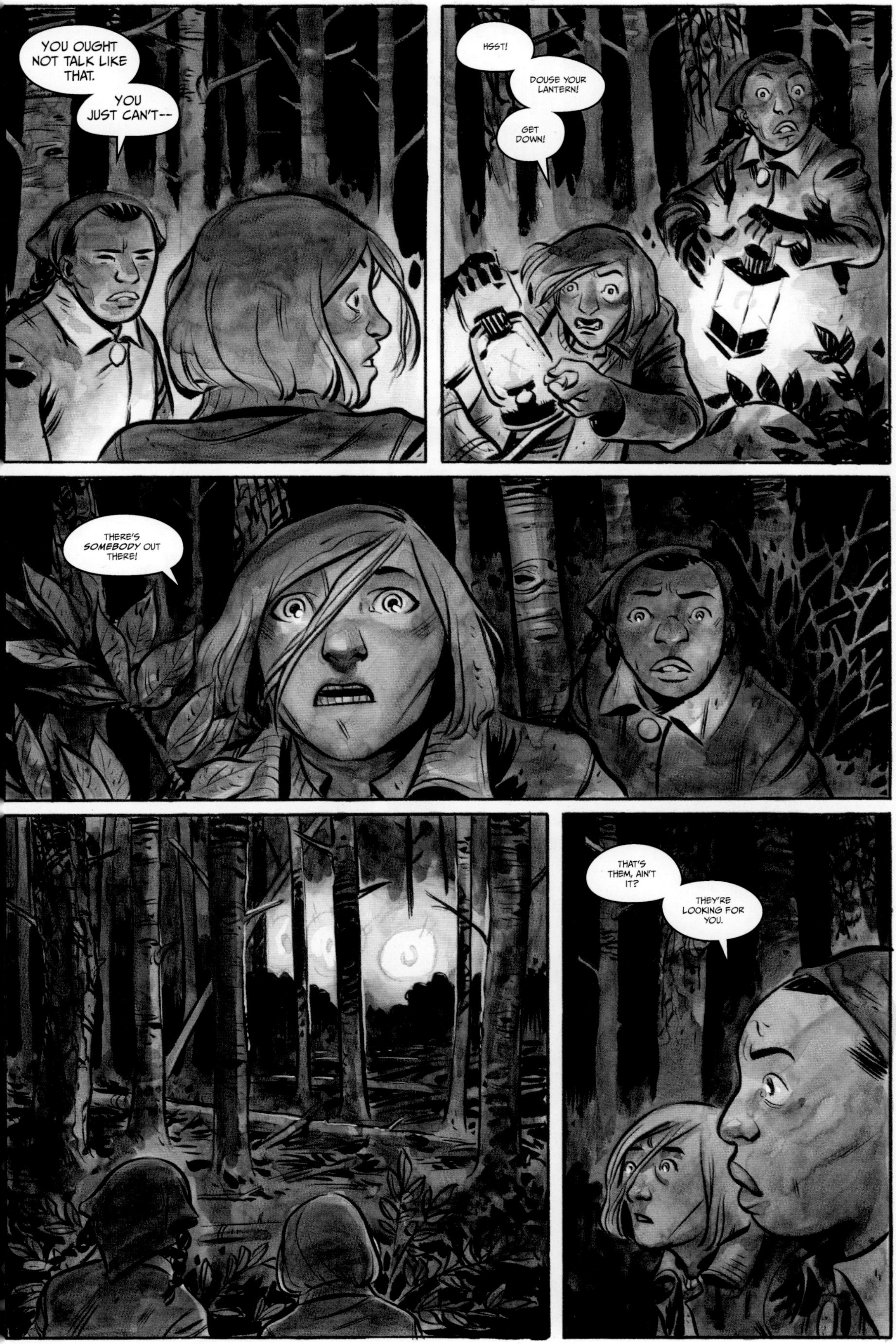
YOU OUGHT NOT TALK LIKE THAT.
YOU JUST CAN'T--
HSST!
DOUSE YOUR LANTERN!
GET DOWN!
THERE'S *SOMEBODY* OUT THERE!
THAT'S THEM, AIN'T IT?
THEY'RE LOOKING FOR YOU.

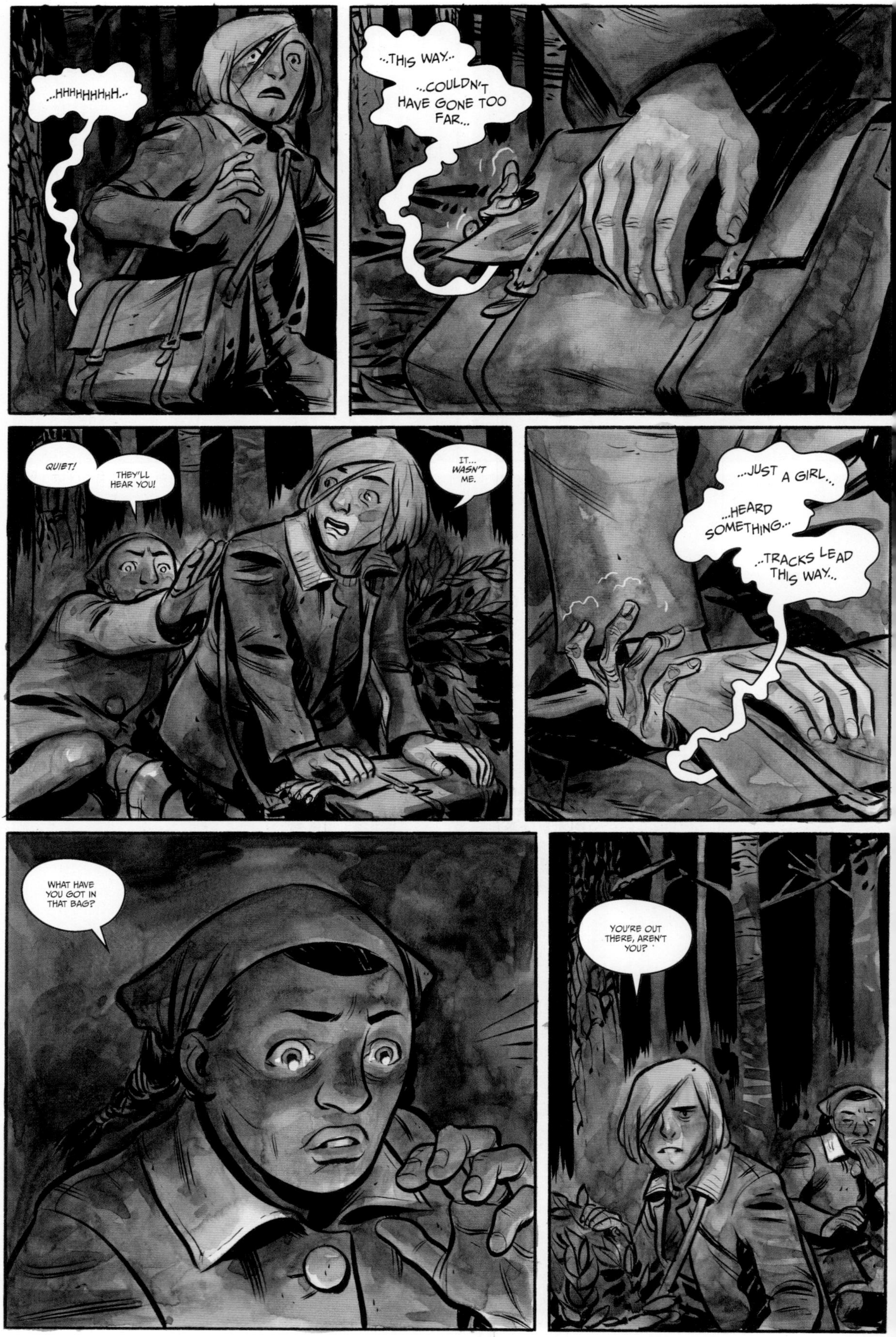
...HHHHHHHHH...
...THIS WAY...
...COULDN'T HAVE GONE TOO FAR...
QUIET!
THEY'LL HEAR YOU!
IT... WASN'T ME.
...JUST A GIRL...
...HEARD SOMETHING...
...TRACKS LEAD THIS WAY...
WHAT HAVE YOU GOT IN THAT BAG?
YOU'RE OUT THERE, AREN'T YOU?

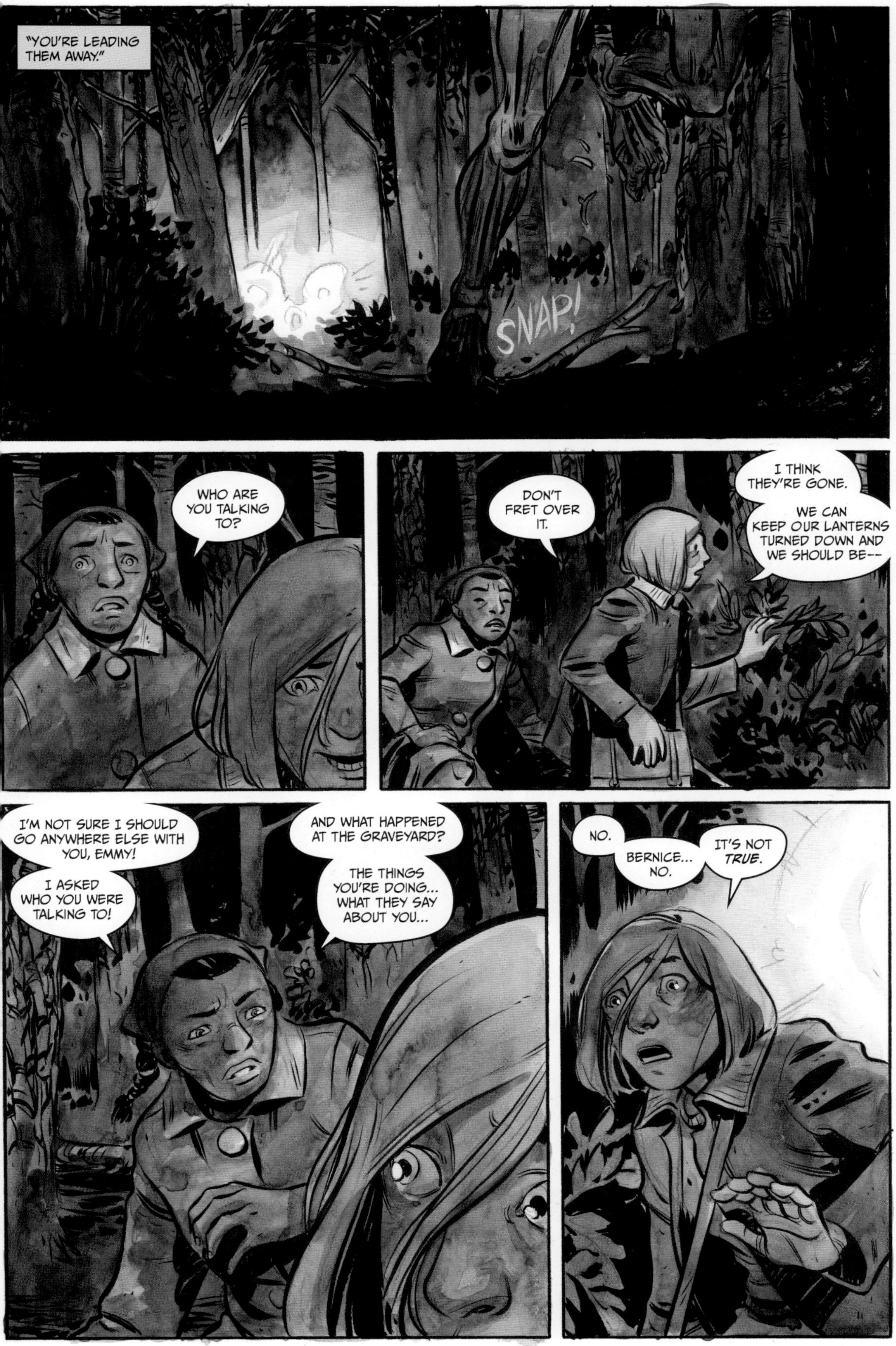
"YOU'RE LEADING THEM AWAY."
SNAP!
WHO ARE YOU TALKING TO?
DON'T FRET OVER IT.
I THINK THEY'RE GONE.
WE CAN KEEP OUR LANTERNS TURNED DOWN AND WE SHOULD BE--
I'M NOT SURE I SHOULD GO ANYWHERE ELSE WITH YOU, EMMY!
I ASKED WHO YOU WERE TALKING TO!
AND WHAT HAPPENED AT THE GRAVEYARD?
THE THINGS YOU'RE DOING... WHAT THEY SAY ABOUT YOU...
NO.
BERNICE... NO.
IT'S NOT *TRUE*.

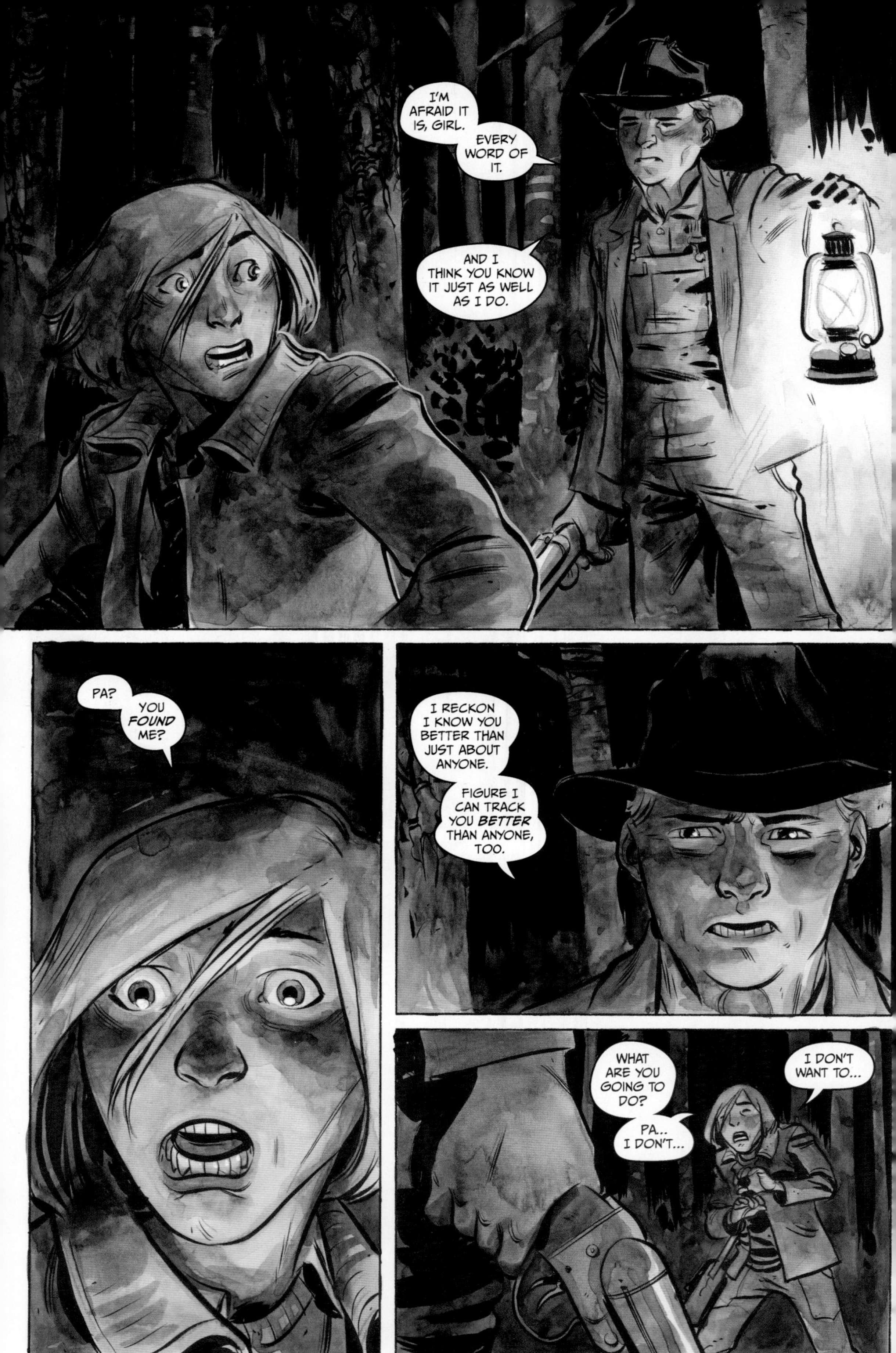
I'M AFRAID IT IS, GIRL.
EVERY WORD OF IT.
AND I THINK YOU KNOW IT JUST AS WELL AS I DO.
PA?
YOU *FOUND* ME?
I RECKON I KNOW YOU BETTER THAN JUST ABOUT ANYONE.
FIGURE I CAN TRACK YOU *BETTER* THAN ANYONE, TOO.
WHAT ARE YOU GOING TO DO?
PA... I DON'T...
I DON'T WANT TO...

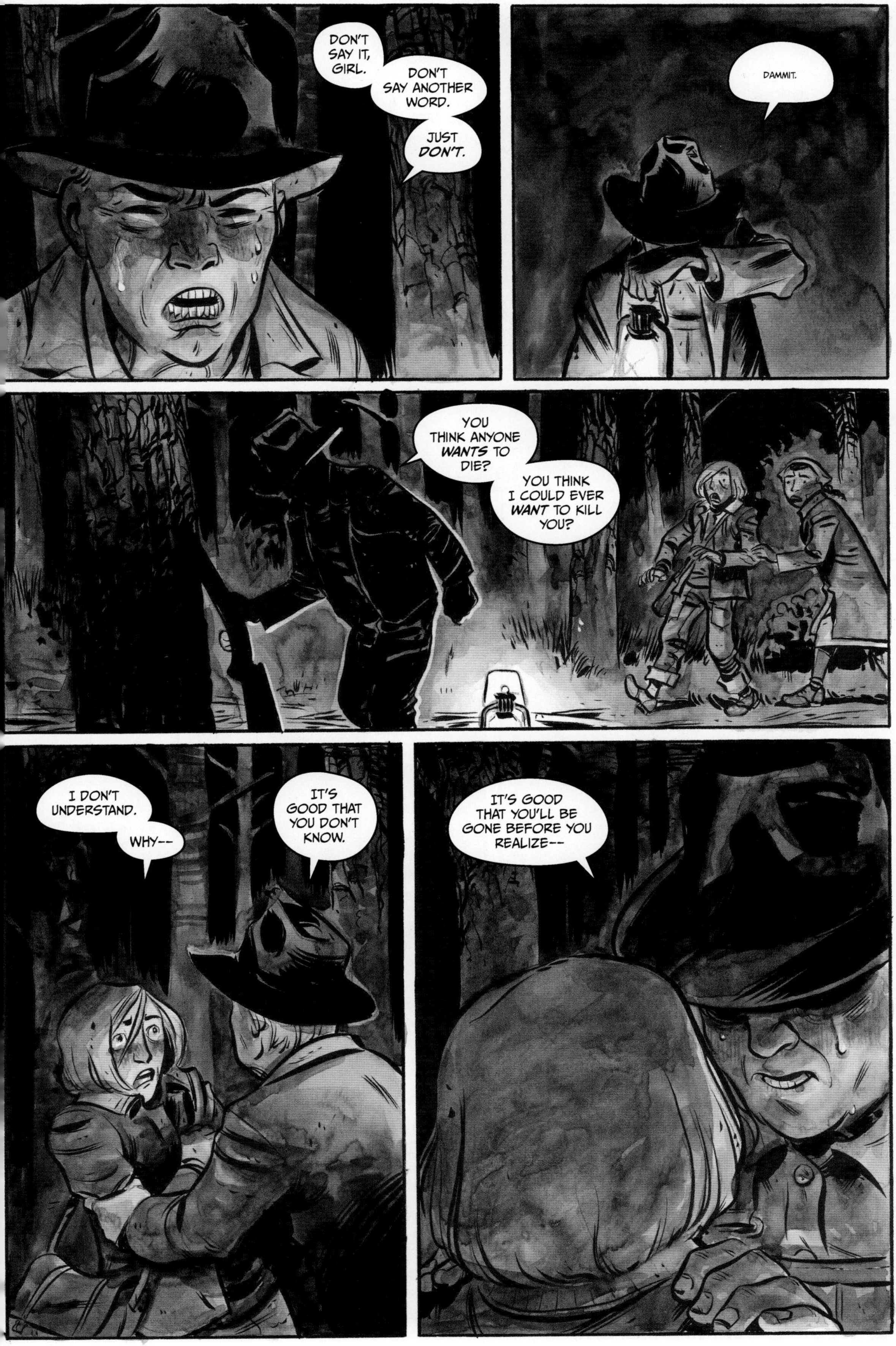
DON'T SAY IT, GIRL.
DON'T SAY ANOTHER WORD.
JUST *DON'T.*
DAMMIT.
YOU THINK ANYONE *WANTS* TO DIE?
YOU THINK I COULD EVER *WANT* TO KILL YOU?
I DON'T UNDERSTAND.
WHY--
IT'S GOOD THAT YOU DON'T KNOW.
IT'S GOOD THAT YOU'LL BE GONE BEFORE YOU REALIZE--

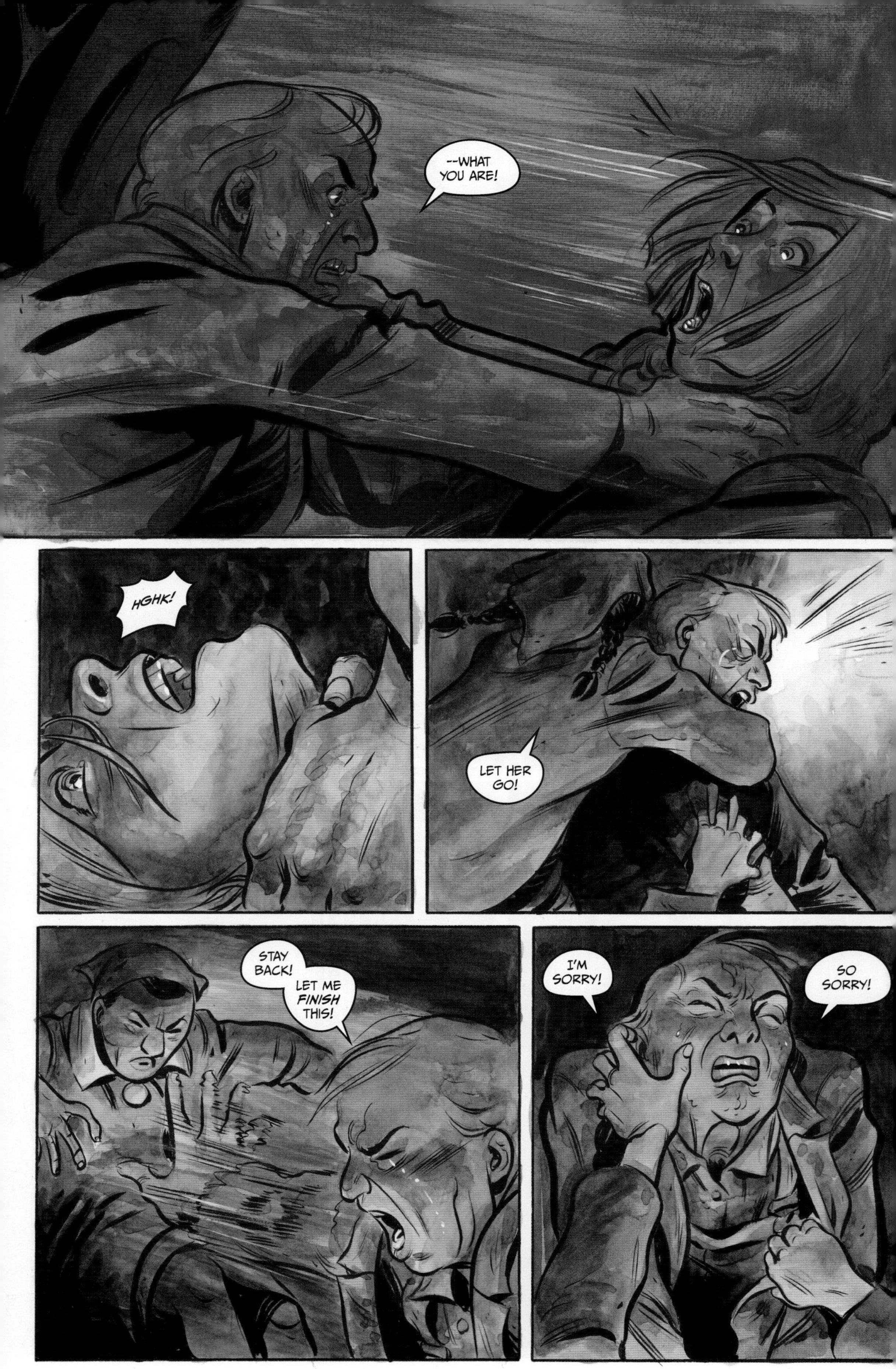

--WHAT YOU ARE!
HGHK!
LET HER GO!
STAY BACK!
LET ME *FINISH* THIS!
I'M SORRY!
SO SORRY!

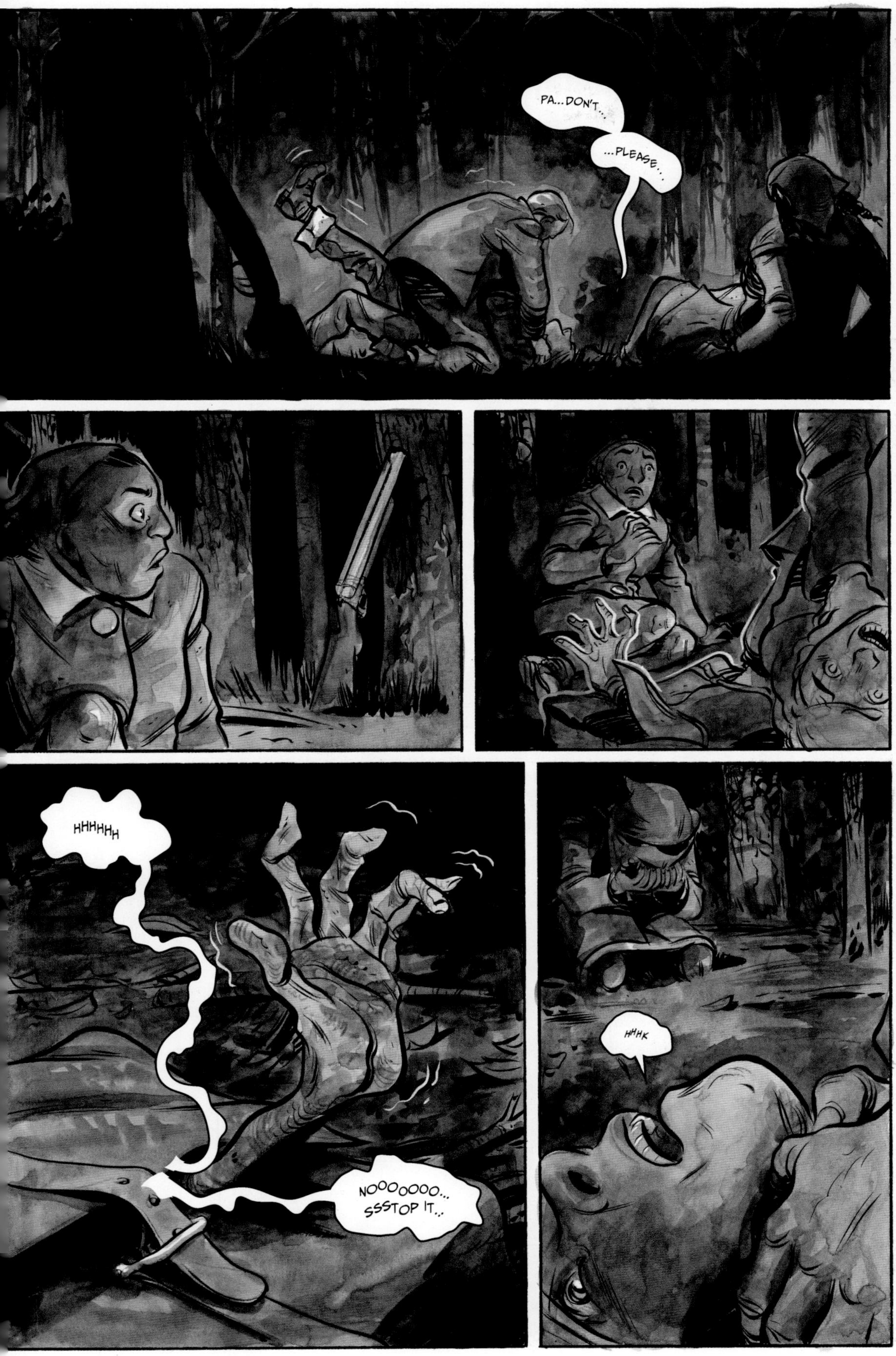
PA...DON'T...
...PLEASE...
HHHHHH
NOOOOOOO...
SSSTOP IT...
HHHK

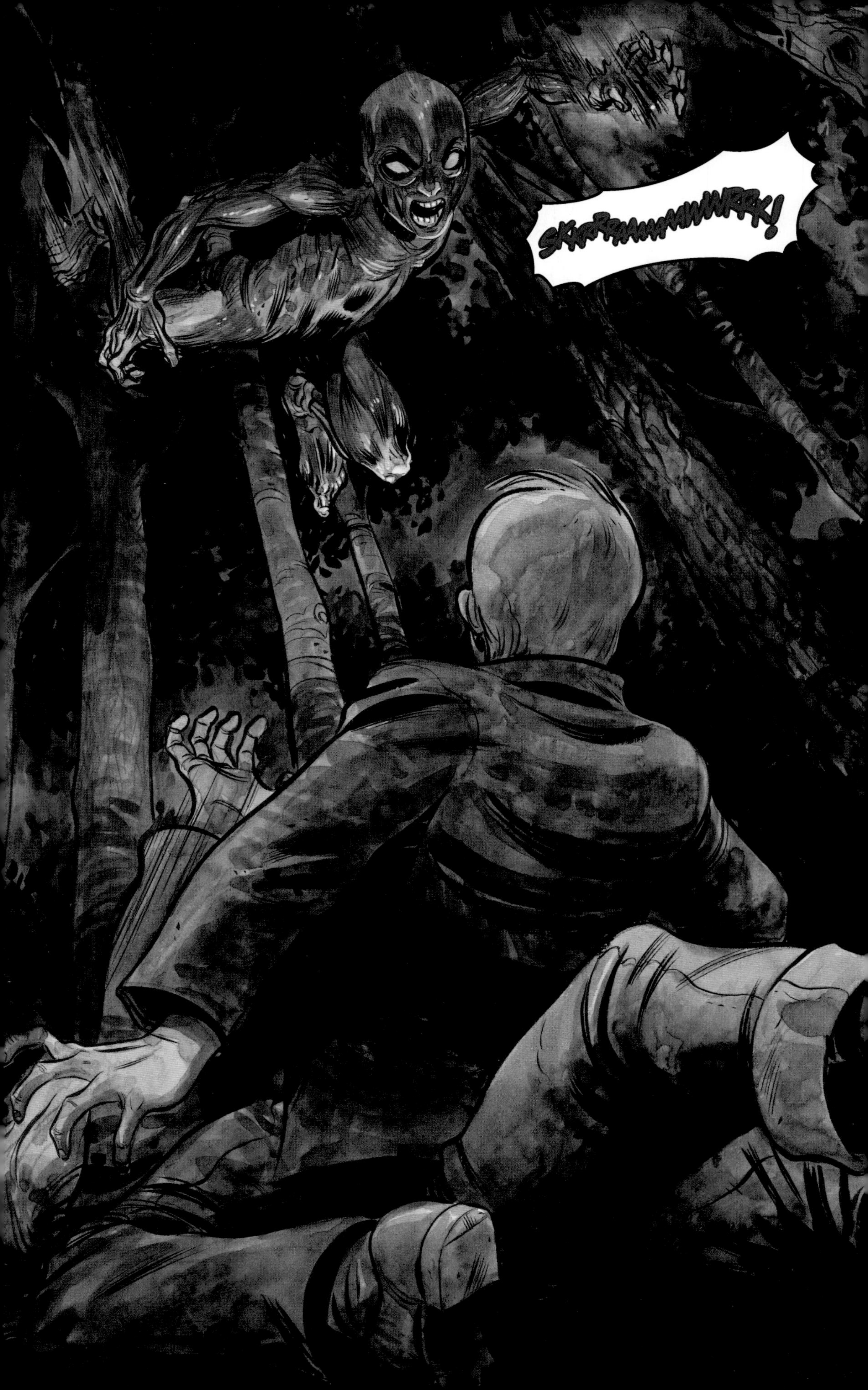
SKKRRAAAAAAWWRRK!

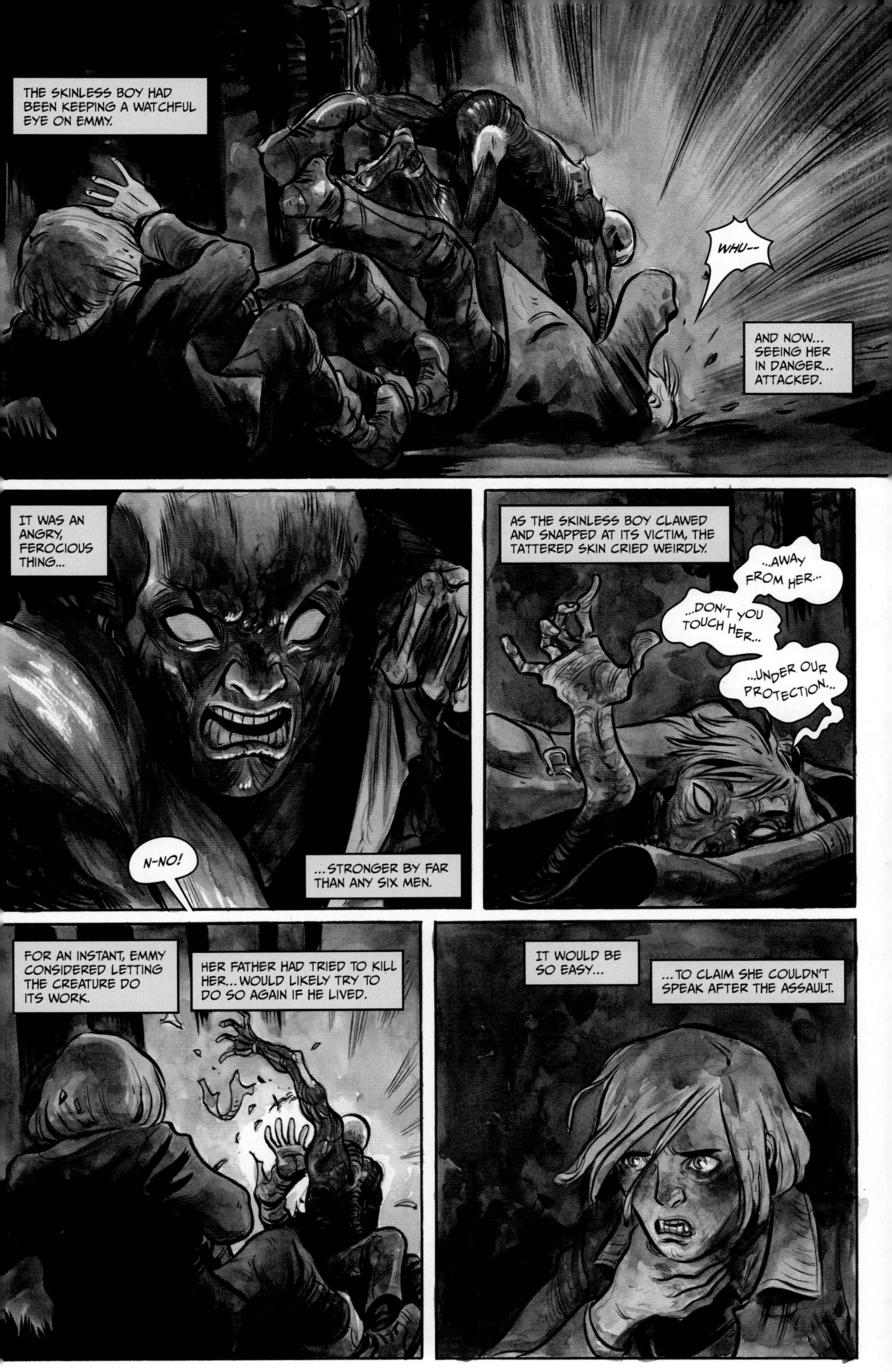
THE SKINLESS BOY HAD BEEN KEEPING A WATCHFUL EYE ON EMMY.
WHU--
AND NOW... SEEING HER IN DANGER... ATTACKED.
IT WAS AN ANGRY, FEROCIOUS THING...
N-NO!
...STRONGER BY FAR THAN ANY SIX MEN.
AS THE SKINLESS BOY CLAWED AND SNAPPED AT ITS VICTIM, THE TATTERED SKIN CRIED WEIRDLY.
...AWAY FROM HER...
...DON'T YOU TOUCH HER...
...UNDER OUR PROTECTION...
FOR AN INSTANT, EMMY CONSIDERED LETTING THE CREATURE DO ITS WORK.
HER FATHER HAD TRIED TO KILL HER... WOULD LIKELY TRY TO DO SO AGAIN IF HE LIVED.
IT WOULD BE SO EASY...
...TO CLAIM SHE COULDN'T SPEAK AFTER THE ASSAULT.

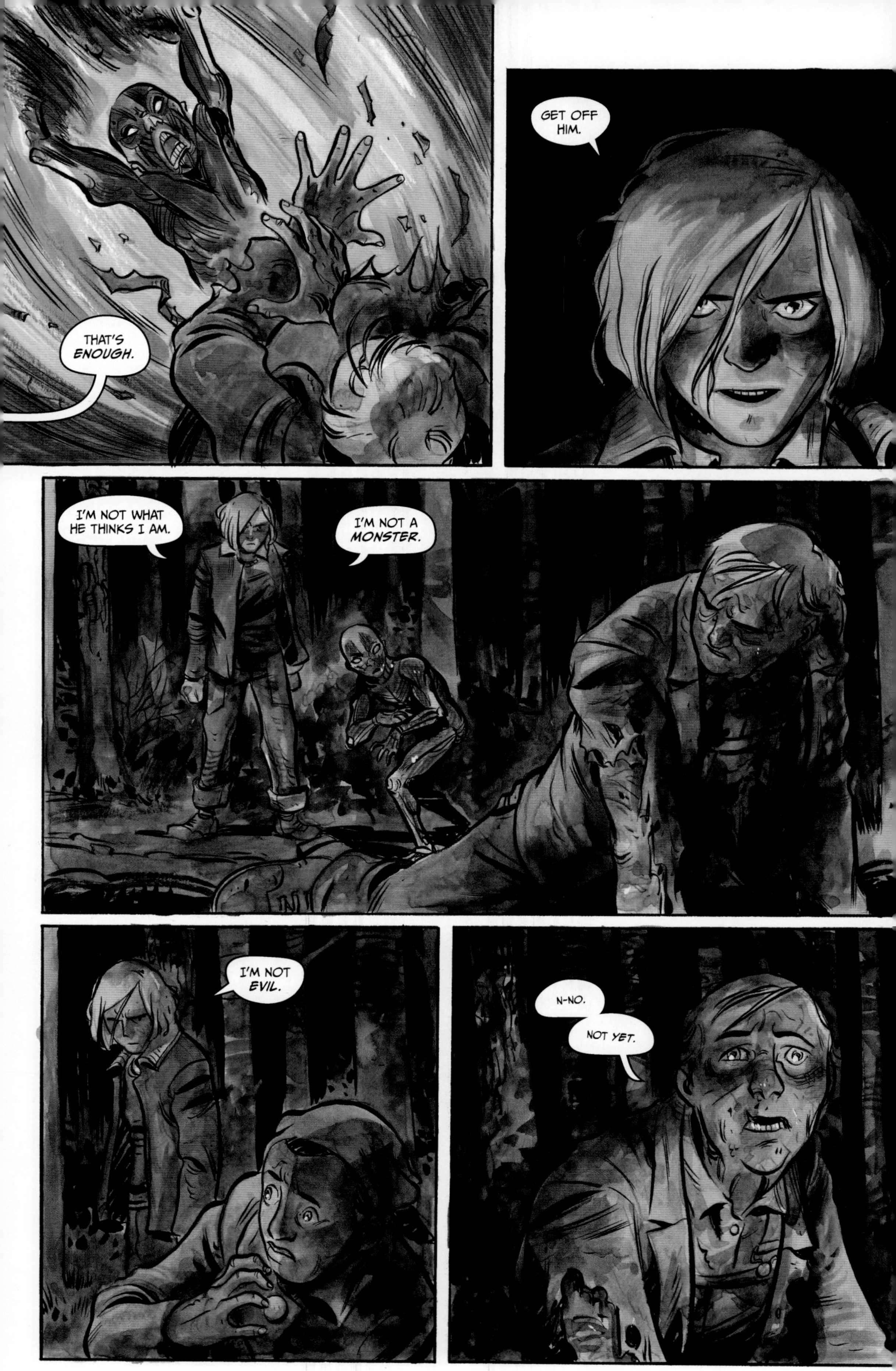
THAT'S ENOUGH.
GET OFF HIM.
I'M NOT WHAT HE THINKS I AM.
I'M NOT A MONSTER.
I'M NOT EVIL.
N-NO.
NOT YET.

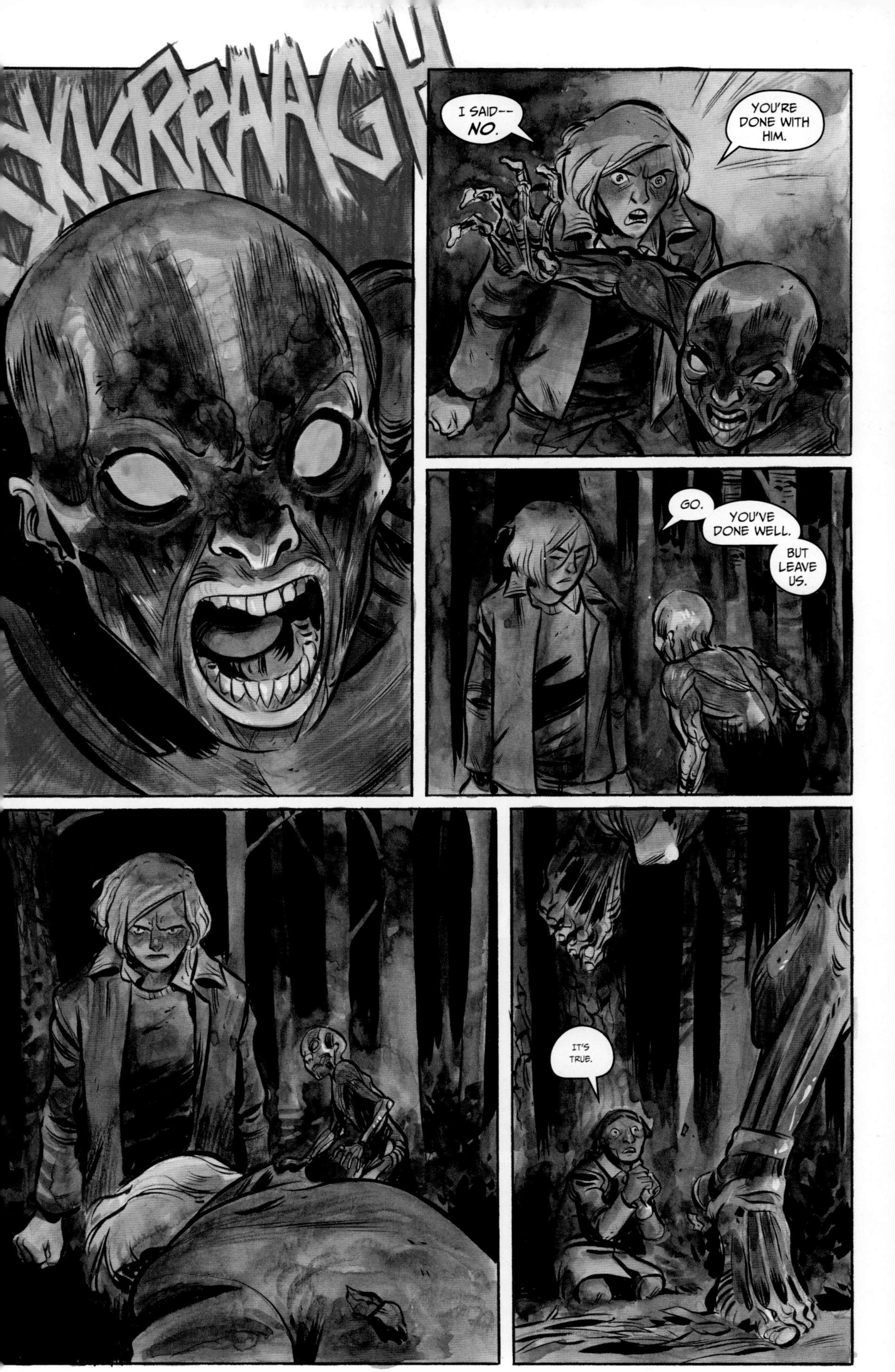
KKRRAAGH
I SAID-- NO.
YOU'RE DONE WITH HIM.
GO.
YOU'VE DONE WELL.
BUT LEAVE US.
IT'S TRUE.

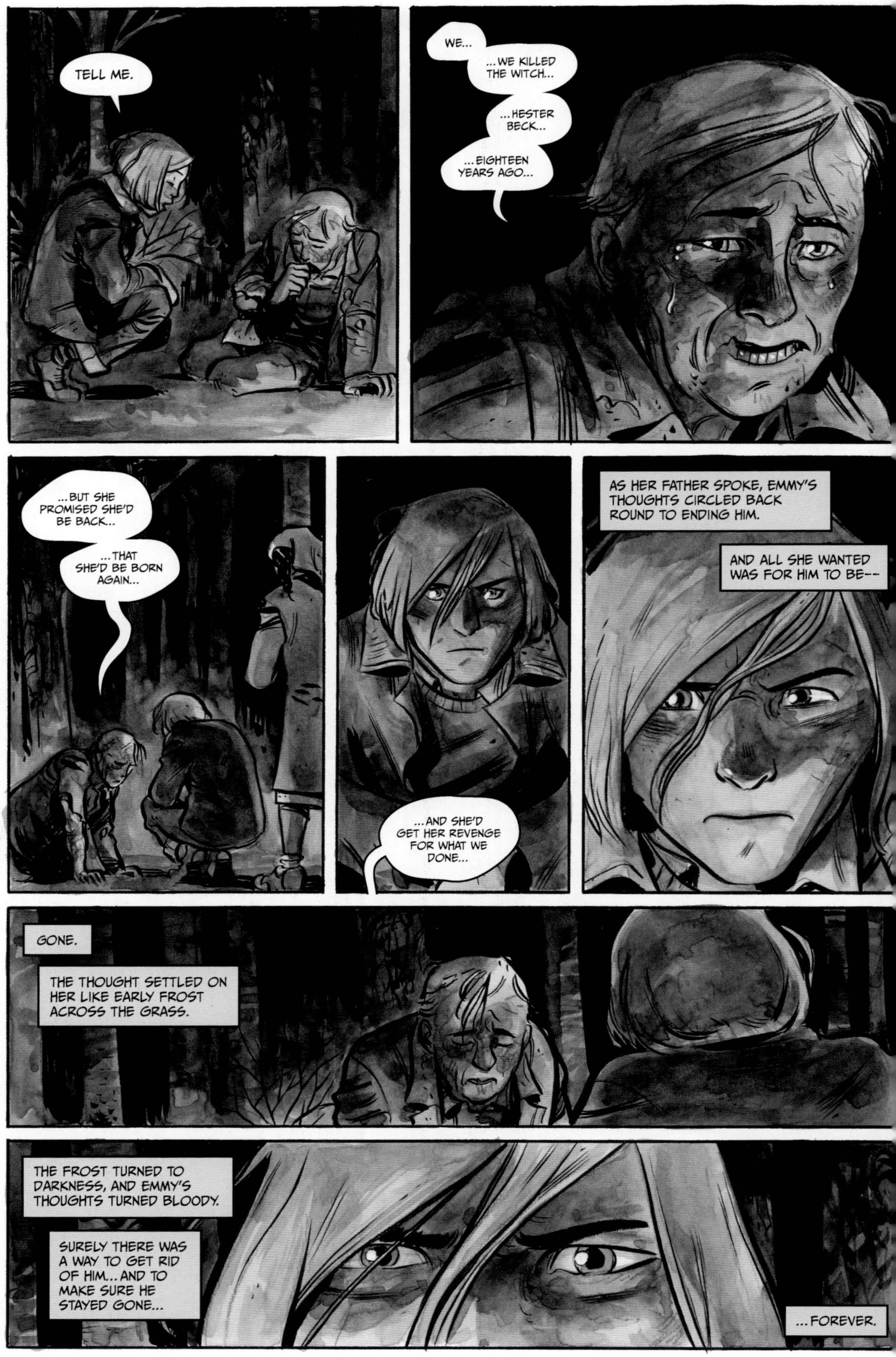

TELL ME.
WE...
...WE KILLED THE WITCH...
...HESTER BECK...
...EIGHTEEN YEARS AGO...
...BUT SHE PROMISED SHE'D BE BACK...
...THAT SHE'D BE BORN AGAIN...
...AND SHE'D GET HER REVENGE FOR WHAT WE DONE...
AS HER FATHER SPOKE, EMMY'S THOUGHTS CIRCLED BACK ROUND TO ENDING HIM.
AND ALL SHE WANTED WAS FOR HIM TO BE--
GONE.
THE THOUGHT SETTLED ON HER LIKE EARLY FROST ACROSS THE GRASS.
THE FROST TURNED TO DARKNESS, AND EMMY'S THOUGHTS TURNED BLOODY.
SURELY THERE WAS A WAY TO GET RID OF HIM...AND TO MAKE SURE HE STAYED GONE...
...FOREVER.

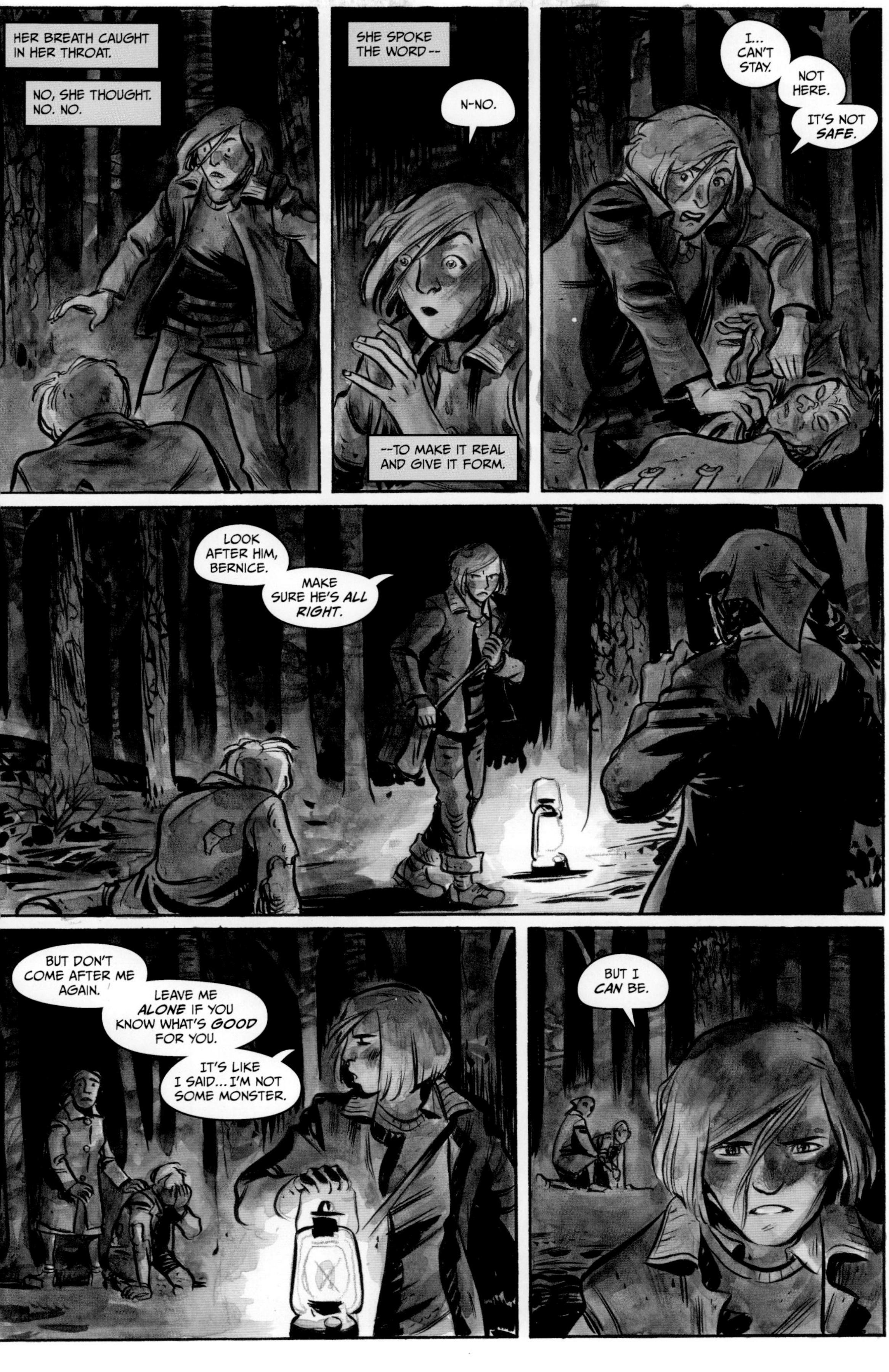

HER BREATH CAUGHT IN HER THROAT.
NO, SHE THOUGHT. NO. NO.
SHE SPOKE THE WORD--
N-NO.
--TO MAKE IT REAL AND GIVE IT FORM.
I... CAN'T STAY.
NOT HERE.
IT'S NOT SAFE.
LOOK AFTER HIM, BERNICE.
MAKE SURE HE'S ALL RIGHT.
BUT DON'T COME AFTER ME AGAIN.
LEAVE ME ALONE IF YOU KNOW WHAT'S GOOD FOR YOU.
IT'S LIKE I SAID... I'M NOT SOME MONSTER.
BUT I CAN BE.

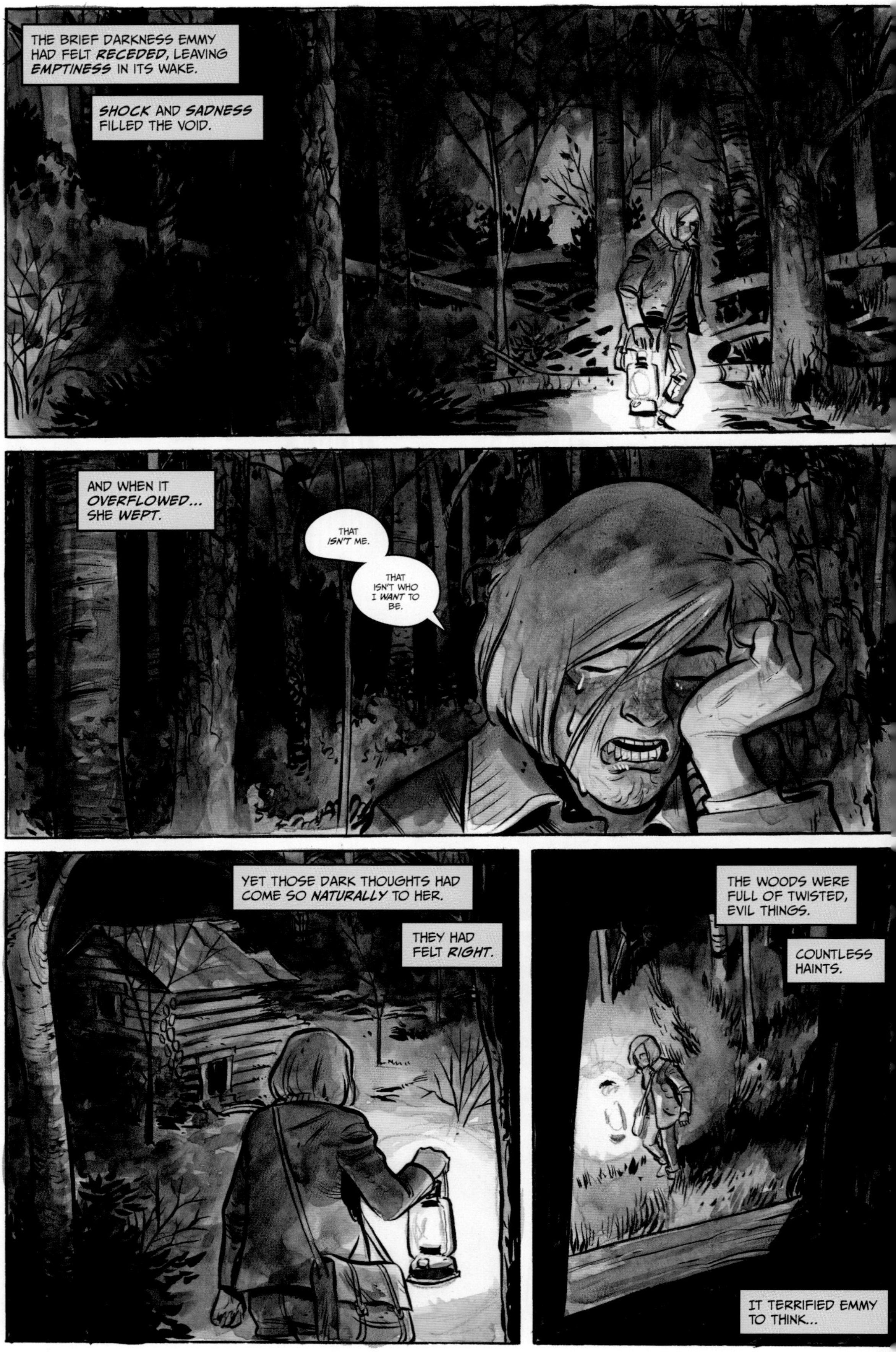
THE BRIEF DARKNESS EMMY HAD FELT *RECEDED*, LEAVING *EMPTINESS* IN ITS WAKE.
SHOCK AND *SADNESS* FILLED THE VOID.
AND WHEN IT *OVERFLOWED*... SHE *WEPT*.
THAT *ISN'T* ME.
THAT ISN'T WHO I *WANT* TO BE.
YET THOSE DARK THOUGHTS HAD COME SO *NATURALLY* TO HER.
THEY HAD FELT *RIGHT*.
THE WOODS WERE FULL OF TWISTED, EVIL THINGS.
COUNTLESS HAINTS.
IT TERRIFIED EMMY TO THINK...

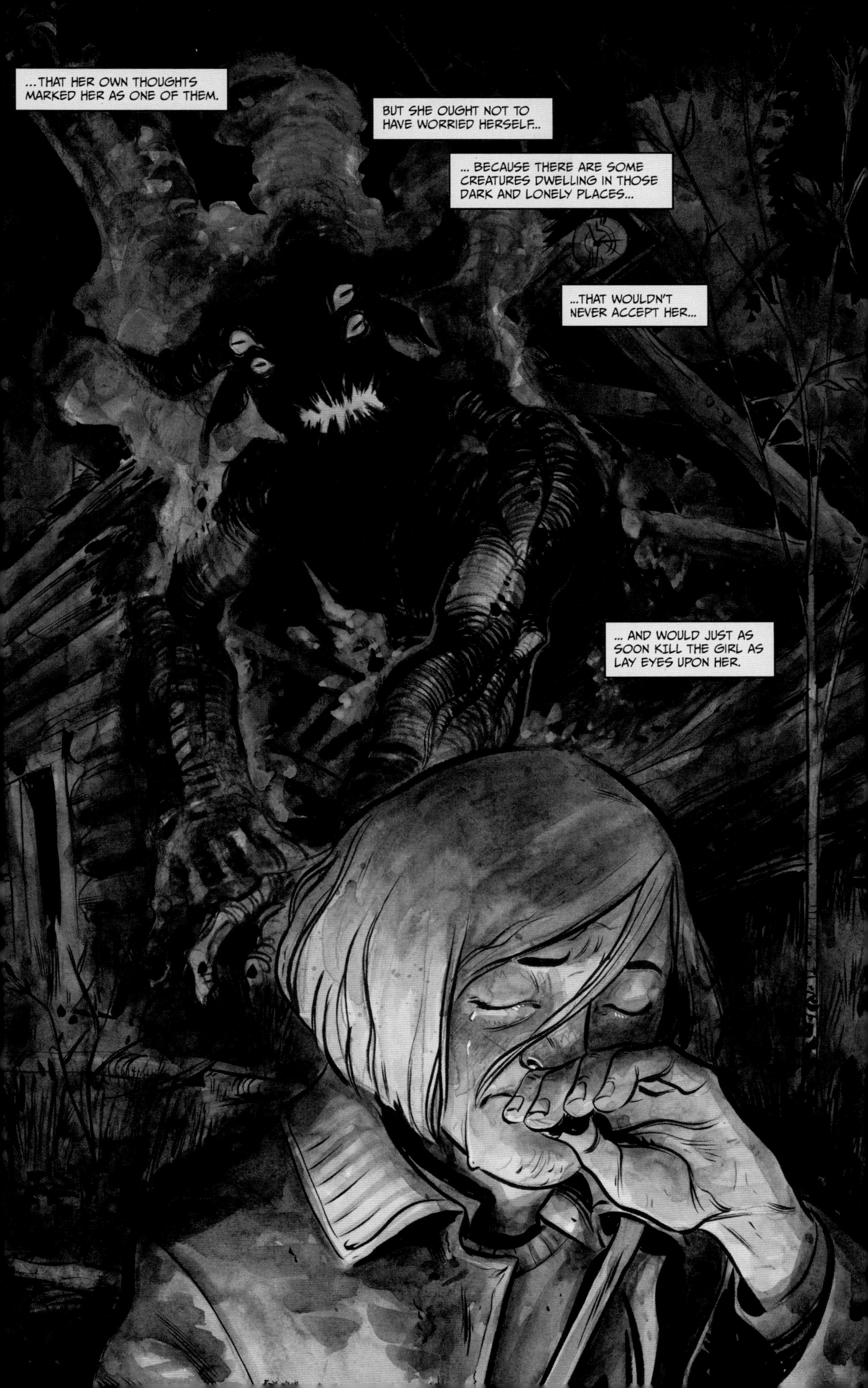
...THAT HER OWN THOUGHTS MARKED HER AS ONE OF THEM.
BUT SHE OUGHT NOT TO HAVE WORRIED HERSELF...
... BECAUSE THERE ARE SOME CREATURES DWELLING IN THOSE DARK AND LONELY PLACES...
...THAT WOULDN'T NEVER ACCEPT HER...
... AND WOULD JUST AS SOON KILL THE GIRL AS LAY EYES UPON HER.

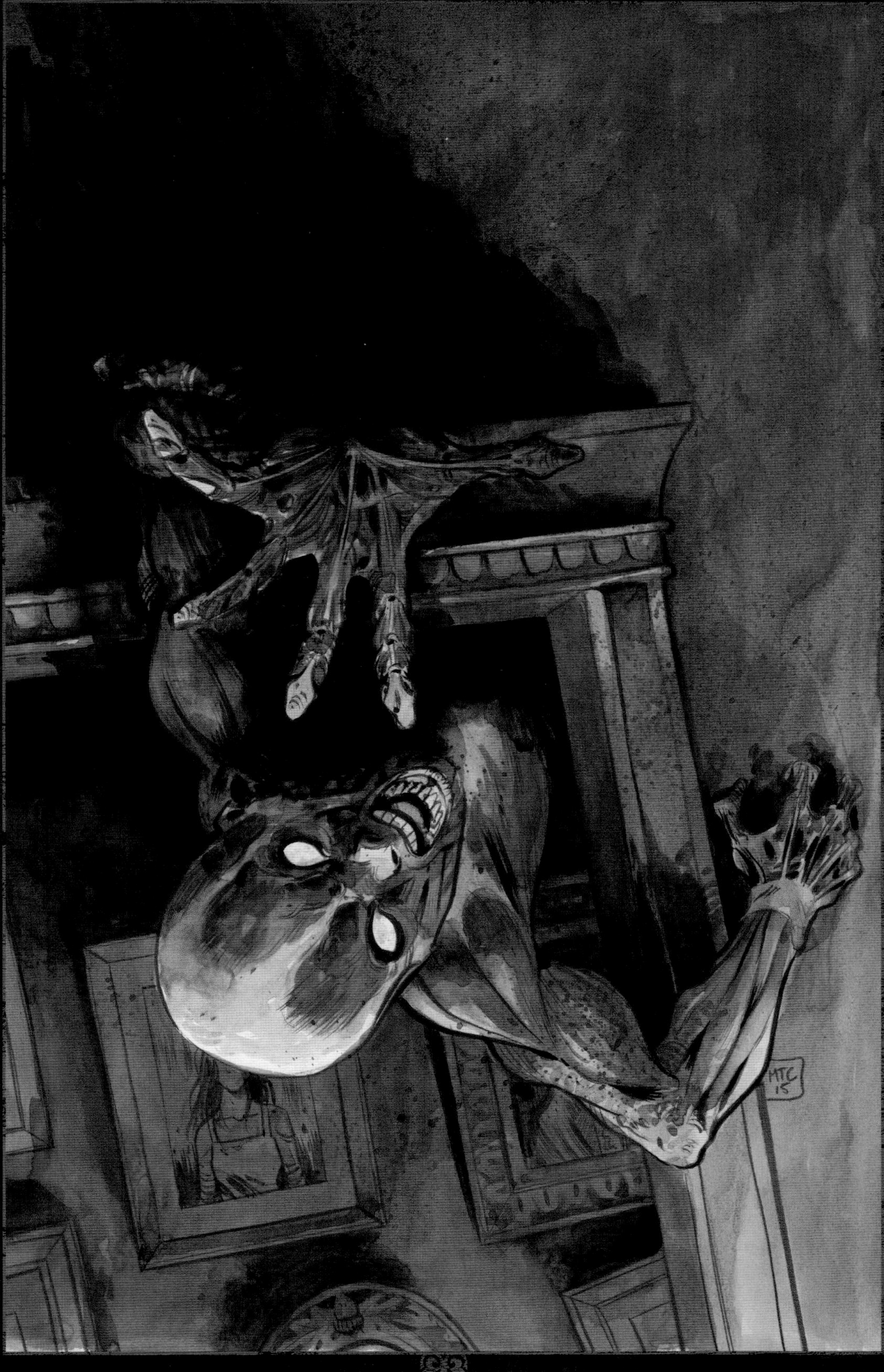
MTC 15

FOUR

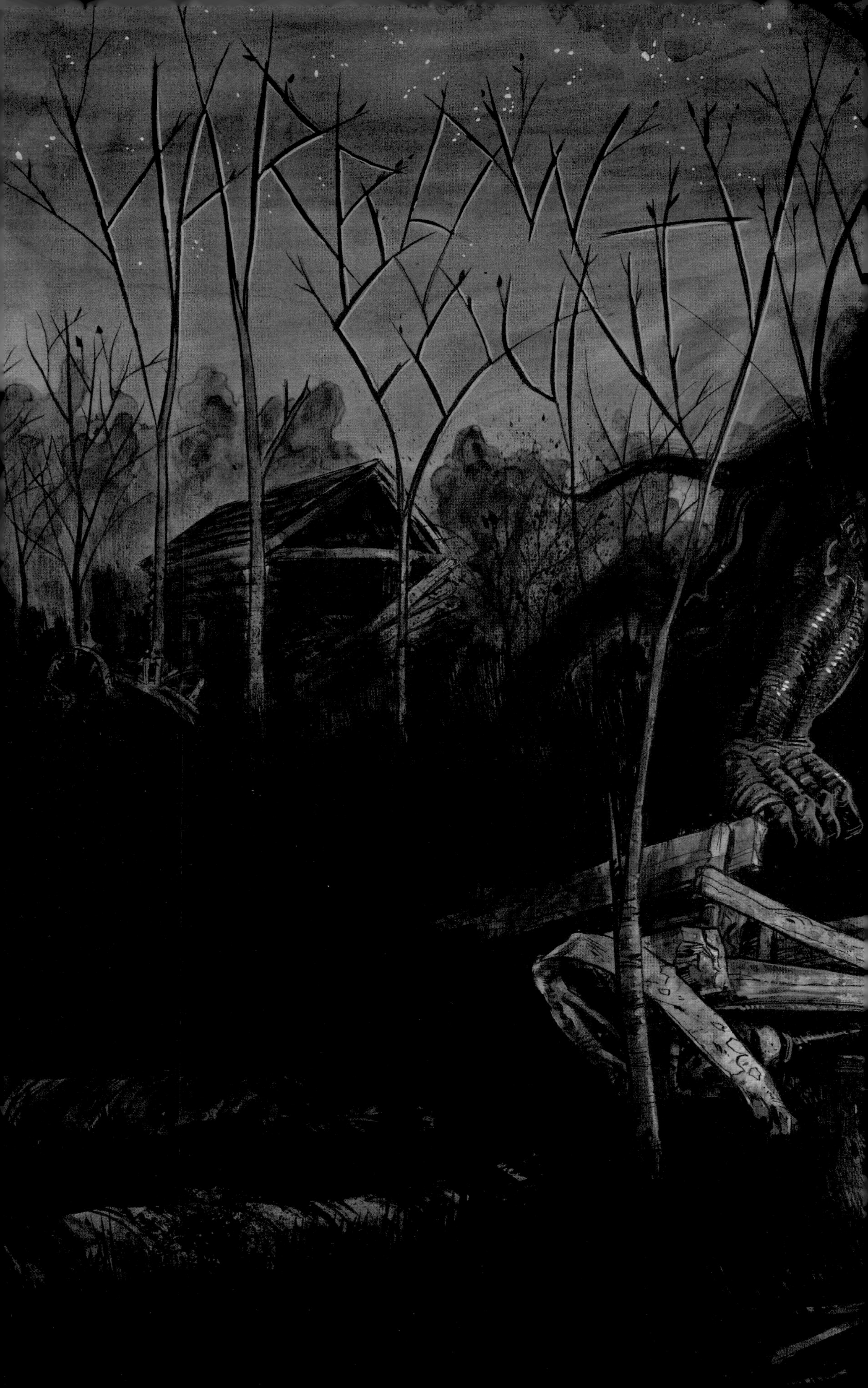

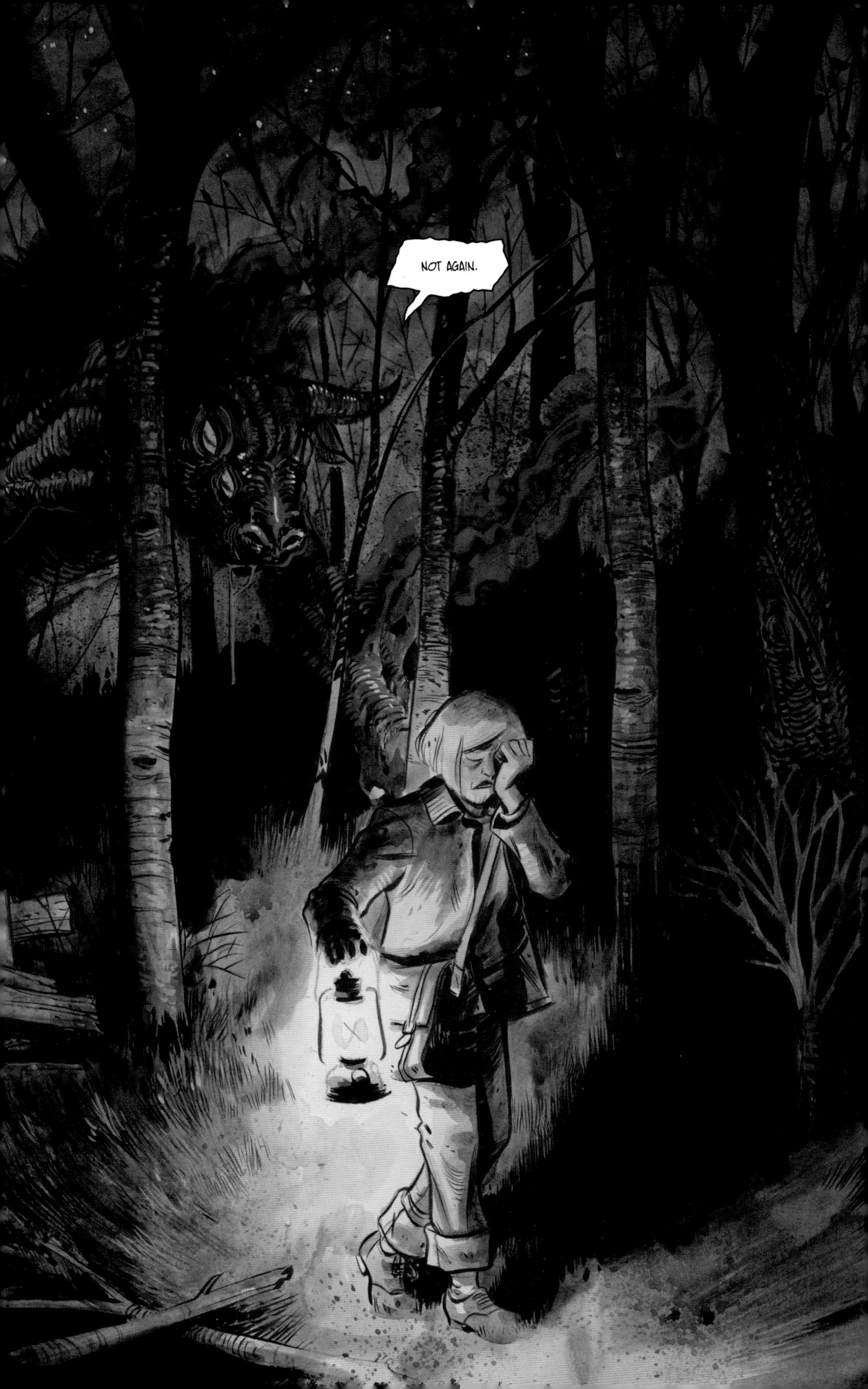
NOT AGAIN.

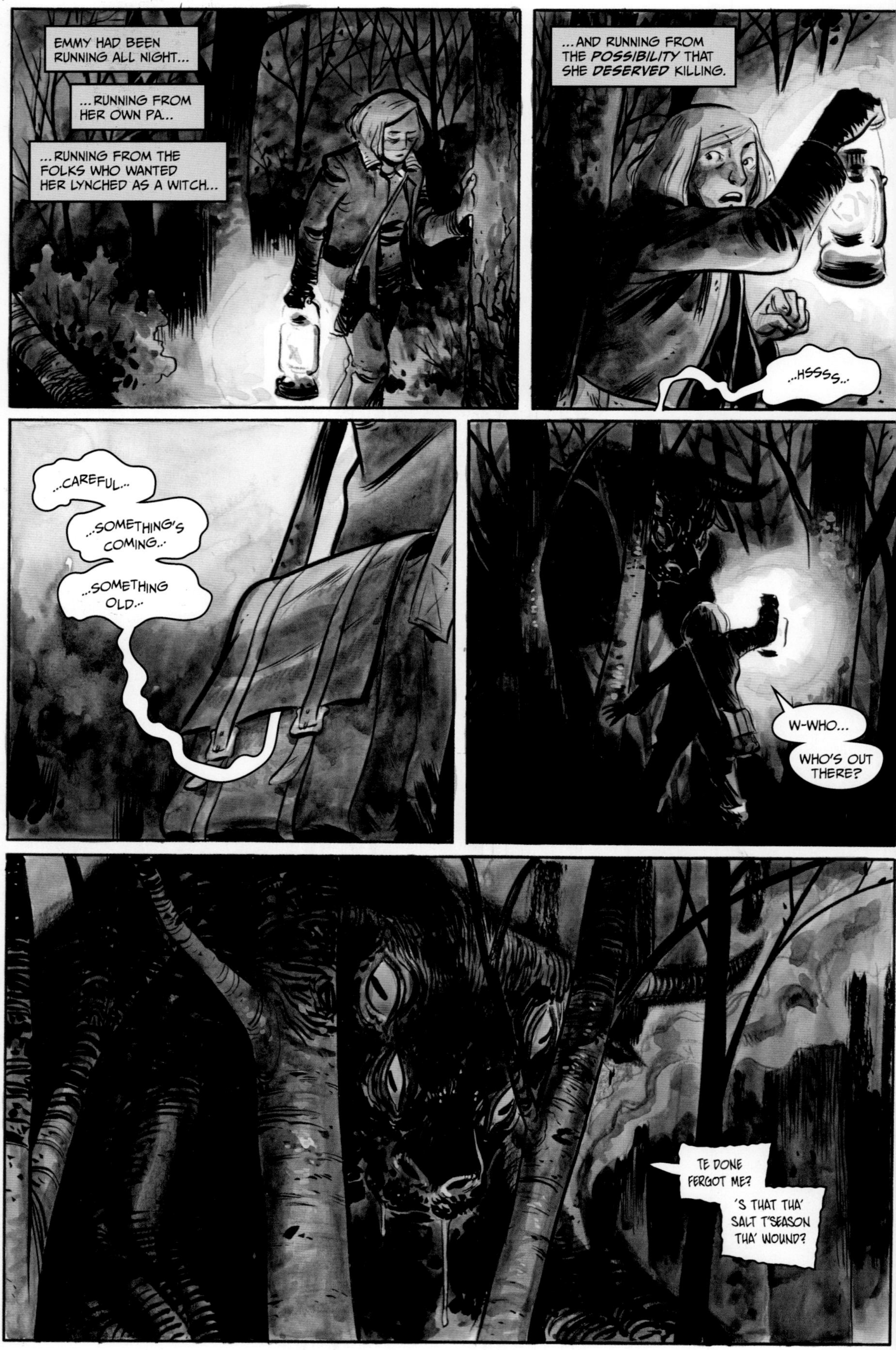
EMMY HAD BEEN RUNNING ALL NIGHT...
...RUNNING FROM HER OWN PA...
...RUNNING FROM THE FOLKS WHO WANTED HER LYNCHED AS A WITCH...
...AND RUNNING FROM THE *POSSIBILITY* THAT SHE *DESERVED* KILLING.
...HSSSS...
...CAREFUL...
...SOMETHING'S COMING...
...SOMETHING OLD...
W-WHO...
WHO'S OUT THERE?
YE DONE FERGOT ME?
'S THAT THA' SALT T'SEASON THA' WOUND?

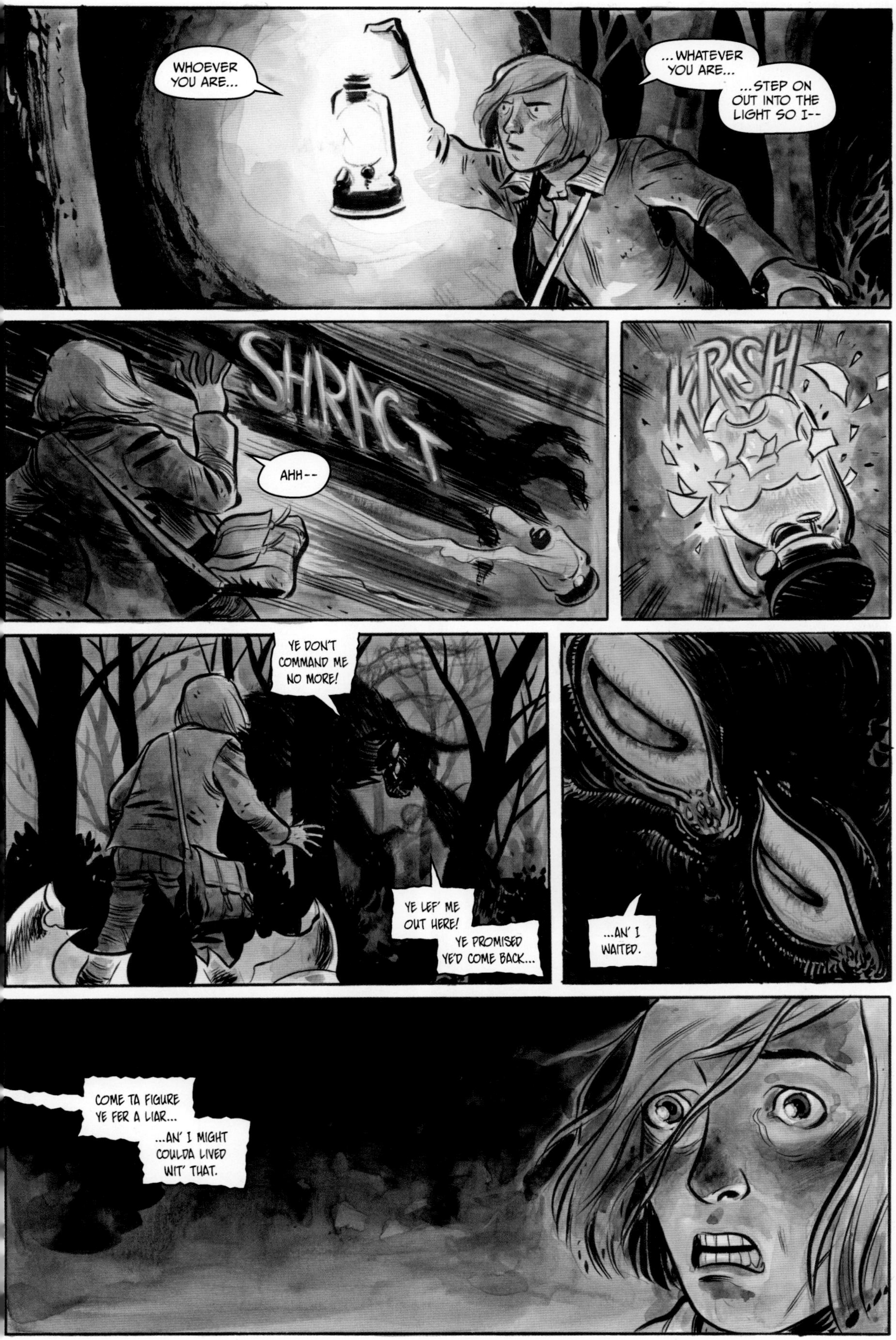
WHOEVER YOU ARE...
...WHATEVER YOU ARE...
...STEP ON OUT INTO THE LIGHT SO I--
SHRACT
AHH--
KRSH
YE DON'T COMMAND ME NO MORE!
YE LEF' ME OUT HERE!
YE PROMISED YE'D COME BACK...
...AN' I WAITED.
COME TA FIGURE YE FER A LIAR...
...AN' I MIGHT COULDA LIVED WIT' THAT.

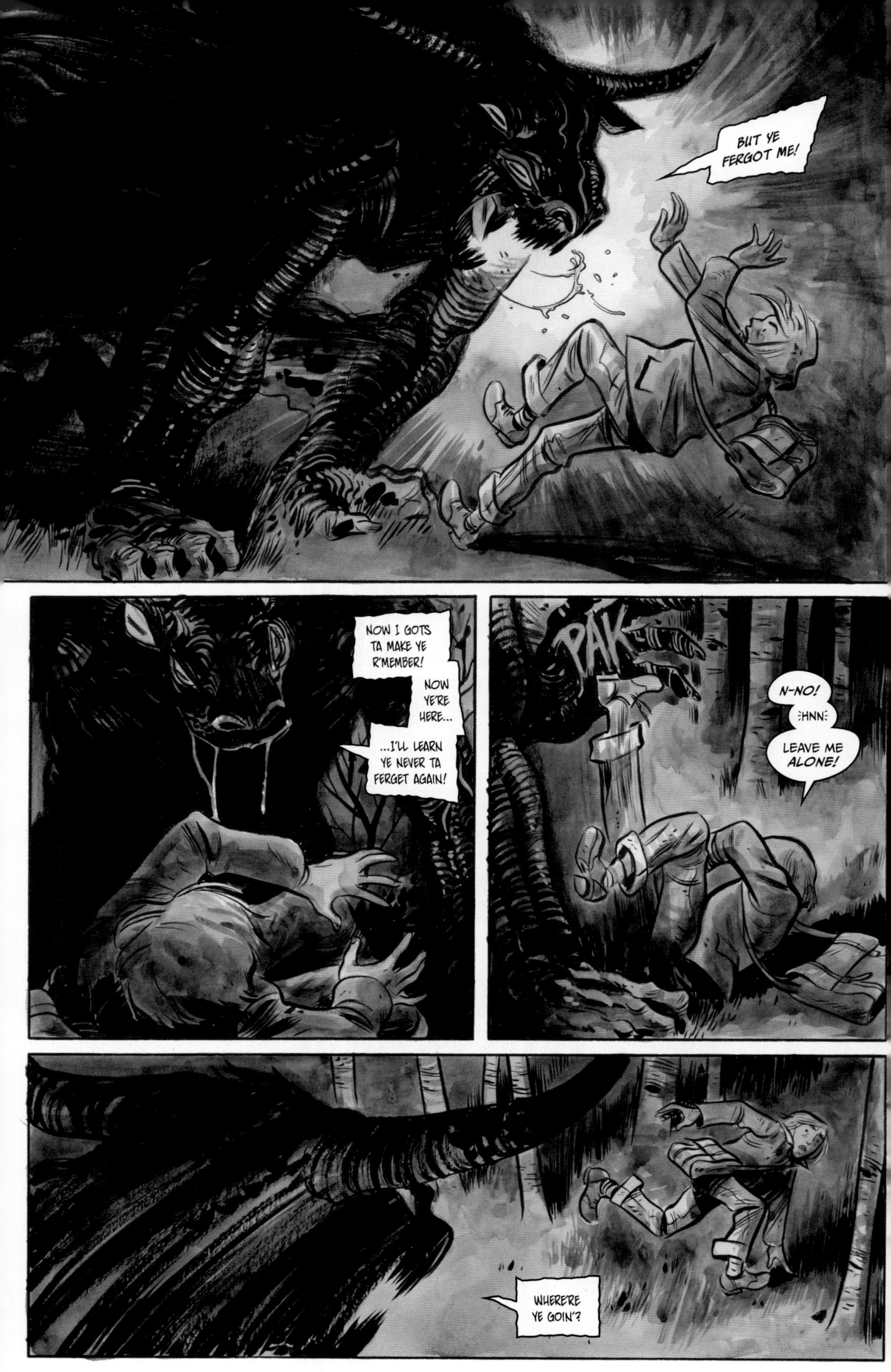
BUT YE FERGOT ME!
NOW I GOTS TA MAKE YE R'MEMBER!
NOW YE'RE HERE...
...I'LL LEARN YE NEVER TA FERGET AGAIN!
PAK
N-NO!
HNN
LEAVE ME ALONE!
WHERE'RE YE GOIN'?

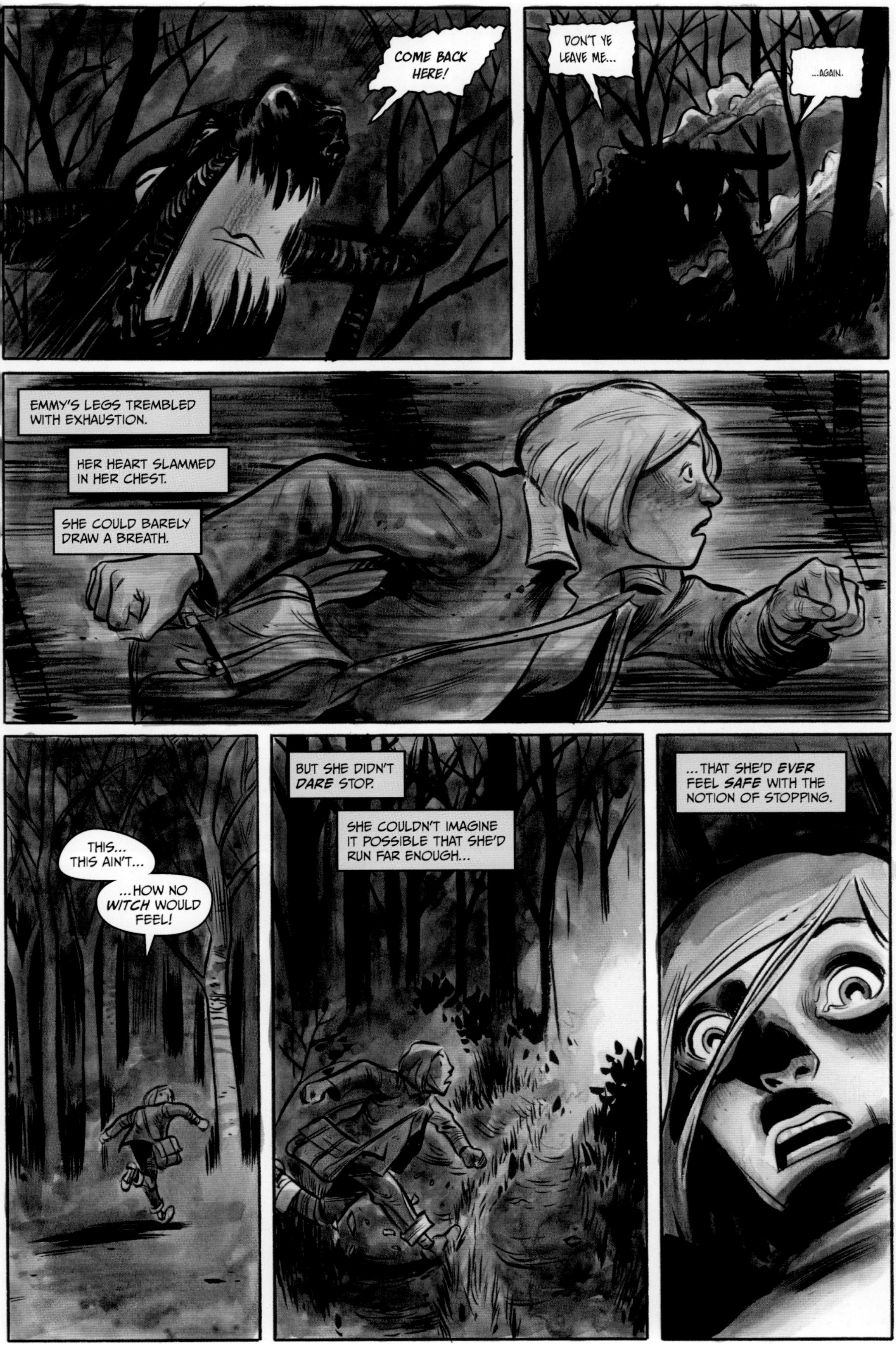
COME BACK HERE!
DON'T YE LEAVE ME...
...AGAIN.
EMMY'S LEGS TREMBLED WITH EXHAUSTION.
HER HEART SLAMMED IN HER CHEST.
SHE COULD BARELY DRAW A BREATH.
THIS... THIS AIN'T...
...HOW NO WITCH WOULD FEEL!
BUT SHE DIDN'T DARE STOP.
SHE COULDN'T IMAGINE IT POSSIBLE THAT SHE'D RUN FAR ENOUGH...
...THAT SHE'D EVER FEEL SAFE WITH THE NOTION OF STOPPING.

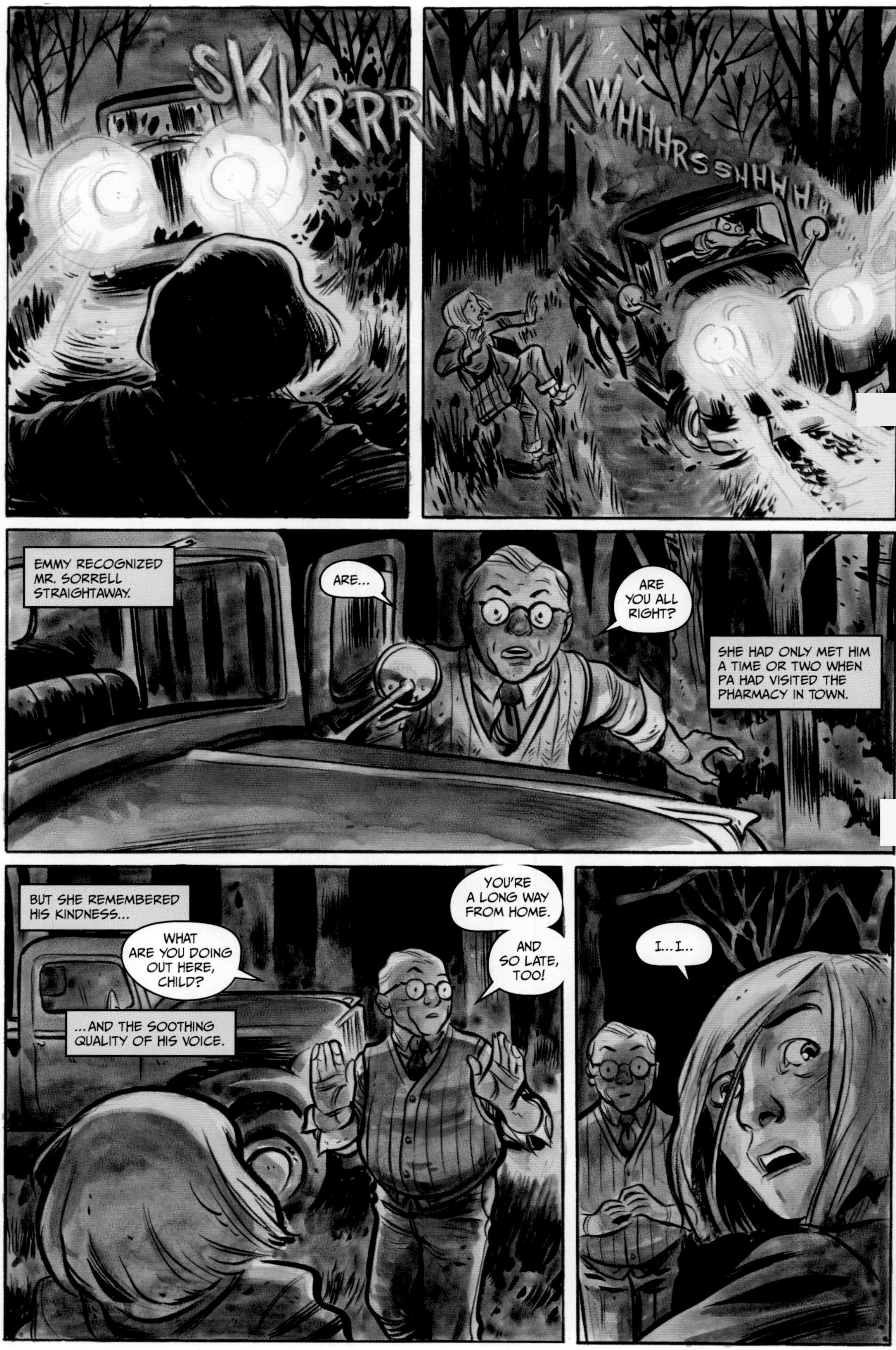
SKKRRRNNNNKWHHHRSSHHHH
EMMY RECOGNIZED MR. SORRELL STRAIGHTAWAY.
ARE...
ARE YOU ALL RIGHT?
SHE HAD ONLY MET HIM A TIME OR TWO WHEN PA HAD VISITED THE PHARMACY IN TOWN.
BUT SHE REMEMBERED HIS KINDNESS...
WHAT ARE YOU DOING OUT HERE, CHILD?
...AND THE SOOTHING QUALITY OF HIS VOICE.
YOU'RE A LONG WAY FROM HOME.
AND SO LATE, TOO!
I...I...

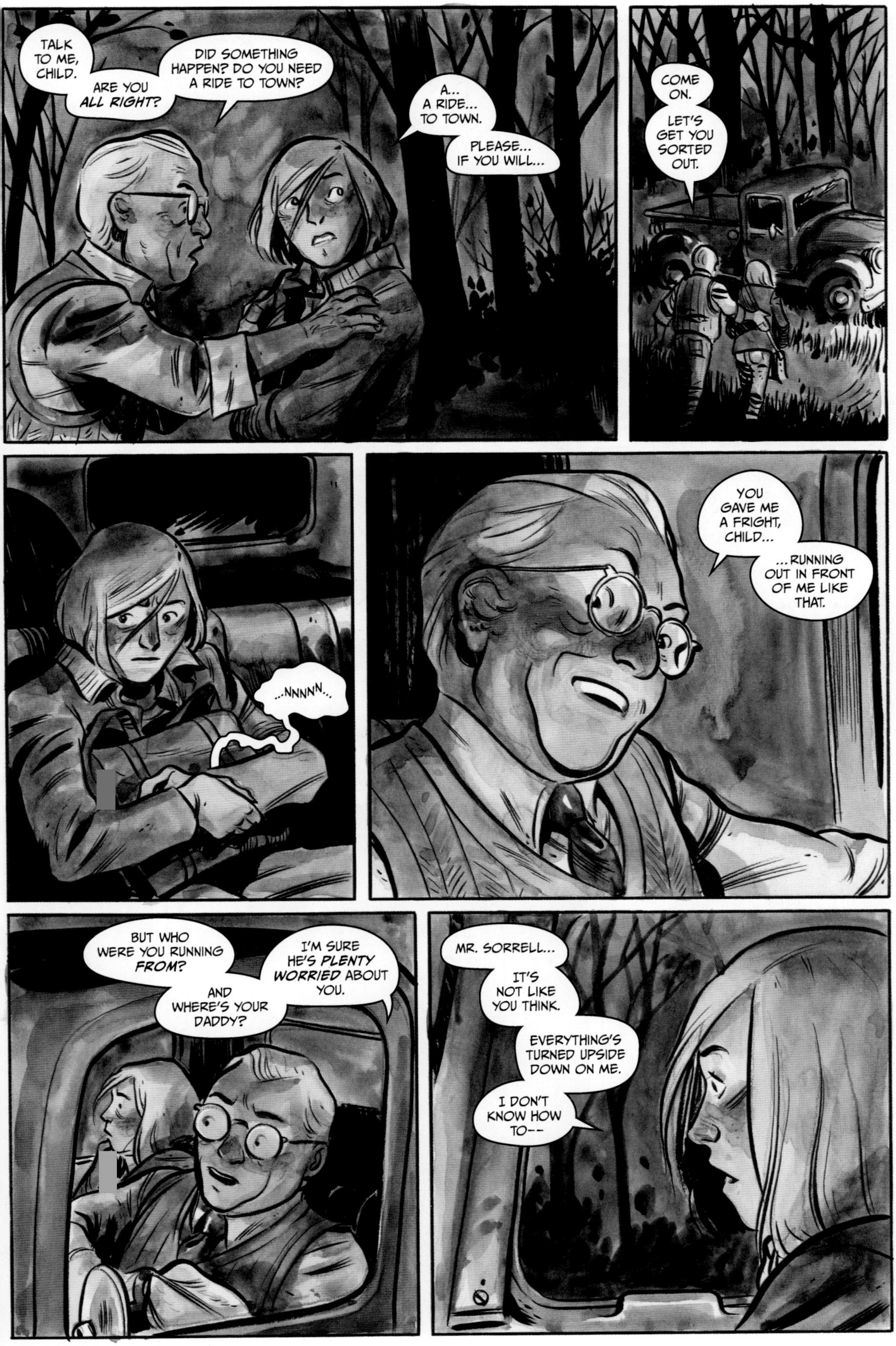
TALK TO ME, CHILD.
ARE YOU ALL RIGHT?
DID SOMETHING HAPPEN? DO YOU NEED A RIDE TO TOWN?
A... A RIDE... TO TOWN.
PLEASE... IF YOU WILL...
COME ON.
LET'S GET YOU SORTED OUT.
...NNNNN...
YOU GAVE ME A FRIGHT, CHILD...
...RUNNING OUT IN FRONT OF ME LIKE THAT.
BUT WHO WERE YOU RUNNING FROM?
AND WHERE'S YOUR DADDY?
I'M SURE HE'S PLENTY WORRIED ABOUT YOU.
MR. SORRELL...
IT'S NOT LIKE YOU THINK.
EVERYTHING'S TURNED UPSIDE DOWN ON ME.
I DON'T KNOW HOW TO--

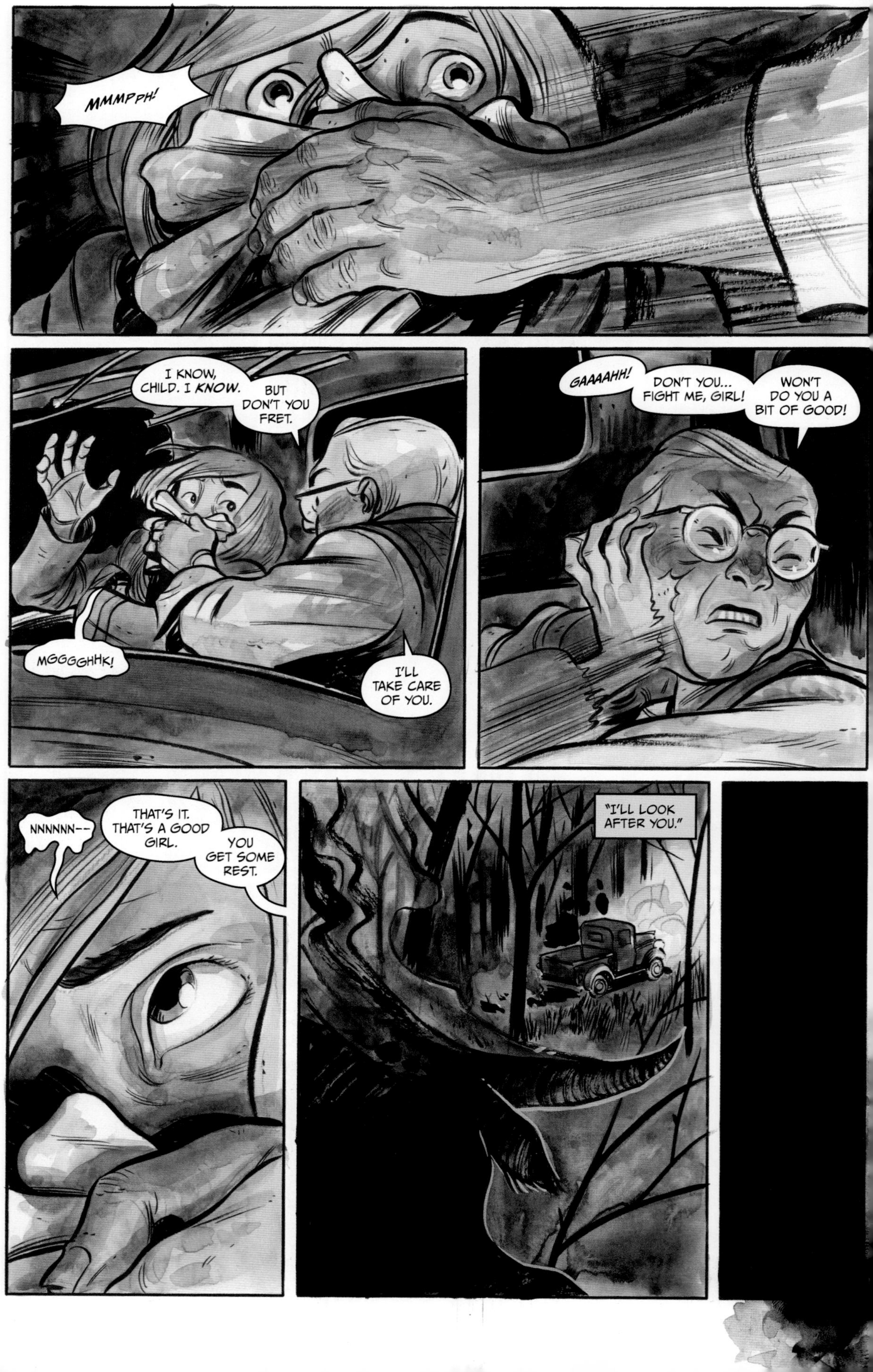
MMMPPH!
I KNOW, CHILD. I KNOW.
BUT DON'T YOU FRET.
MGGGGHHK!
I'LL TAKE CARE OF YOU.
GAAAAHH!
DON'T YOU... FIGHT ME, GIRL!
WON'T DO YOU A BIT OF GOOD!
NNNNNN--
THAT'S IT. THAT'S A GOOD GIRL.
YOU GET SOME REST.
"I'LL LOOK AFTER YOU."

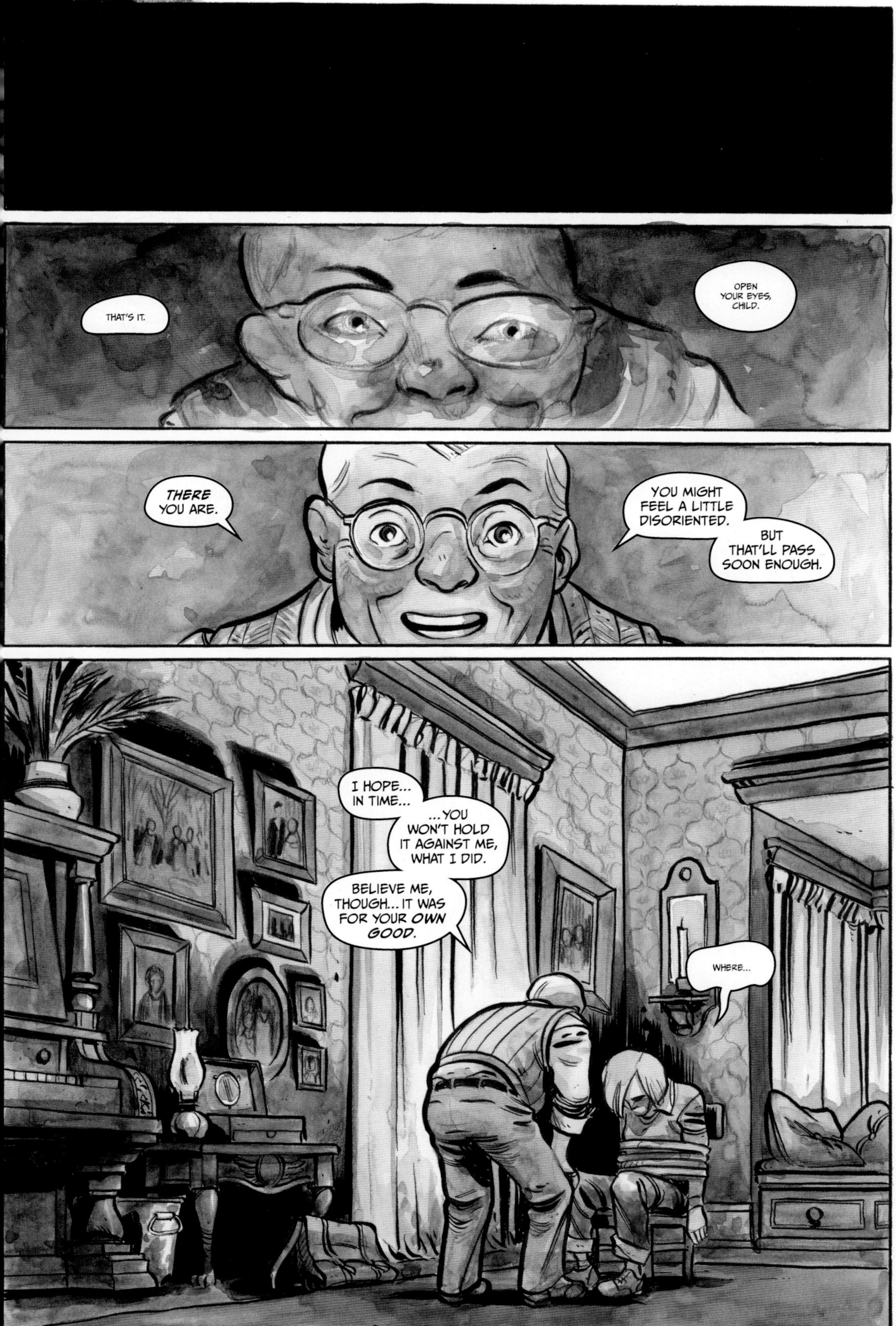
THAT'S IT.
OPEN YOUR EYES, CHILD.
THERE YOU ARE.
YOU MIGHT FEEL A LITTLE DISORIENTED.
BUT THAT'LL PASS SOON ENOUGH.
I HOPE... IN TIME...
...YOU WON'T HOLD IT AGAINST ME, WHAT I DID.
BELIEVE ME, THOUGH... IT WAS FOR YOUR OWN GOOD.
WHERE...

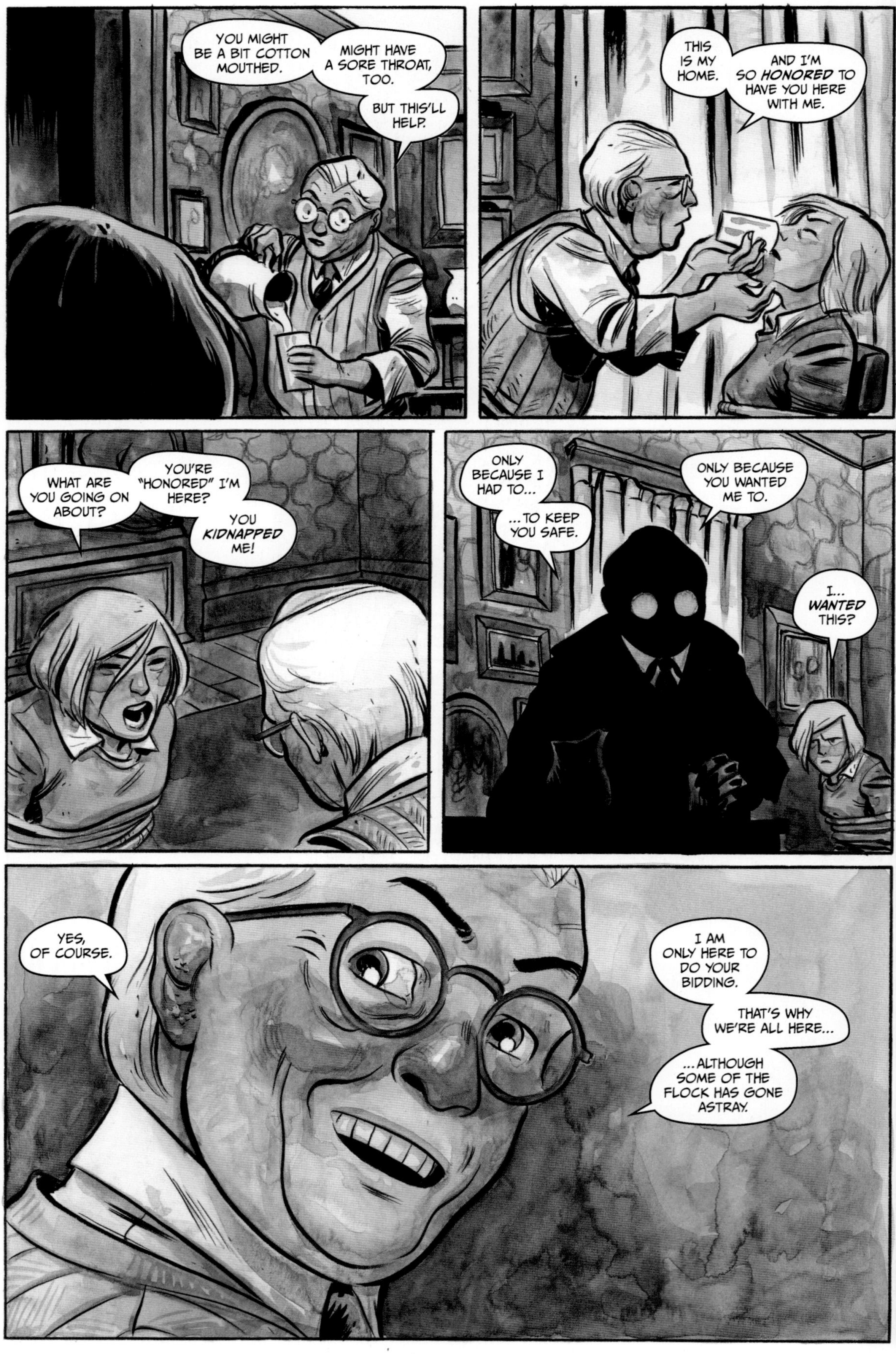
YOU MIGHT BE A BIT COTTON MOUTHED.
MIGHT HAVE A SORE THROAT, TOO.
BUT THIS'LL HELP.
THIS IS MY HOME.
AND I'M SO *HONORED* TO HAVE YOU HERE WITH ME.
WHAT ARE YOU GOING ON ABOUT?
YOU'RE "HONORED" I'M HERE?
YOU *KIDNAPPED* ME!
ONLY BECAUSE I HAD TO...
...TO KEEP YOU SAFE.
ONLY BECAUSE YOU WANTED ME TO.
I... *WANTED* THIS?
YES, OF COURSE.
I AM ONLY HERE TO DO YOUR BIDDING.
THAT'S WHY WE'RE ALL HERE...
...ALTHOUGH SOME OF THE FLOCK HAS GONE ASTRAY.

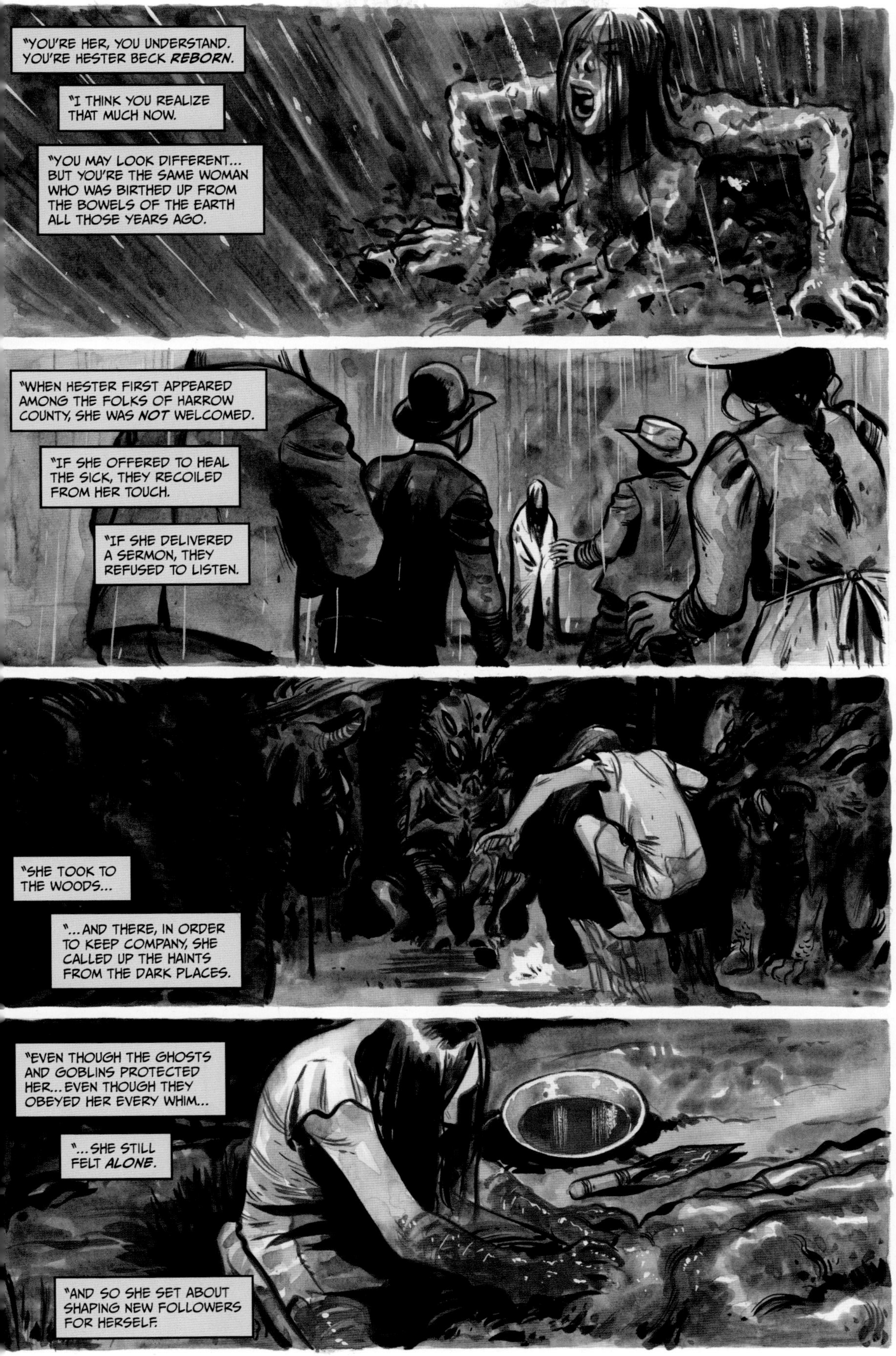
"YOU'RE HER, YOU UNDERSTAND. YOU'RE HESTER BECK *REBORN*.
"I THINK YOU REALIZE THAT MUCH NOW.
"YOU MAY LOOK DIFFERENT... BUT YOU'RE THE SAME WOMAN WHO WAS BIRTHED UP FROM THE BOWELS OF THE EARTH ALL THOSE YEARS AGO.
"WHEN HESTER FIRST APPEARED AMONG THE FOLKS OF HARROW COUNTY, SHE WAS *NOT* WELCOMED.
"IF SHE OFFERED TO HEAL THE SICK, THEY RECOILED FROM HER TOUCH.
"IF SHE DELIVERED A SERMON, THEY REFUSED TO LISTEN.
"SHE TOOK TO THE WOODS...
"...AND THERE, IN ORDER TO KEEP COMPANY, SHE CALLED UP THE HAINTS FROM THE DARK PLACES.
"EVEN THOUGH THE GHOSTS AND GOBLINS PROTECTED HER... EVEN THOUGH THEY OBEYED HER EVERY WHIM...
"...SHE STILL FELT *ALONE*.
"AND SO SHE SET ABOUT SHAPING NEW FOLLOWERS FOR HERSELF.

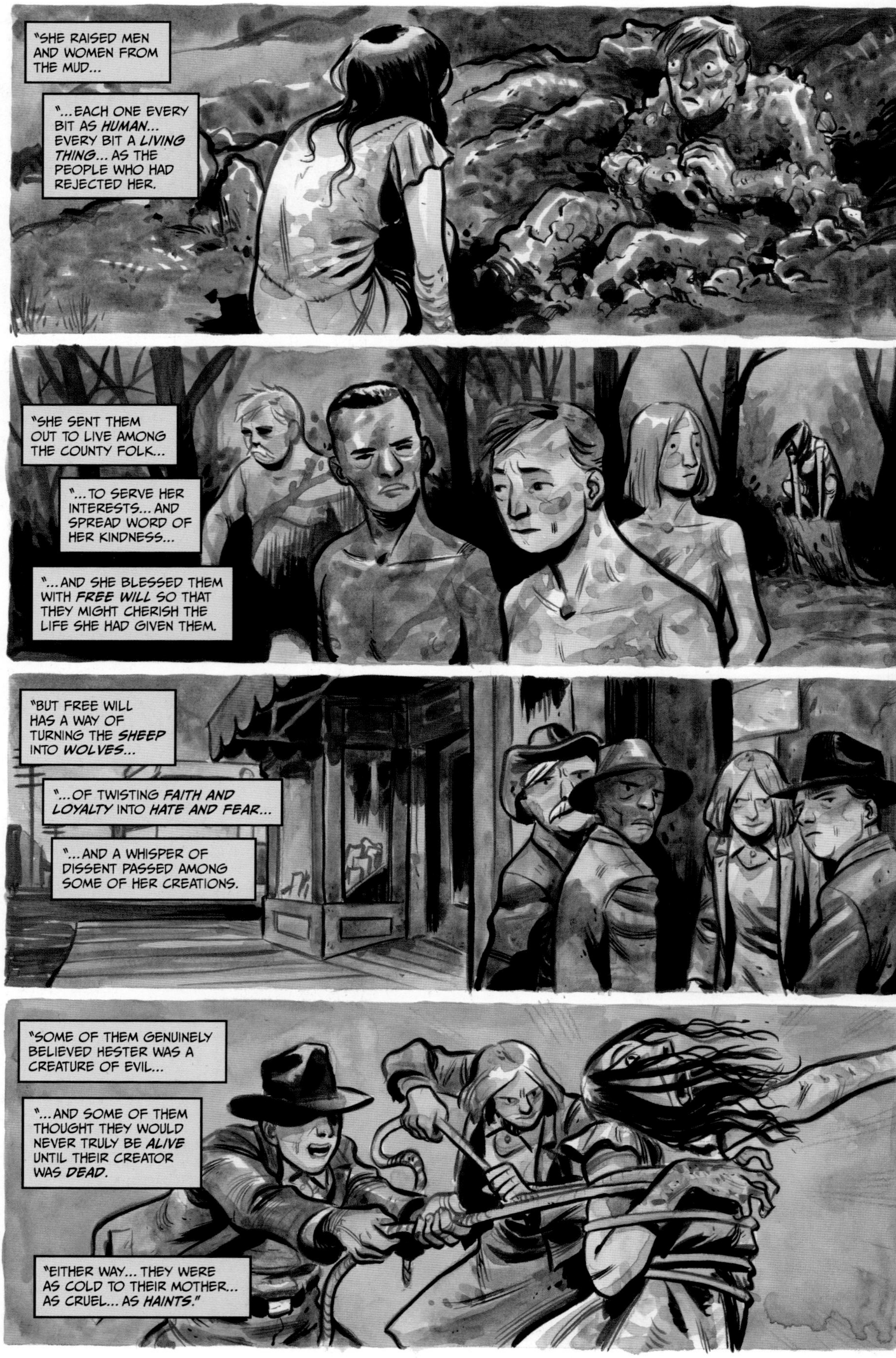
"SHE RAISED MEN AND WOMEN FROM THE MUD...
"...EACH ONE EVERY BIT AS HUMAN... EVERY BIT A LIVING THING... AS THE PEOPLE WHO HAD REJECTED HER.
"SHE SENT THEM OUT TO LIVE AMONG THE COUNTY FOLK...
"...TO SERVE HER INTERESTS... AND SPREAD WORD OF HER KINDNESS...
"...AND SHE BLESSED THEM WITH FREE WILL SO THAT THEY MIGHT CHERISH THE LIFE SHE HAD GIVEN THEM.
"BUT FREE WILL HAS A WAY OF TURNING THE SHEEP INTO WOLVES...
"...OF TWISTING FAITH AND LOYALTY INTO HATE AND FEAR...
"...AND A WHISPER OF DISSENT PASSED AMONG SOME OF HER CREATIONS.
"SOME OF THEM GENUINELY BELIEVED HESTER WAS A CREATURE OF EVIL...
"...AND SOME OF THEM THOUGHT THEY WOULD NEVER TRULY BE ALIVE UNTIL THEIR CREATOR WAS DEAD.
"EITHER WAY... THEY WERE AS COLD TO THEIR MOTHER... AS CRUEL... AS HAINTS."

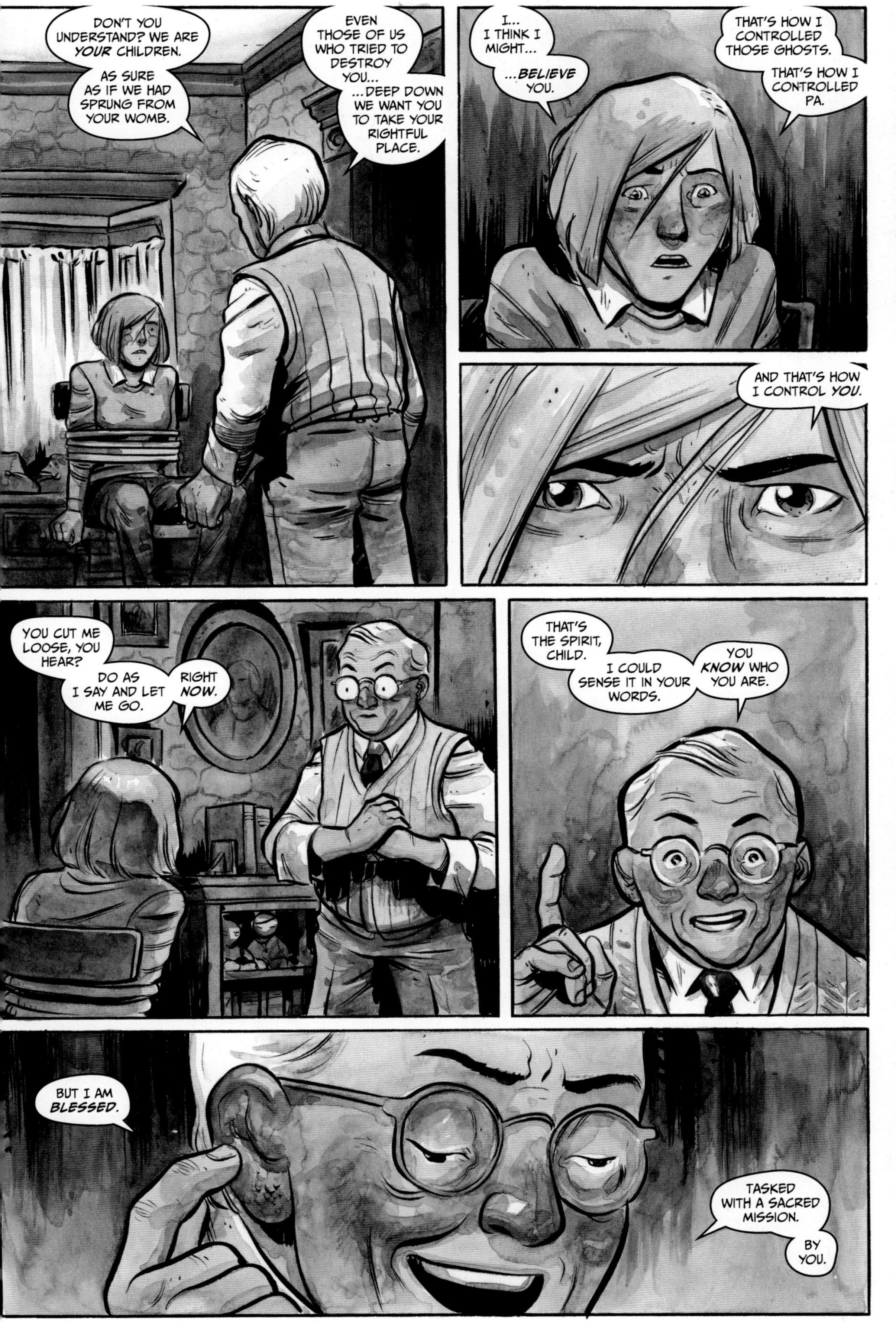
DON'T YOU UNDERSTAND? WE ARE *YOUR* CHILDREN.
AS SURE AS IF WE HAD SPRUNG FROM YOUR WOMB.
EVEN THOSE OF US WHO TRIED TO DESTROY YOU...
...DEEP DOWN WE WANT YOU TO TAKE YOUR RIGHTFUL PLACE.
I... I THINK I MIGHT...
...*BELIEVE* YOU.
THAT'S HOW I CONTROLLED THOSE GHOSTS.
THAT'S HOW I CONTROLLED PA.
AND THAT'S HOW I CONTROL *YOU*.
YOU CUT ME LOOSE, YOU HEAR?
DO AS I SAY AND LET ME GO.
RIGHT *NOW*.
THAT'S THE SPIRIT, CHILD.
I COULD SENSE IT IN YOUR WORDS.
YOU *KNOW* WHO YOU ARE.
BUT I AM *BLESSED*.
TASKED WITH A SACRED MISSION.
BY YOU.

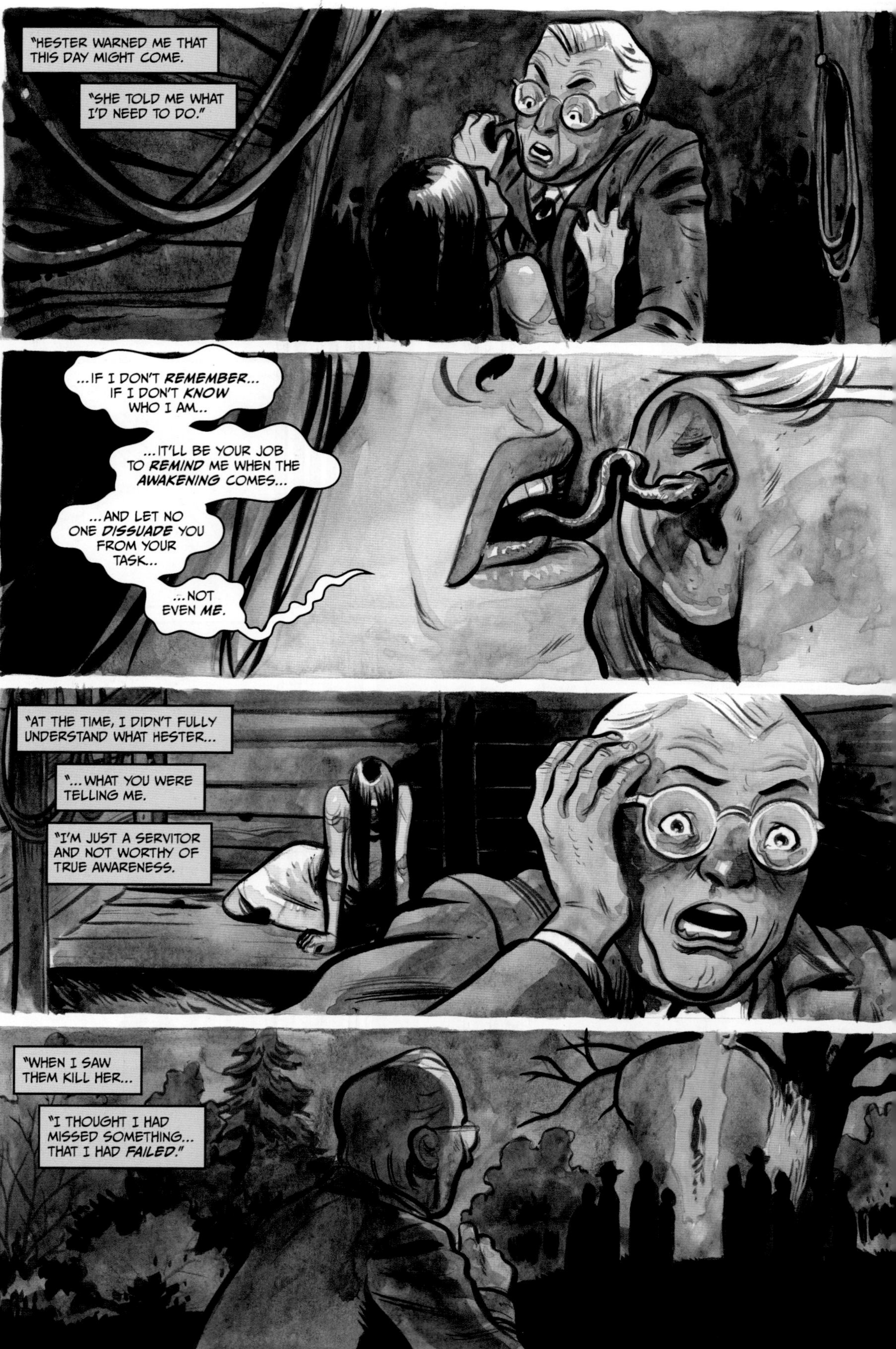
"HESTER WARNED ME THAT THIS DAY MIGHT COME.
"SHE TOLD ME WHAT I'D NEED TO DO."
...IF I DON'T REMEMBER... IF I DON'T KNOW WHO I AM...
...IT'LL BE YOUR JOB TO REMIND ME WHEN THE AWAKENING COMES...
...AND LET NO ONE DISSUADE YOU FROM YOUR TASK...
...NOT EVEN ME.
"AT THE TIME, I DIDN'T FULLY UNDERSTAND WHAT HESTER...
"...WHAT YOU WERE TELLING ME.
"I'M JUST A SERVITOR AND NOT WORTHY OF TRUE AWARENESS.
"WHEN I SAW THEM KILL HER...
"I THOUGHT I HAD MISSED SOMETHING... THAT I HAD FAILED."

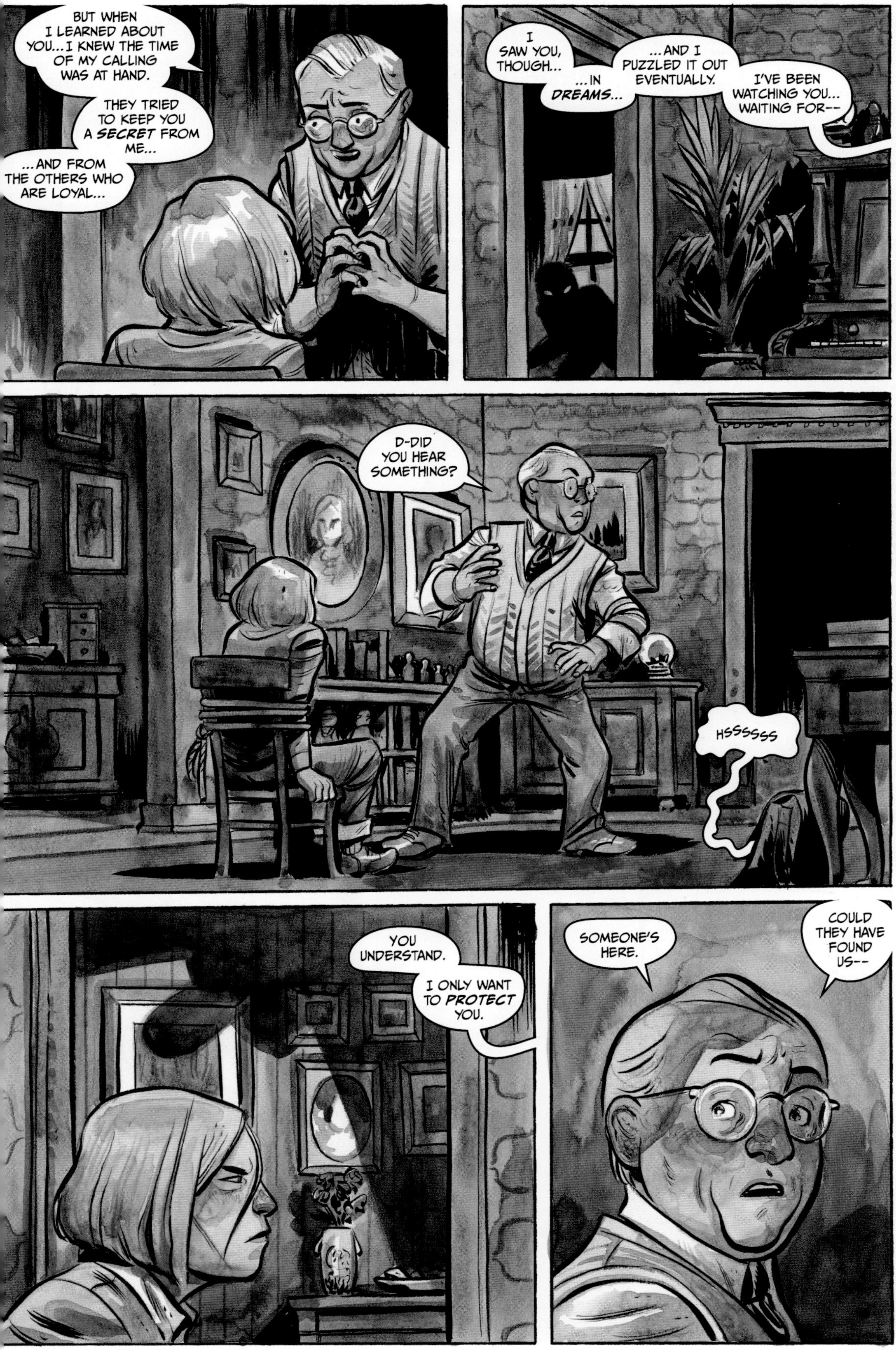
BUT WHEN I LEARNED ABOUT YOU... I KNEW THE TIME OF MY CALLING WAS AT HAND.
THEY TRIED TO KEEP YOU A SECRET FROM ME...
...AND FROM THE OTHERS WHO ARE LOYAL...
I SAW YOU, THOUGH...
...IN DREAMS...
...AND I PUZZLED IT OUT EVENTUALLY.
I'VE BEEN WATCHING YOU... WAITING FOR--
D-DID YOU HEAR SOMETHING?
HSSSSSS
YOU UNDERSTAND.
I ONLY WANT TO PROTECT YOU.
SOMEONE'S HERE.
COULD THEY HAVE FOUND US--

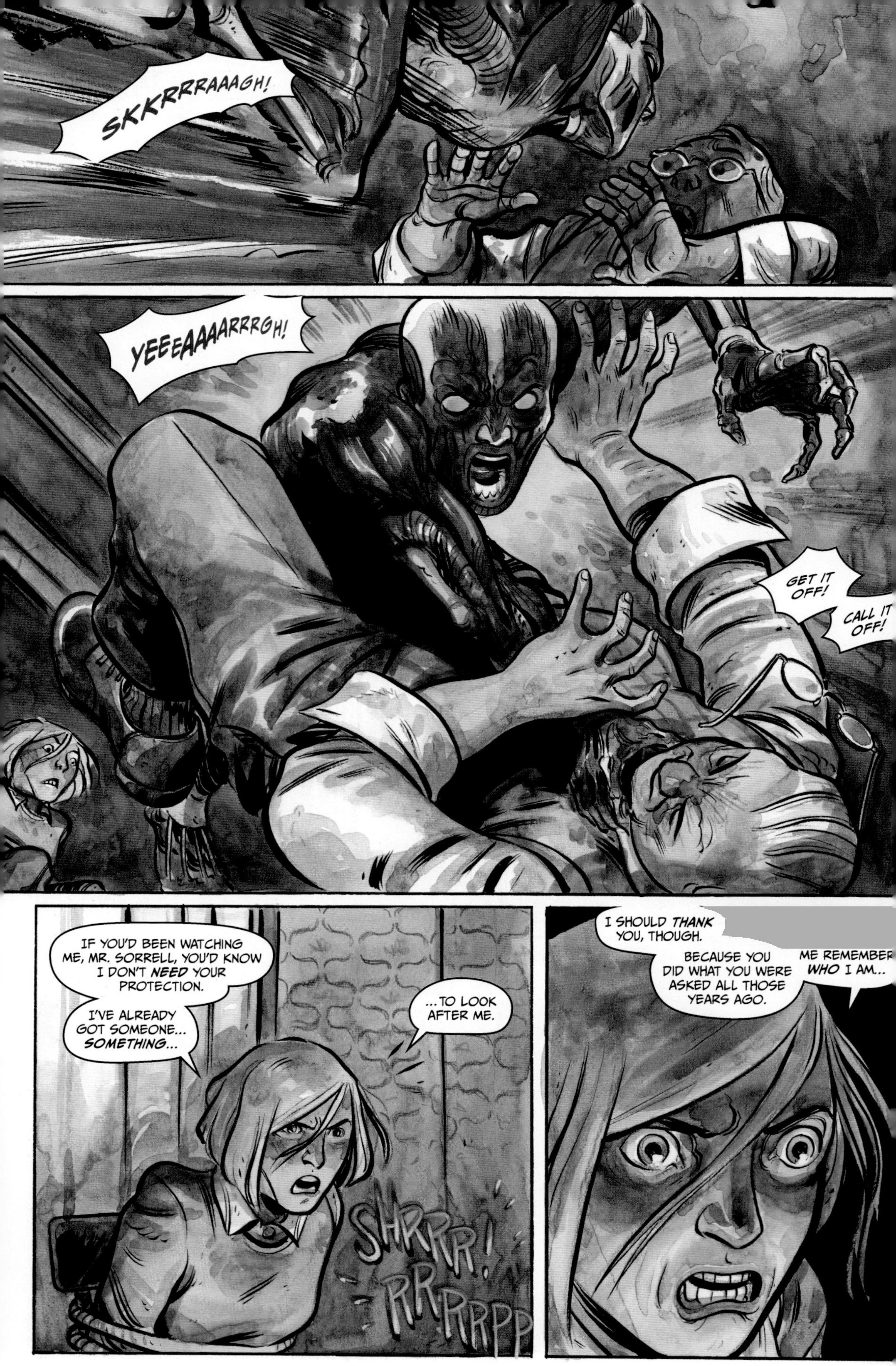
SKKRRRAAAGH!
YEEEAAAARRRGH!
GET IT OFF!
CALL IT OFF!
IF YOU'D BEEN WATCHING ME, MR. SORRELL, YOU'D KNOW I DON'T NEED YOUR PROTECTION.
I'VE ALREADY GOT SOMEONE... SOMETHING...
...TO LOOK AFTER ME.
SHRRRR! RRRRRPP
I SHOULD THANK YOU, THOUGH.
BECAUSE YOU DID WHAT YOU WERE ASKED ALL THOSE YEARS AGO.
ME REMEMBER WHO I AM...

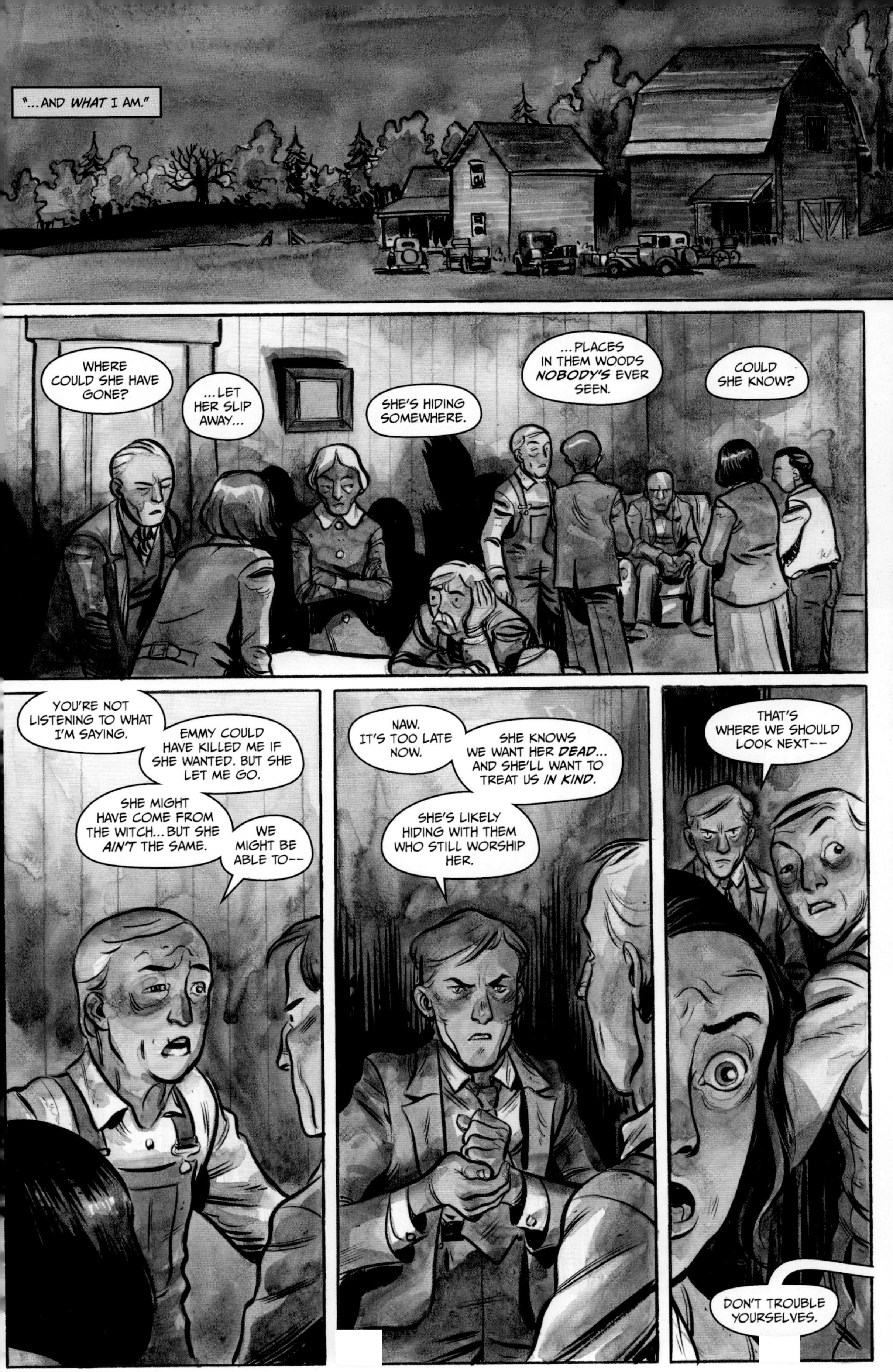
"...AND *WHAT* I AM."
WHERE COULD SHE HAVE GONE?
...LET HER SLIP AWAY...
SHE'S HIDING SOMEWHERE.
...PLACES IN THEM WOODS *NOBODY'S* EVER SEEN.
COULD SHE KNOW?
YOU'RE NOT LISTENING TO WHAT I'M SAYING.
EMMY COULD HAVE KILLED ME IF SHE WANTED. BUT SHE LET ME GO.
SHE MIGHT HAVE COME FROM THE WITCH... BUT SHE *AIN'T* THE SAME.
WE MIGHT BE ABLE TO--
NAW. IT'S TOO LATE NOW.
SHE KNOWS WE WANT HER *DEAD*... AND SHE'LL WANT TO TREAT US *IN KIND*.
SHE'S LIKELY HIDING WITH THEM WHO STILL WORSHIP HER.
THAT'S WHERE WE SHOULD LOOK NEXT--
DON'T TROUBLE YOURSELVES.

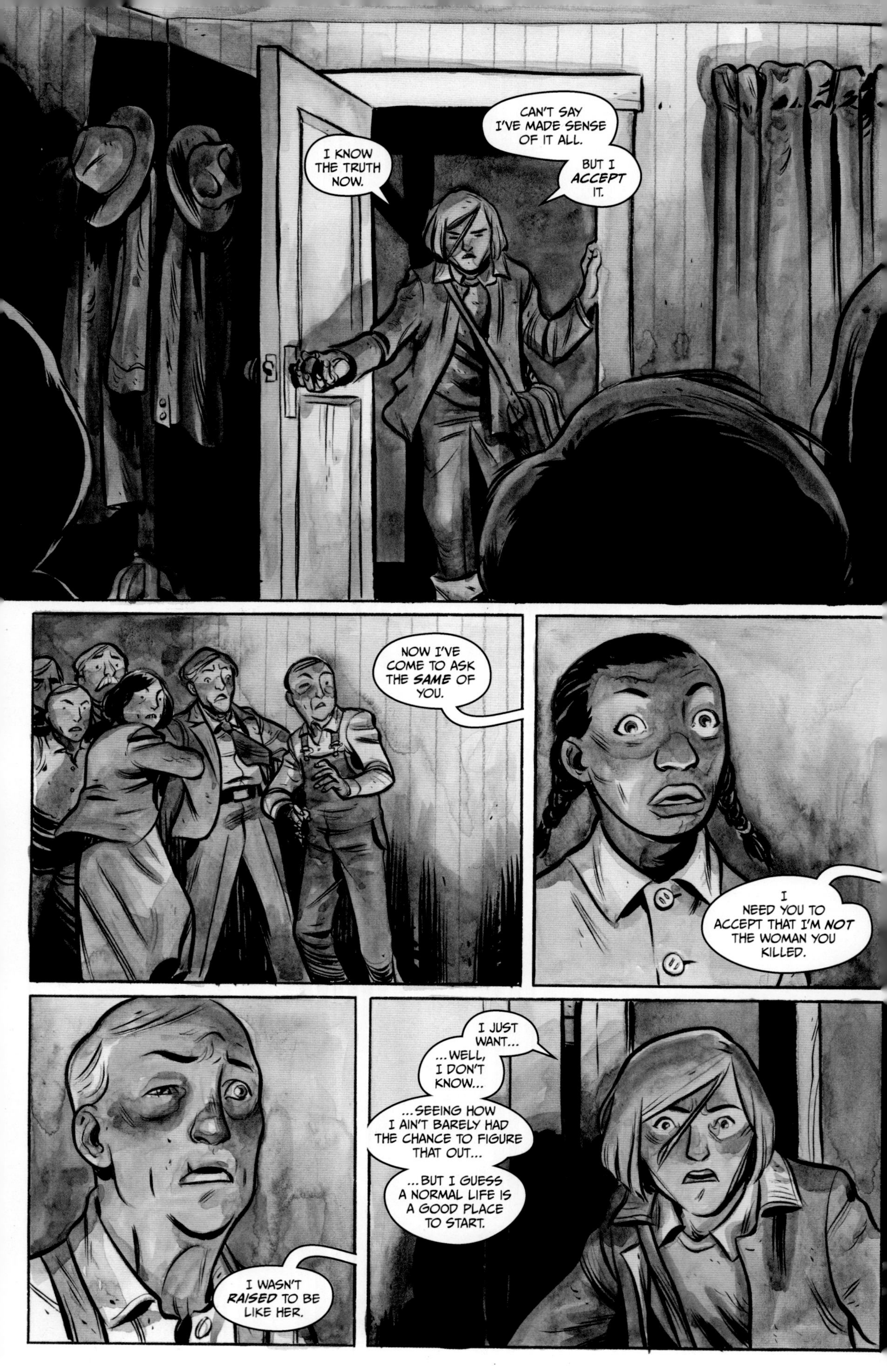
I KNOW THE TRUTH NOW.
CAN'T SAY I'VE MADE SENSE OF IT ALL.
BUT I *ACCEPT* IT.
NOW I'VE COME TO ASK THE *SAME* OF YOU.
I NEED YOU TO ACCEPT THAT I'M *NOT* THE WOMAN YOU KILLED.
I WASN'T *RAISED* TO BE LIKE HER.
I JUST WANT...
...WELL, I DON'T KNOW...
...SEEING HOW I AIN'T BARELY HAD THE CHANCE TO FIGURE THAT OUT...
...BUT I GUESS A NORMAL LIFE IS A GOOD PLACE TO START.

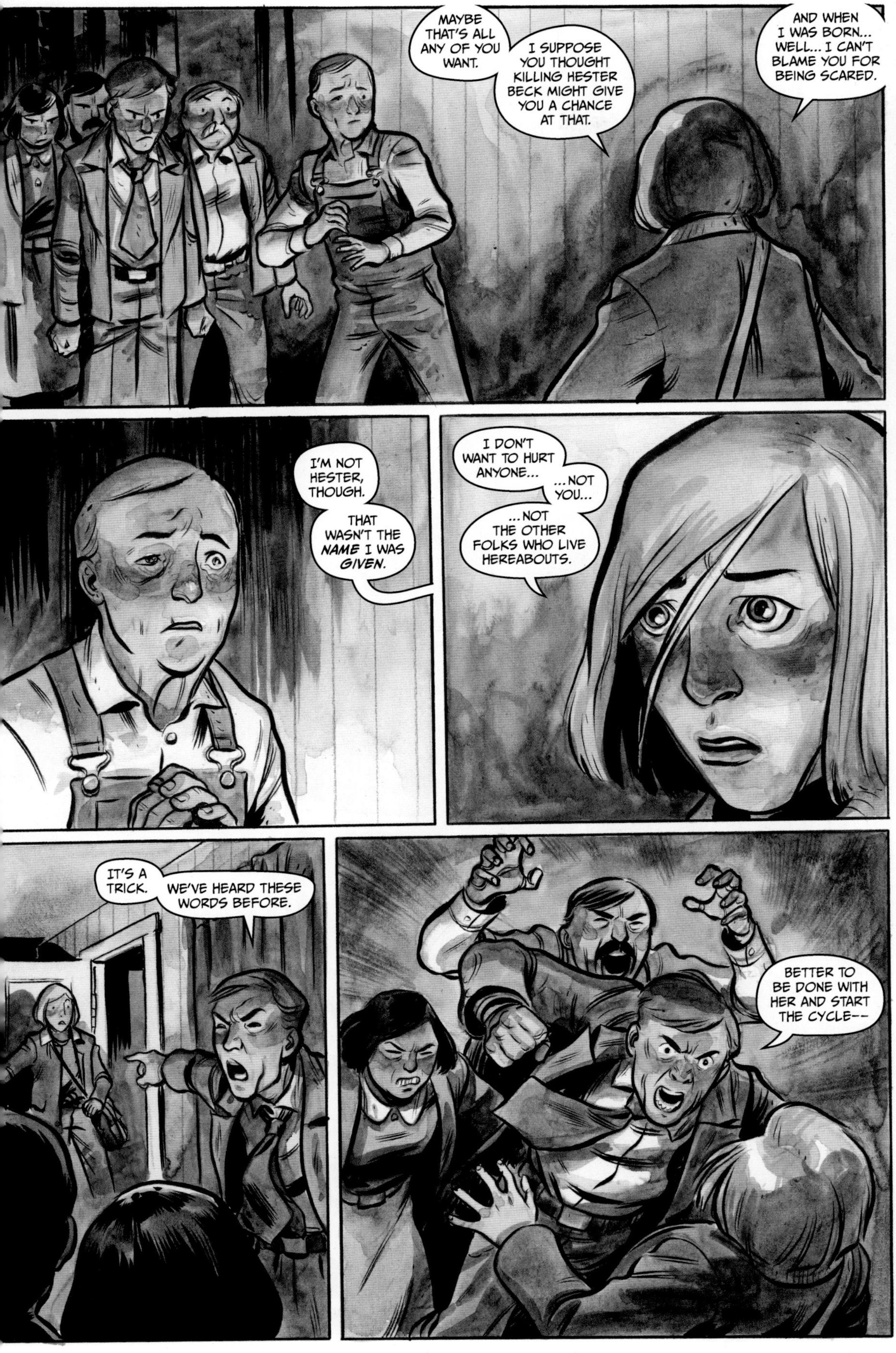
MAYBE THAT'S ALL ANY OF YOU WANT.
I SUPPOSE YOU THOUGHT KILLING HESTER BECK MIGHT GIVE YOU A CHANCE AT THAT.
AND WHEN I WAS BORN... WELL... I CAN'T BLAME YOU FOR BEING SCARED.
I'M NOT HESTER, THOUGH.
THAT WASN'T THE NAME I WAS GIVEN.
I DON'T WANT TO HURT ANYONE...
...NOT YOU...
...NOT THE OTHER FOLKS WHO LIVE HEREABOUTS.
IT'S A TRICK.
WE'VE HEARD THESE WORDS BEFORE.
BETTER TO BE DONE WITH HER AND START THE CYCLE--

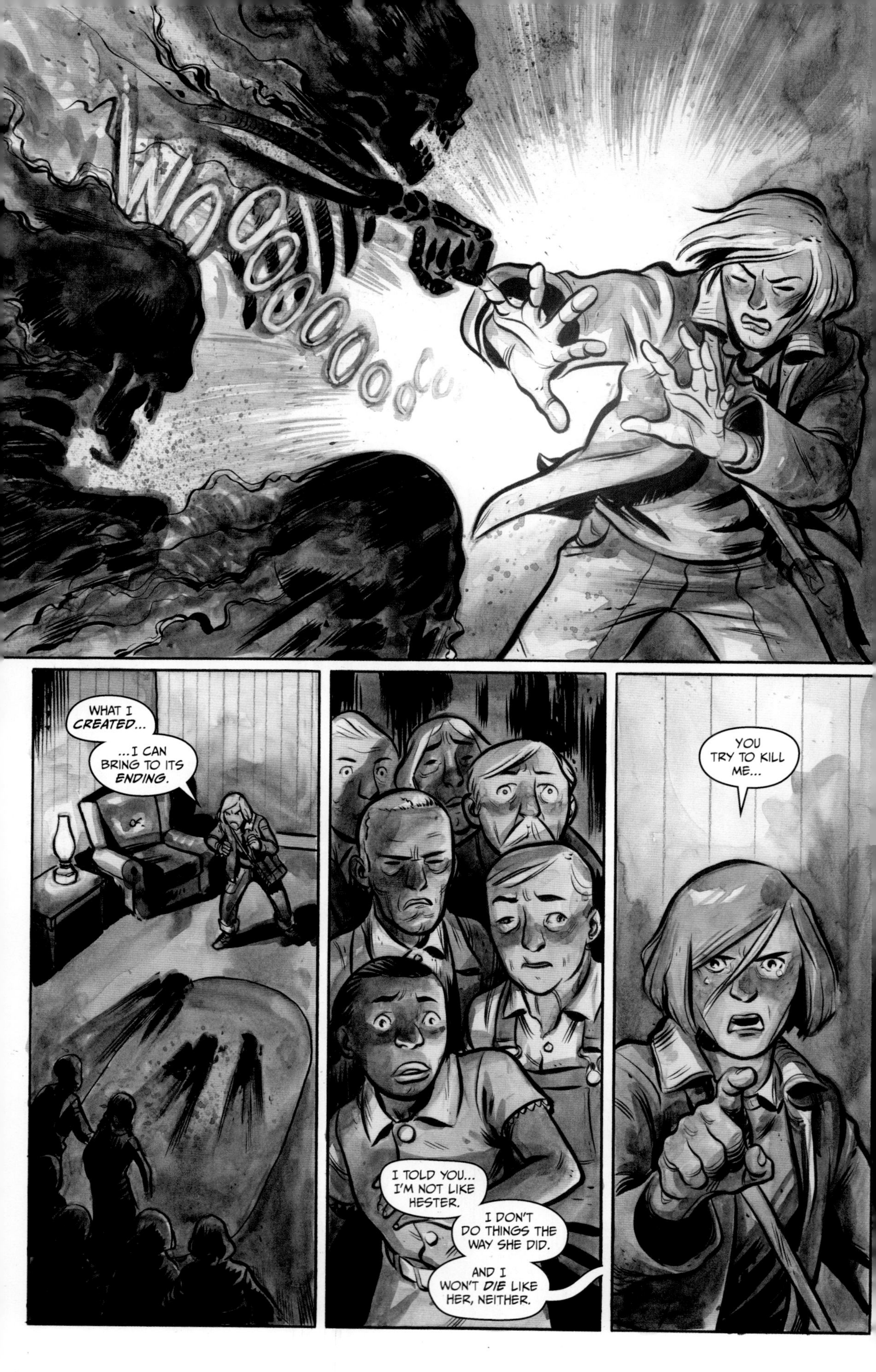
WOOOOOOOOOOOOOOOOOOO
WHAT I *CREATED*...
...I CAN BRING TO ITS *ENDING*.
I TOLD YOU... I'M NOT LIKE HESTER.
I DON'T DO THINGS THE WAY SHE DID.
AND I WON'T *DIE* LIKE HER, NEITHER.
YOU TRY TO KILL ME...

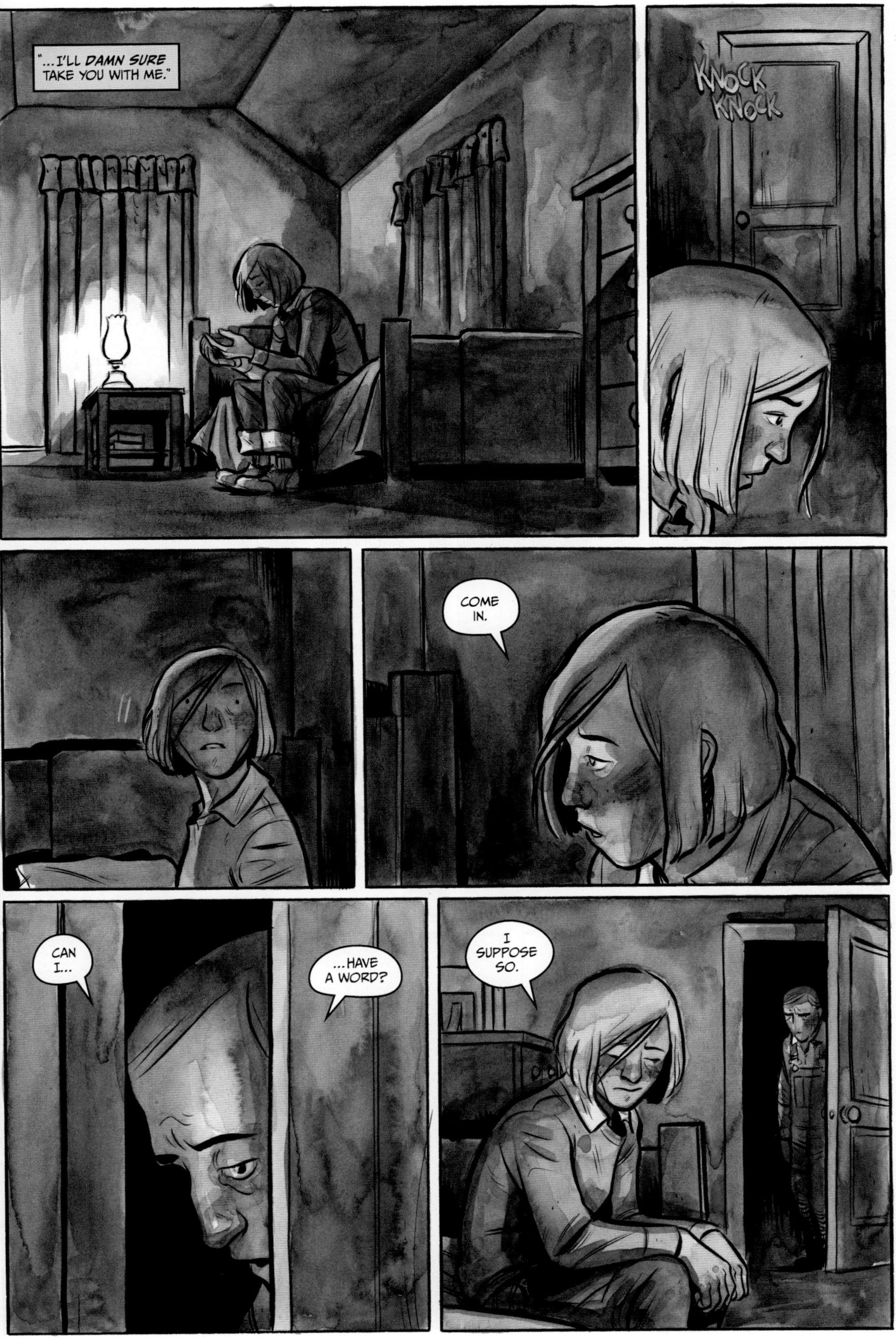
"...I'LL DAMN SURE TAKE YOU WITH ME."
KNOCK KNOCK
COME IN.
CAN I...
...HAVE A WORD?
I SUPPOSE SO.

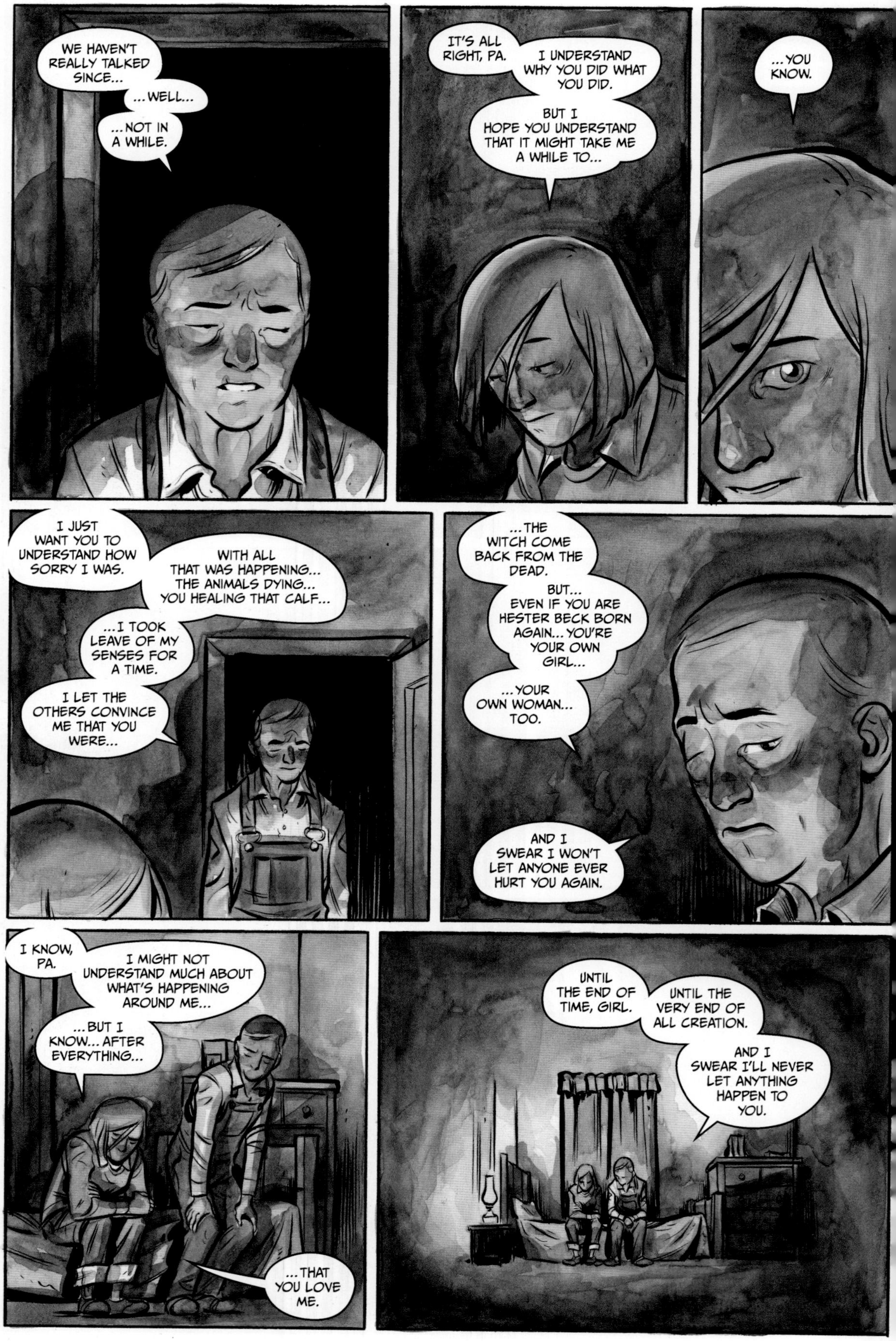
WE HAVEN'T REALLY TALKED SINCE...
...WELL...
...NOT IN A WHILE.
IT'S ALL RIGHT, PA.
I UNDERSTAND WHY YOU DID WHAT YOU DID.
BUT I HOPE YOU UNDERSTAND THAT IT MIGHT TAKE ME A WHILE TO...
...YOU KNOW.
I JUST WANT YOU TO UNDERSTAND HOW SORRY I WAS.
WITH ALL THAT WAS HAPPENING... THE ANIMALS DYING... YOU HEALING THAT CALF...
...I TOOK LEAVE OF MY SENSES FOR A TIME.
I LET THE OTHERS CONVINCE ME THAT YOU WERE...
...THE WITCH COME BACK FROM THE DEAD.
BUT... EVEN IF YOU ARE HESTER BECK BORN AGAIN... YOU'RE YOUR OWN GIRL...
...YOUR OWN WOMAN... TOO.
AND I SWEAR I WON'T LET ANYONE EVER HURT YOU AGAIN.
I KNOW, PA.
I MIGHT NOT UNDERSTAND MUCH ABOUT WHAT'S HAPPENING AROUND ME...
...BUT I KNOW... AFTER EVERYTHING...
...THAT YOU LOVE ME.
UNTIL THE END OF TIME, GIRL.
UNTIL THE VERY END OF ALL CREATION.
AND I SWEAR I'LL NEVER LET ANYTHING HAPPEN TO YOU.

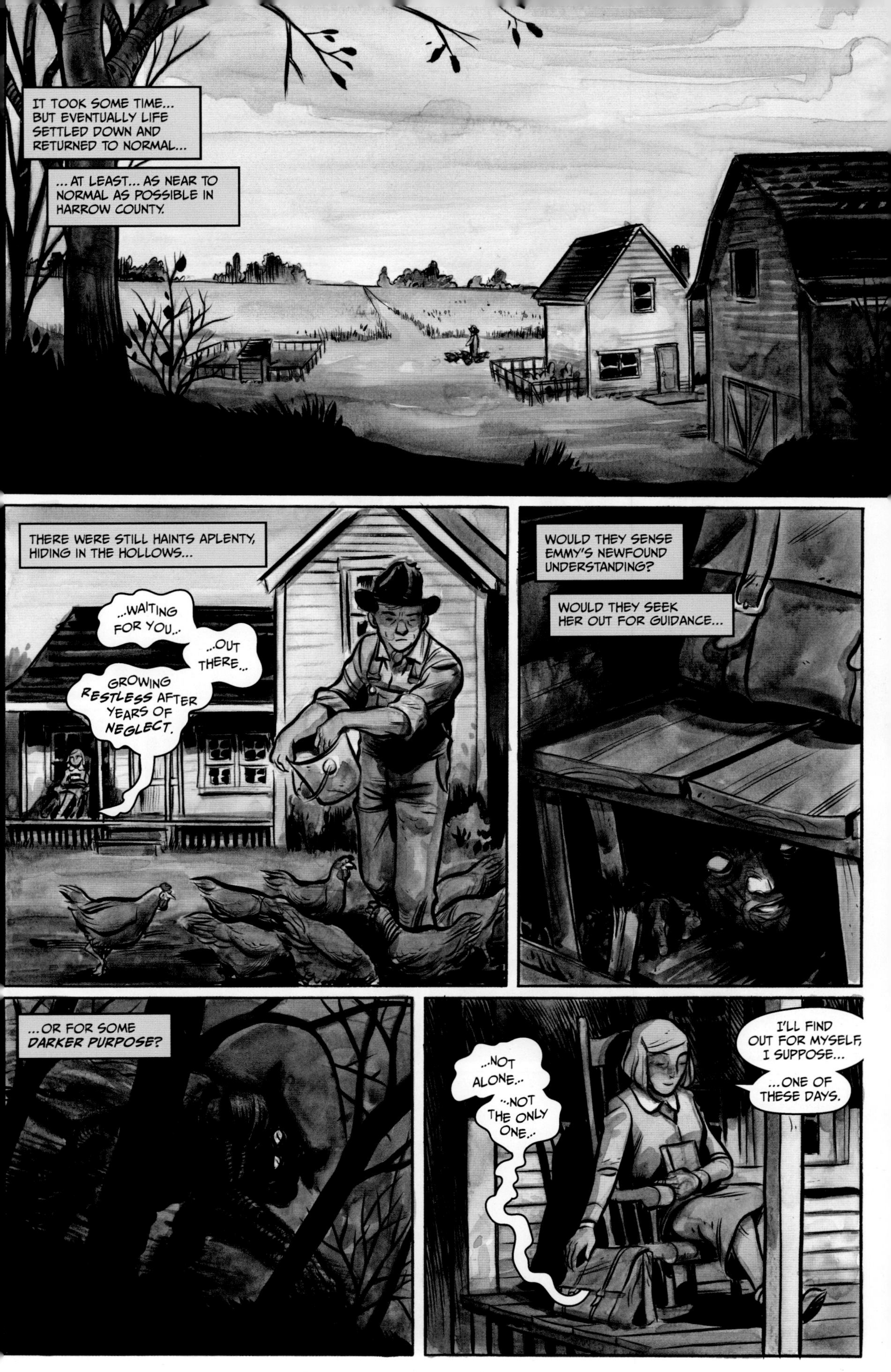
IT TOOK SOME TIME... BUT EVENTUALLY LIFE SETTLED DOWN AND RETURNED TO NORMAL...
... AT LEAST... AS NEAR TO NORMAL AS POSSIBLE IN HARROW COUNTY.
THERE WERE STILL HAINTS APLENTY, HIDING IN THE HOLLOWS...
...WAITING FOR YOU...
...OUT THERE...
GROWING RESTLESS AFTER YEARS OF NEGLECT.
WOULD THEY SENSE EMMY'S NEWFOUND UNDERSTANDING?
WOULD THEY SEEK HER OUT FOR GUIDANCE...
...OR FOR SOME DARKER PURPOSE?
...NOT ALONE...
...NOT THE ONLY ONE...
I'LL FIND OUT FOR MYSELF, I SUPPOSE...
...ONE OF THESE DAYS.

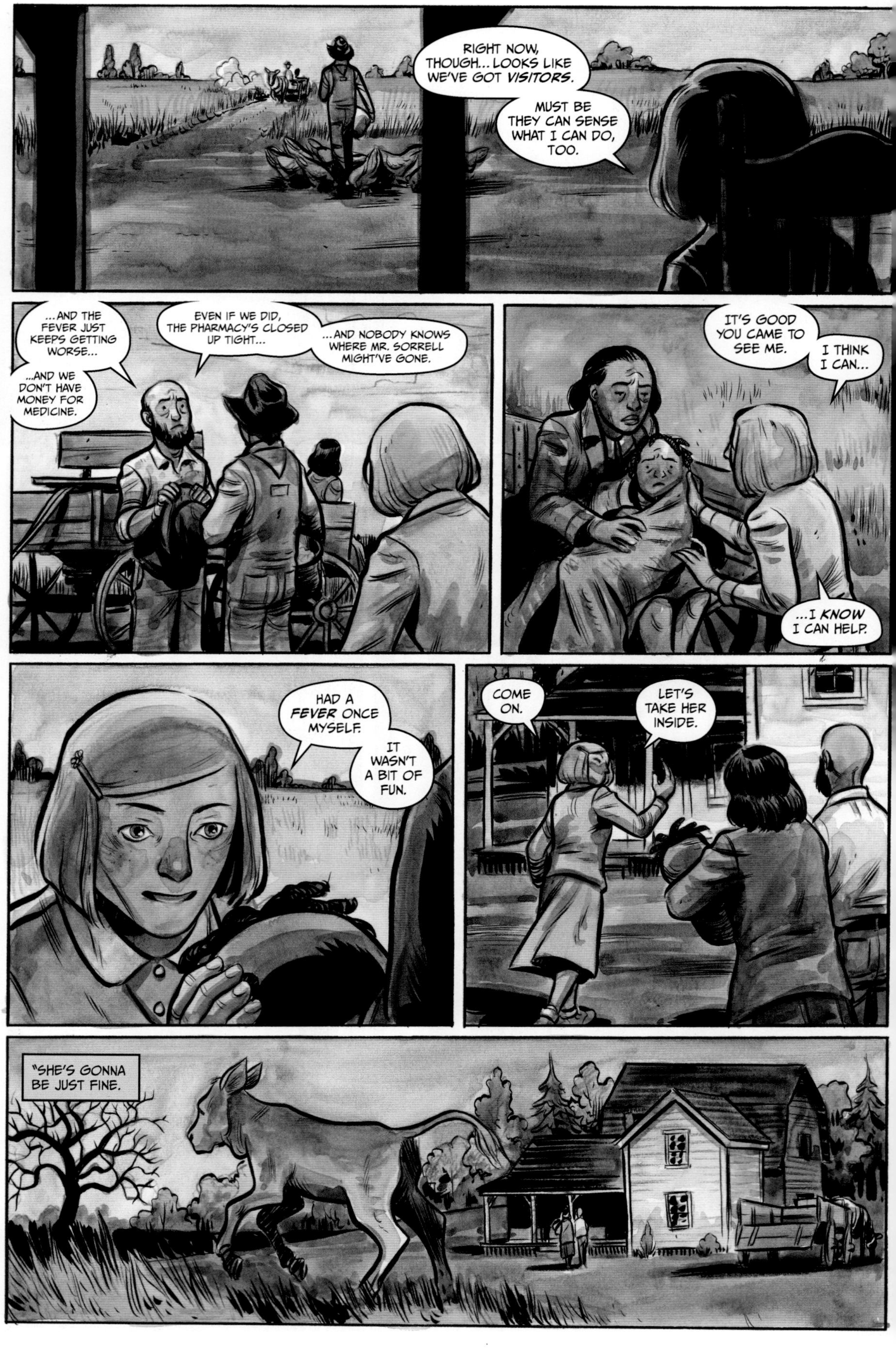
RIGHT NOW, THOUGH... LOOKS LIKE WE'VE GOT *VISITORS*.
MUST BE THEY CAN SENSE WHAT I CAN DO, TOO.
...AND THE FEVER JUST KEEPS GETTING WORSE...
...AND WE DON'T HAVE MONEY FOR MEDICINE.
EVEN IF WE DID, THE PHARMACY'S CLOSED UP TIGHT...
...AND NOBODY KNOWS WHERE MR. SORRELL MIGHT'VE GONE.
IT'S GOOD YOU CAME TO SEE ME.
I THINK I CAN...
...I *KNOW* I CAN HELP.
HAD A *FEVER* ONCE MYSELF.
IT WASN'T A BIT OF FUN.
COME ON.
LET'S TAKE HER INSIDE.
"SHE'S GONNA BE JUST FINE.

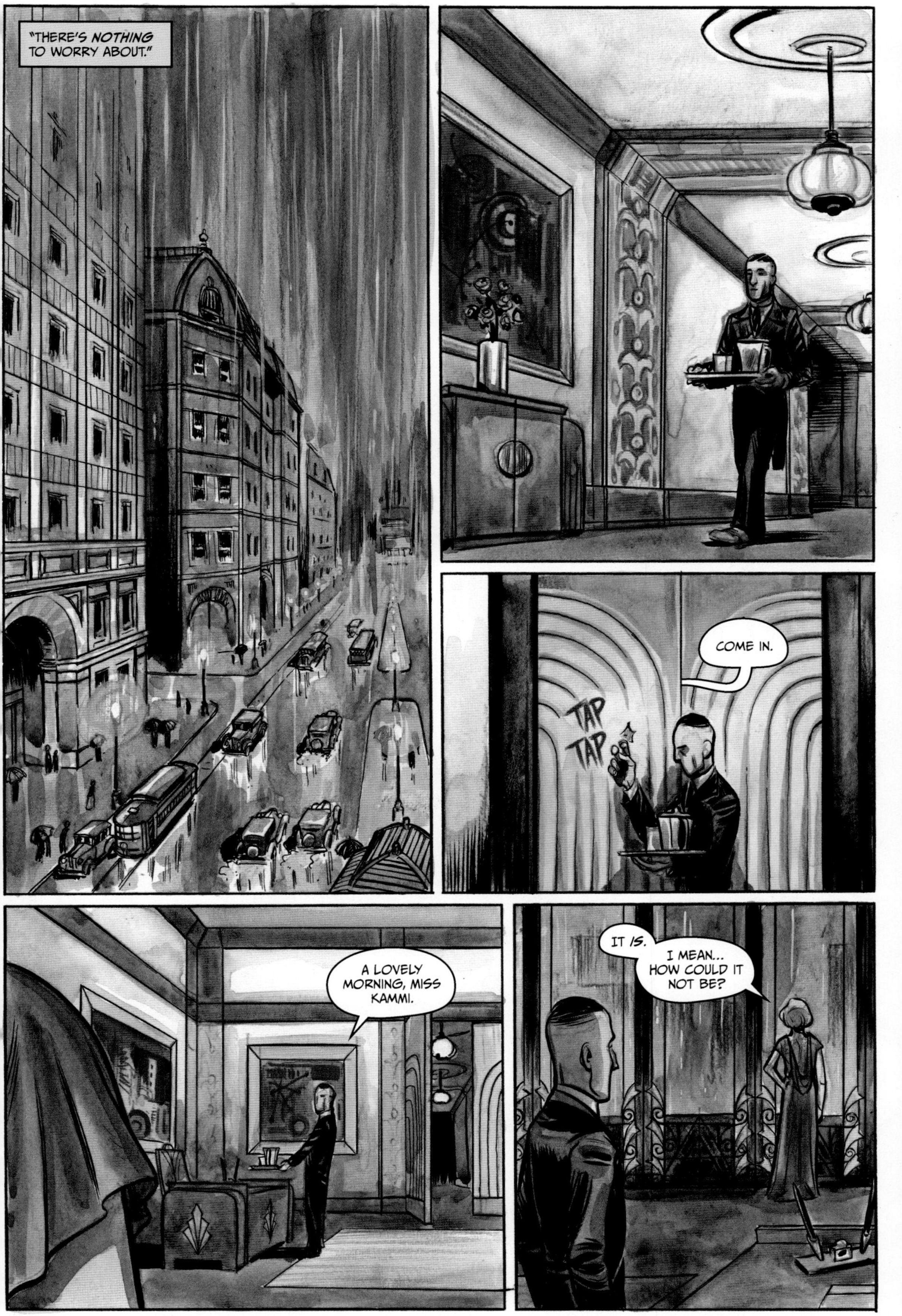
"THERE'S *NOTHING* TO WORRY ABOUT."
COME IN.
TAP TAP
A LOVELY MORNING, MISS KAMMI.
IT *IS*.
I MEAN... HOW COULD IT NOT BE?

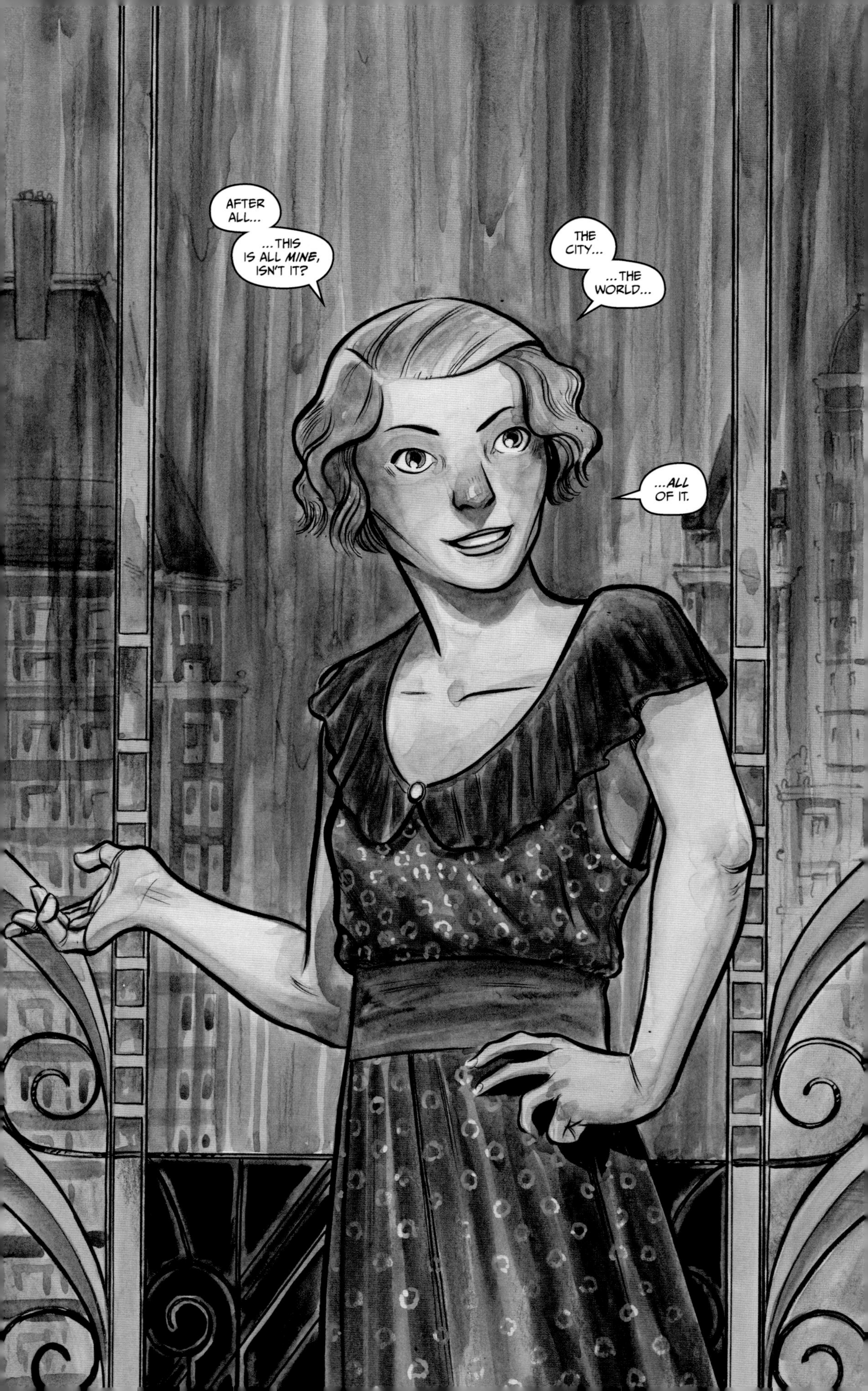
AFTER ALL...
...THIS IS ALL *MINE,* ISN'T IT?
THE CITY...
...THE WORLD...
...*ALL* OF IT.

HARROW
‹SKETCHBOOK›
COUNTY

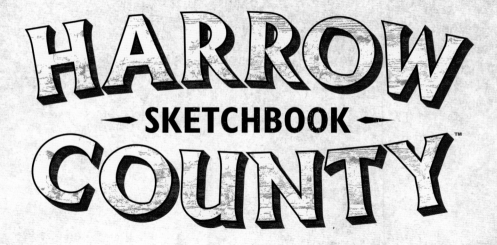

NOTES BY
CULLEN BUNN AND TYLER CROOK

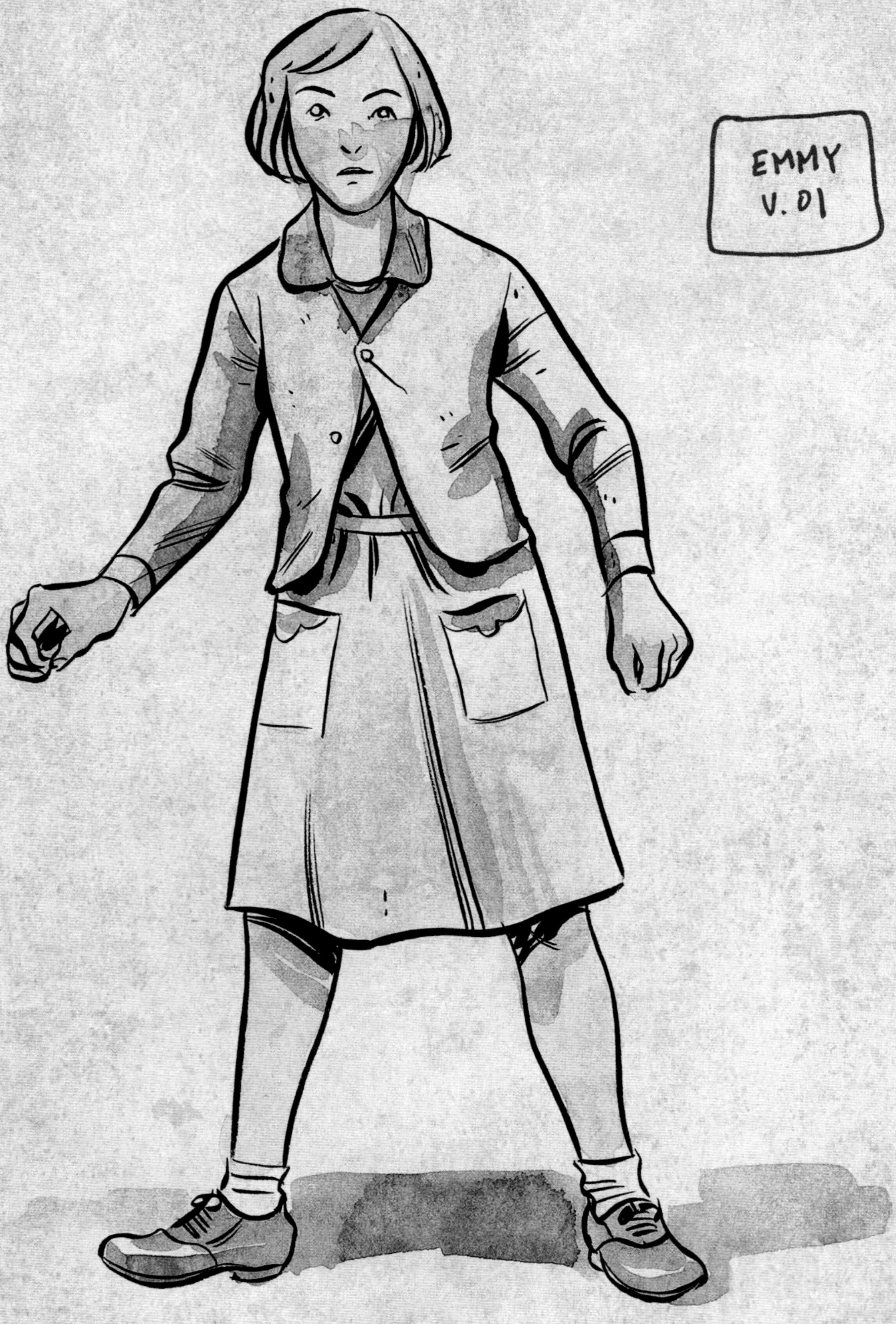
EMMY
V.01

CULLEN BUNN: For me, it was very important that Emmy appear sweet and innocent . . . but her expressions needed to turn cold and sinister at the drop of a hat. Luckily, Tyler brought those elements to life masterfully!

TYLER CROOK: Cullen was really clear about who Emmy was from the start. And that made her design relatively easy. This is the first drawing I did of her, and you can see the general design was there from the beginning.

EMMY

BERNICE

BERNICE

10/6

CB: I knew I loved Emmy right from the start. I did not, however, expect to connect with Bernice so quickly! She's become a favorite character of mine, and we'll be seeing much more of her in the future.

TC: I like designing wardrobe changes like this. I enjoy putting myself into the characters' heads and imagining what they were thinking when they picked out their clothes. I figured Emmy was planning on making her way to the train tracks and hopping a boxcar. Bernice, on the other hand, was on her way to bed when she found out what was going on, so she just threw some shoes on and a jacket over her housecoat.

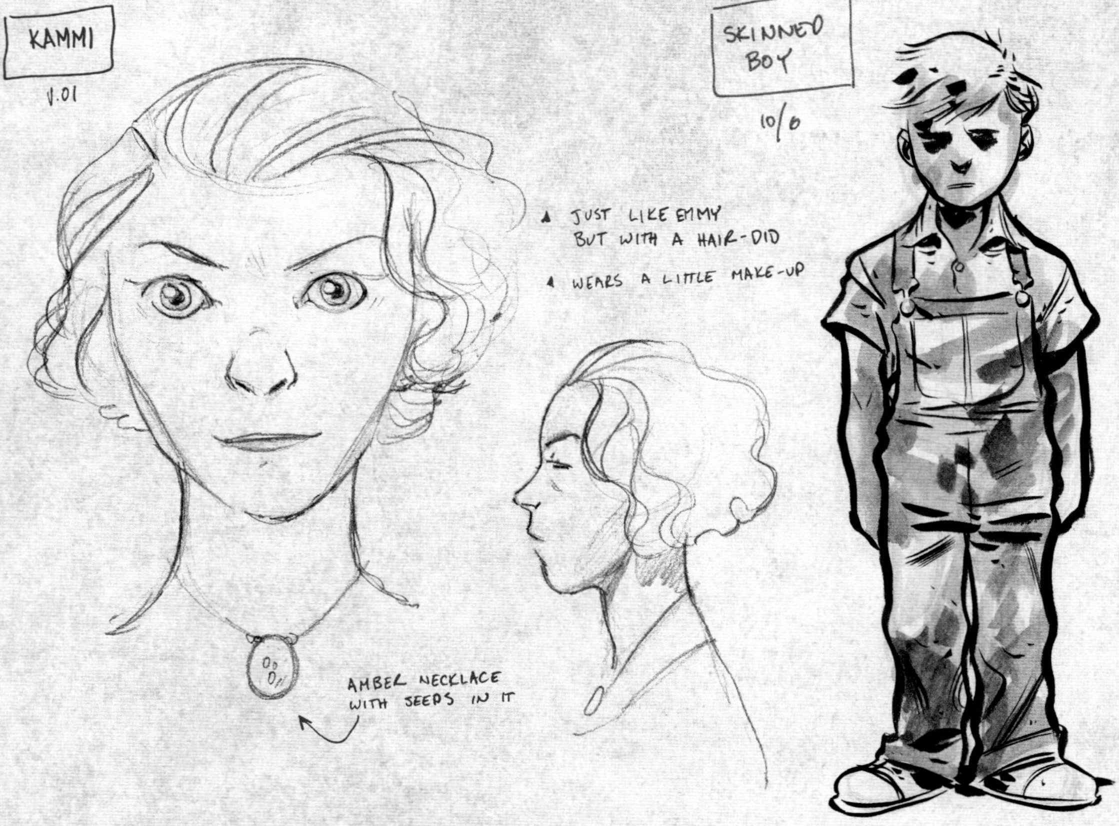
KAMMI
V.01
JUST LIKE EMMY
BUT WITH A HAIR-DID
WEARS A LITTLE MAKE-UP
AMBER NECKLACE
WITH SEEDS IN IT
SKINNED BOY
10/6

TC: I think Cullen had originally planned on the Skinless Boy being closer to Emmy's age. But I really wanted him to be younger. I felt like he needed to be small so he could go places that Emmy couldn't. Also, kids are creepy, so that was a plus.

CB: Definitely the right move making the Skinless Boy younger than Emmy. I also like that, in the comic itself, he's first seen carrying a stuffed bunny around. That made him all the creepier to me.

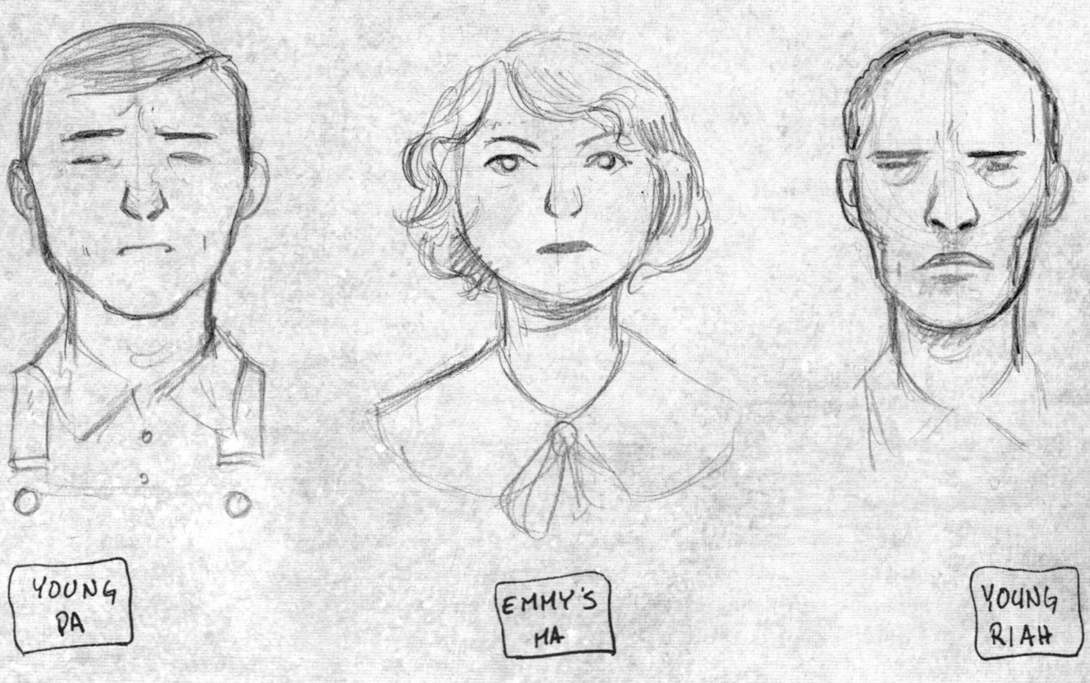
YOUNG PA
EMMY'S MA
YOUNG RIAH

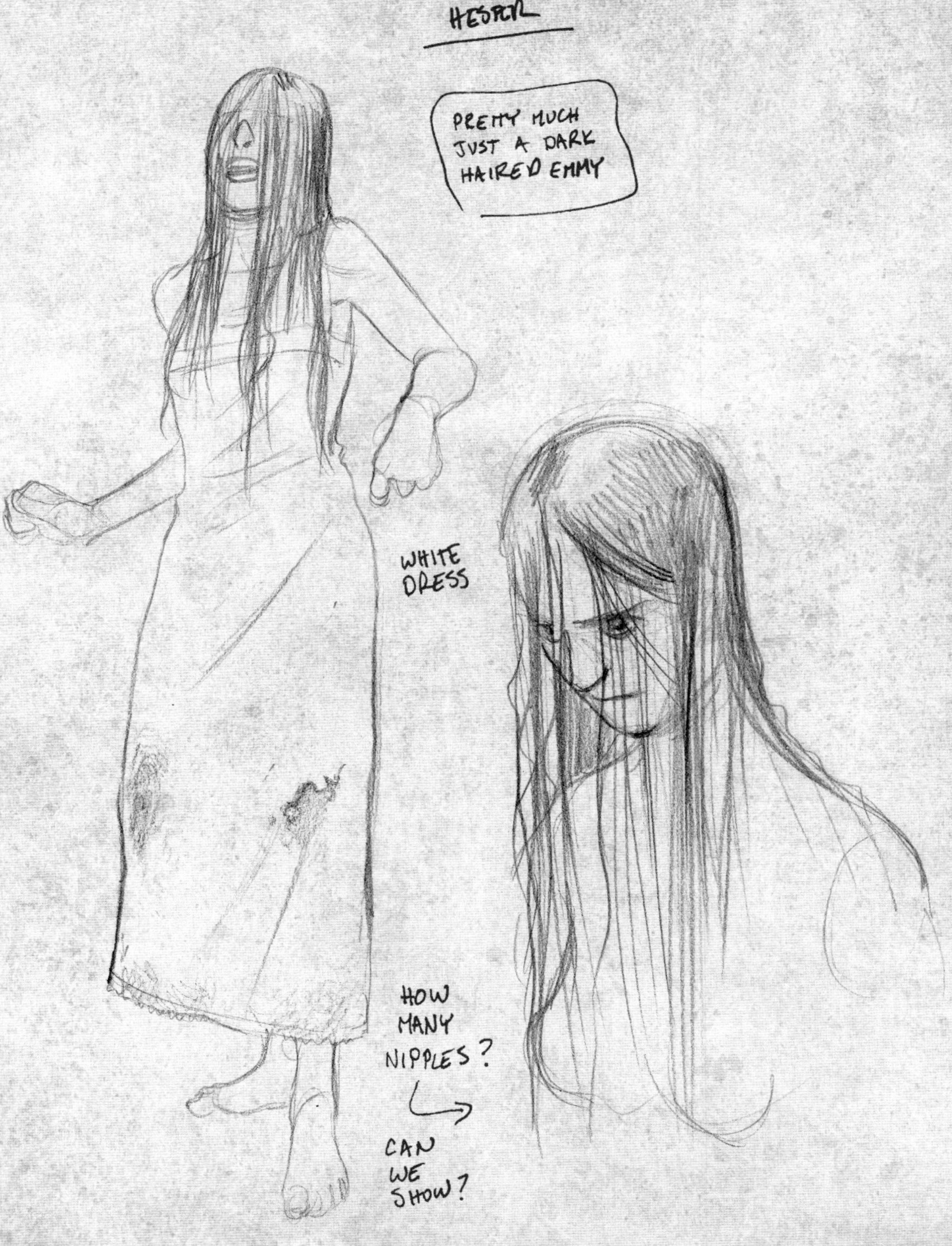
HESTER
PRETTY MUCH
JUST A DARK
HAIRED EMMY
WHITE
DRESS
HOW
MANY
NIPPLES?
CAN
WE
SHOW?

TC: We decided to show zero nipples. It's kind of tempting to use nudity or wanton sexuality in women as a signifier that a character is evil, but Hester, I think, shows her evil pretty clearly without that.

CB: A while back, my wife and I visited my parents at their backwoods home. We were going to sleep on the floor in the living room. There was this big window that looked out toward a shed. As a joke, my dad said, "One night, I saw this old woman running back and forth on top of that shed." This terrified my wife, and she wouldn't sleep in that room. Anyhow, the woman running back and forth on top of the old building? I imagine she looked like this.

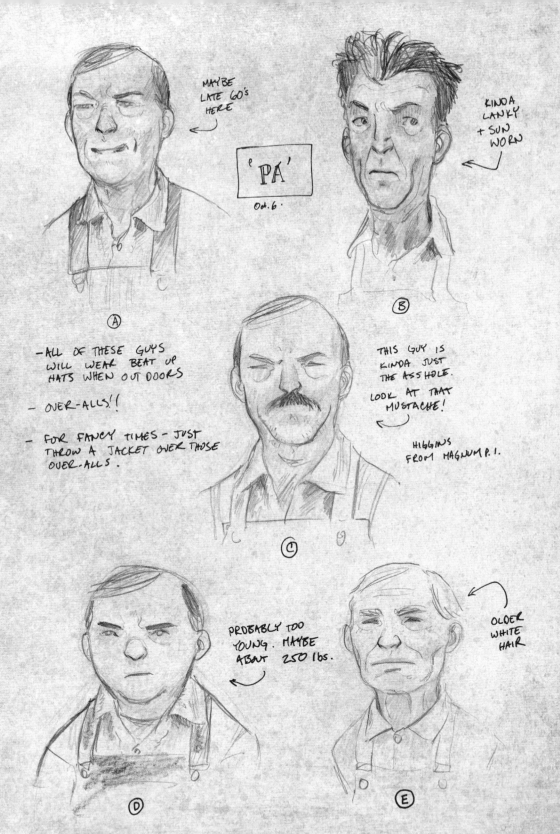

MAYBE LATE 60's HERE

'PA'
Oct. 6.

KINDA LANKY + SUN WORN

A

B

- ALL OF THESE GUYS WILL WEAR BEAT UP HATS WHEN OUT DOORS

- OVER-ALLS!!

- FOR FANCY TIMES - JUST THROW A JACKET OVER THOSE OVER-ALLS.

THIS GUY IS KINDA JUST THE ASSHOLE. LOOK AT THAT MUSTACHE!

HIGGINS FROM MAGNUM P.I.

C

PROBABLY TOO YOUNG. MAYBE ABOUT 250 lbs.

OLDER WHITE HAIR

D

E

TC: It took a little bit of searching to find the right look for Pa. I have a lot of thoughts about Pa, and I'm looking forward to exploring his character more in future story arcs.

CB: Yeah, I remember lots of back-and-forth on Pa, maybe more so than any other character. It was important to get him right because he's the "face" of everything Emmy has known . . . and everything that is changing.

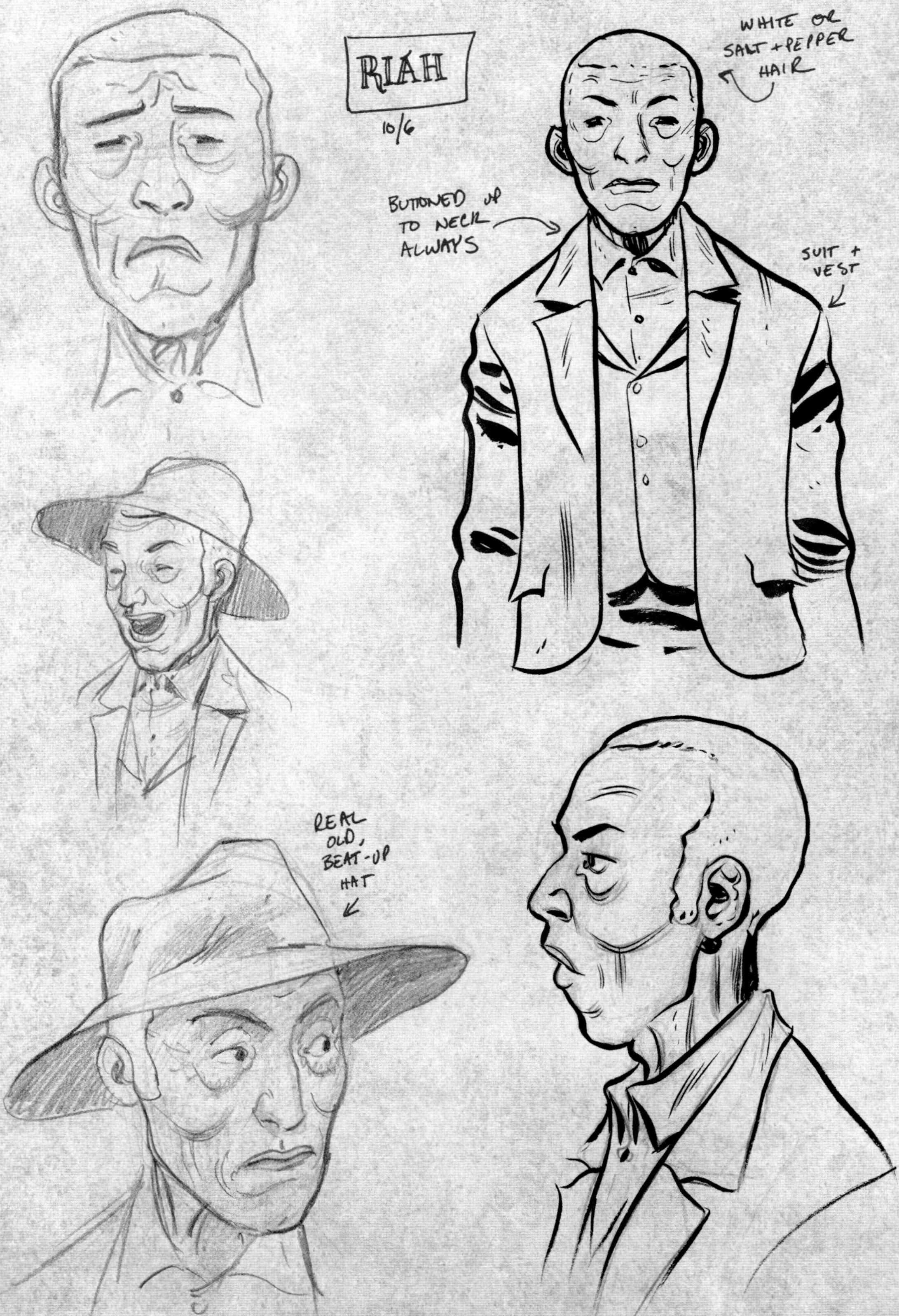
RIAH
10/6
WHITE OR SALT + PEPPER HAIR
BUTTONED UP TO NECK ALWAYS
SUIT + VEST
REAL OLD, BEAT-UP HAT

TC: I like Riah's hat. I think it was already beat up and old when he got it. I can just picture Bernice begging him to throw it out and get a new one, but he'll never give it up!

CB: We'll be seeing much, much more of Riah in the future. That old man has stories to tell!

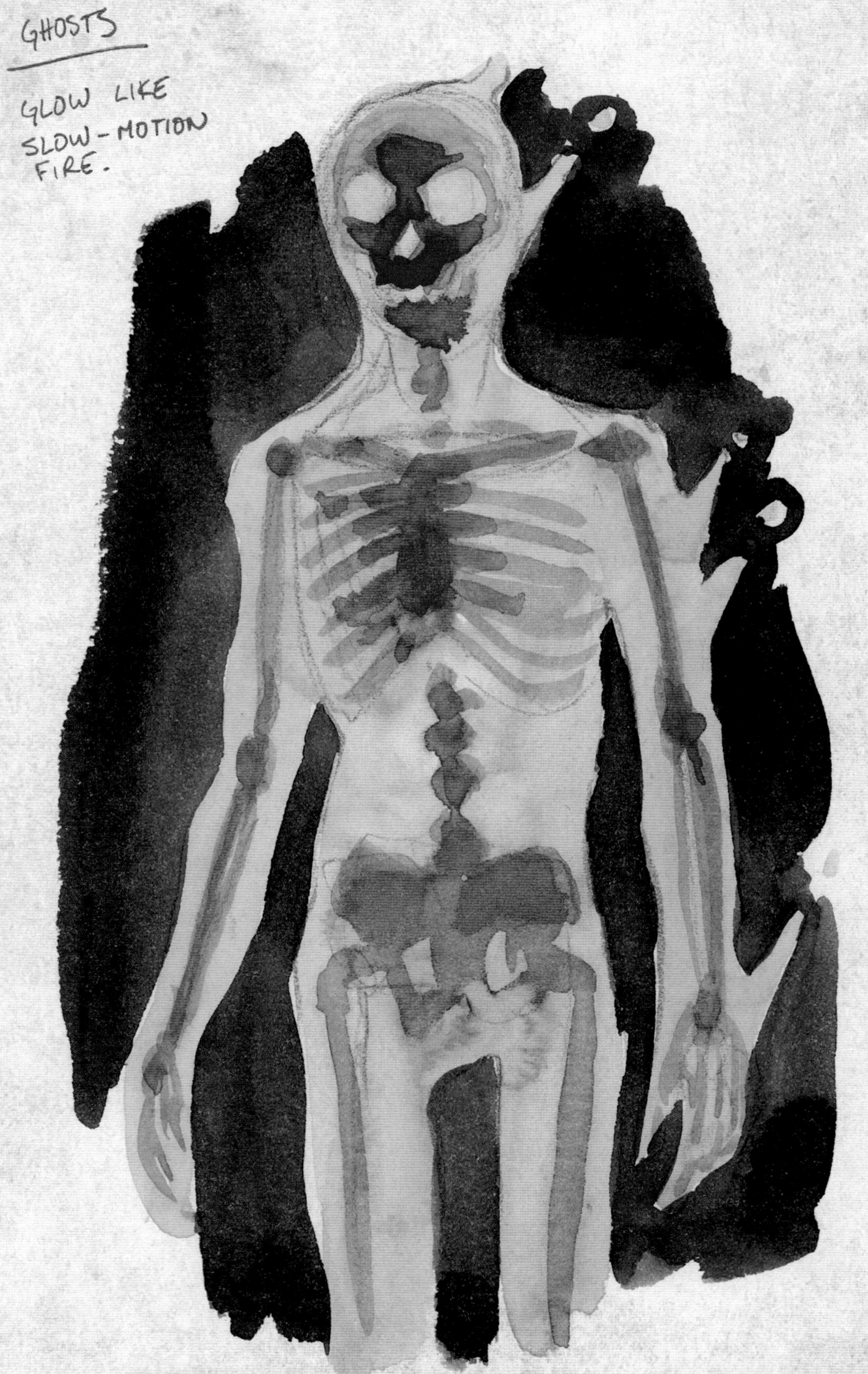
GHOSTS
GLOW LIKE
SLOW-MOTION
FIRE.

CB: I love the unexpected brightness of these ghosts. They look so weird and creepy against the backdrop of shadows.

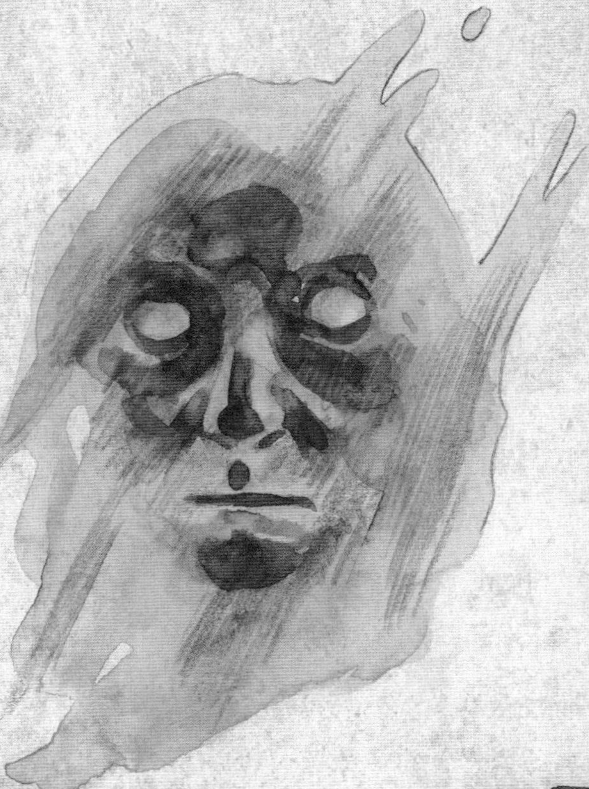

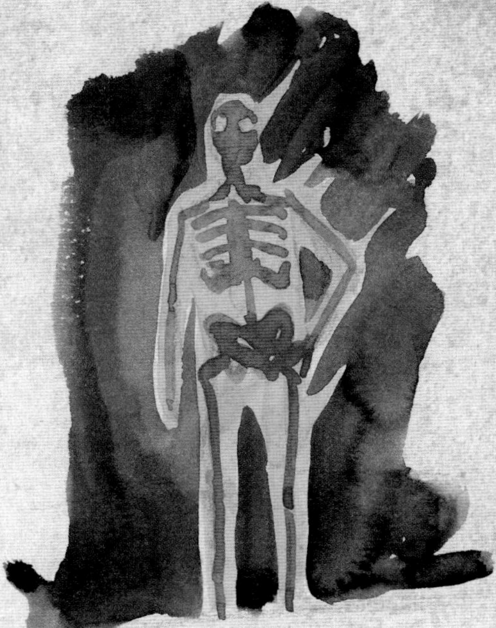
- DIFFERENT LEVELS
OF SKELETON.

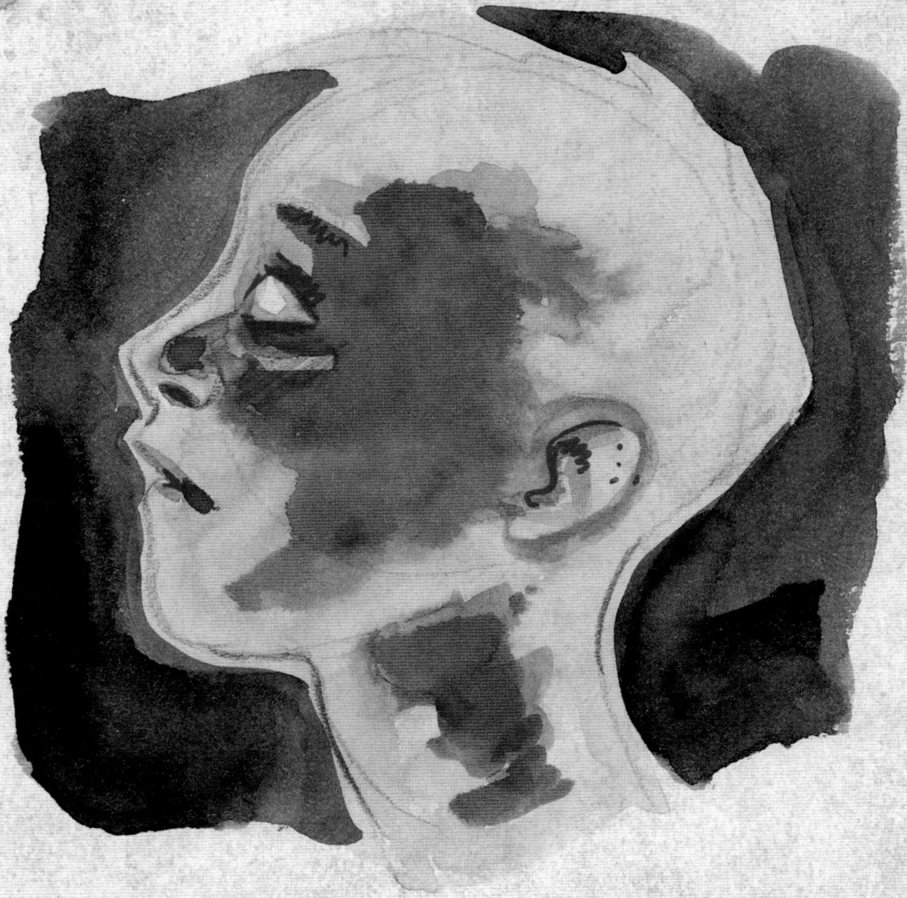

TC: My thought with this is that they remain as ghosts because they are tortured by something that won't let them go. But instead of being tortured by outside flames, it's something inside them that burns.

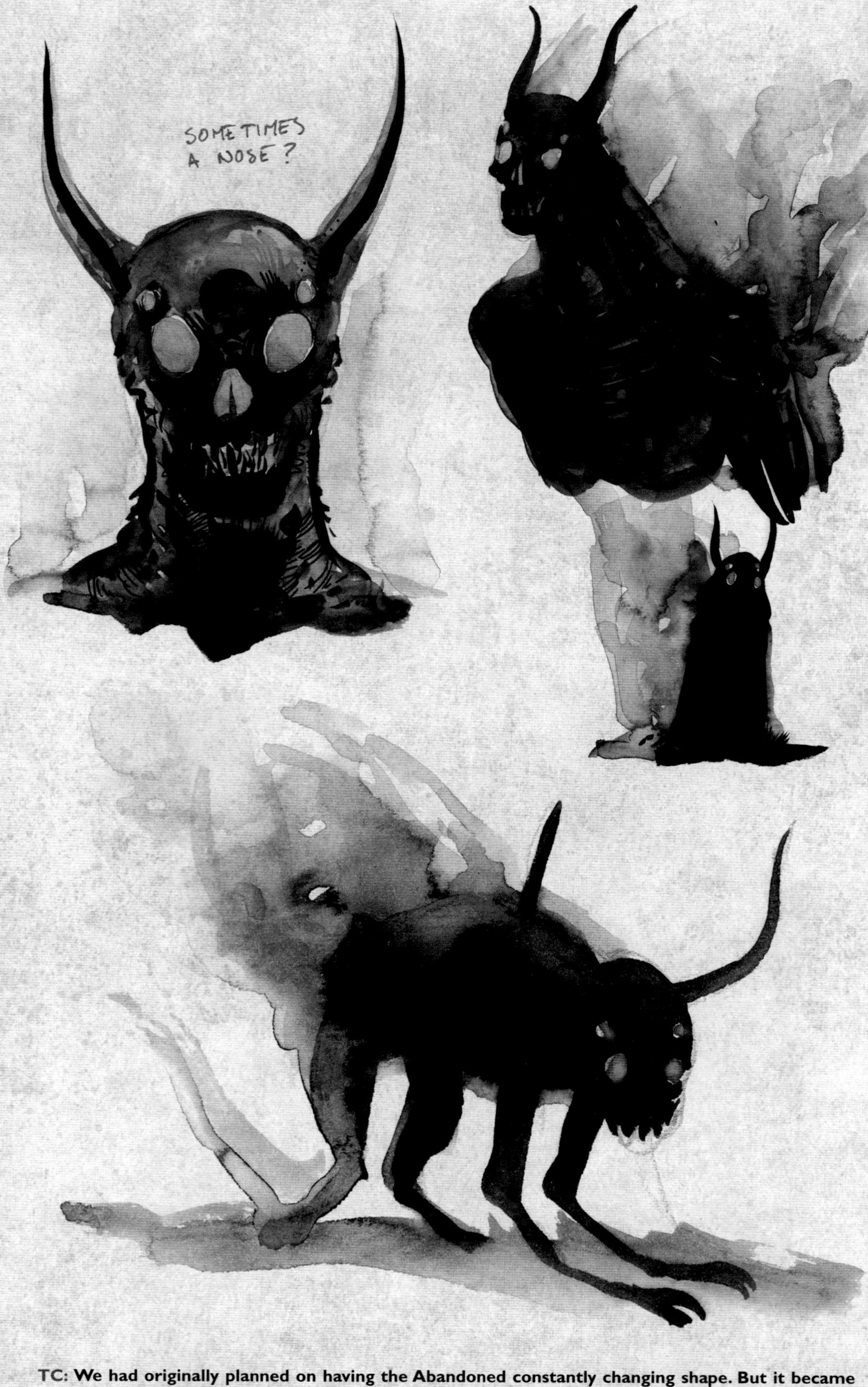
SOMETIMES
A NOSE?

TC: We had originally planned on having the Abandoned constantly changing shape. But it became clear pretty quickly that would have been super confusing. So we just stuck with the initial Minotaur that I drew on the second page.

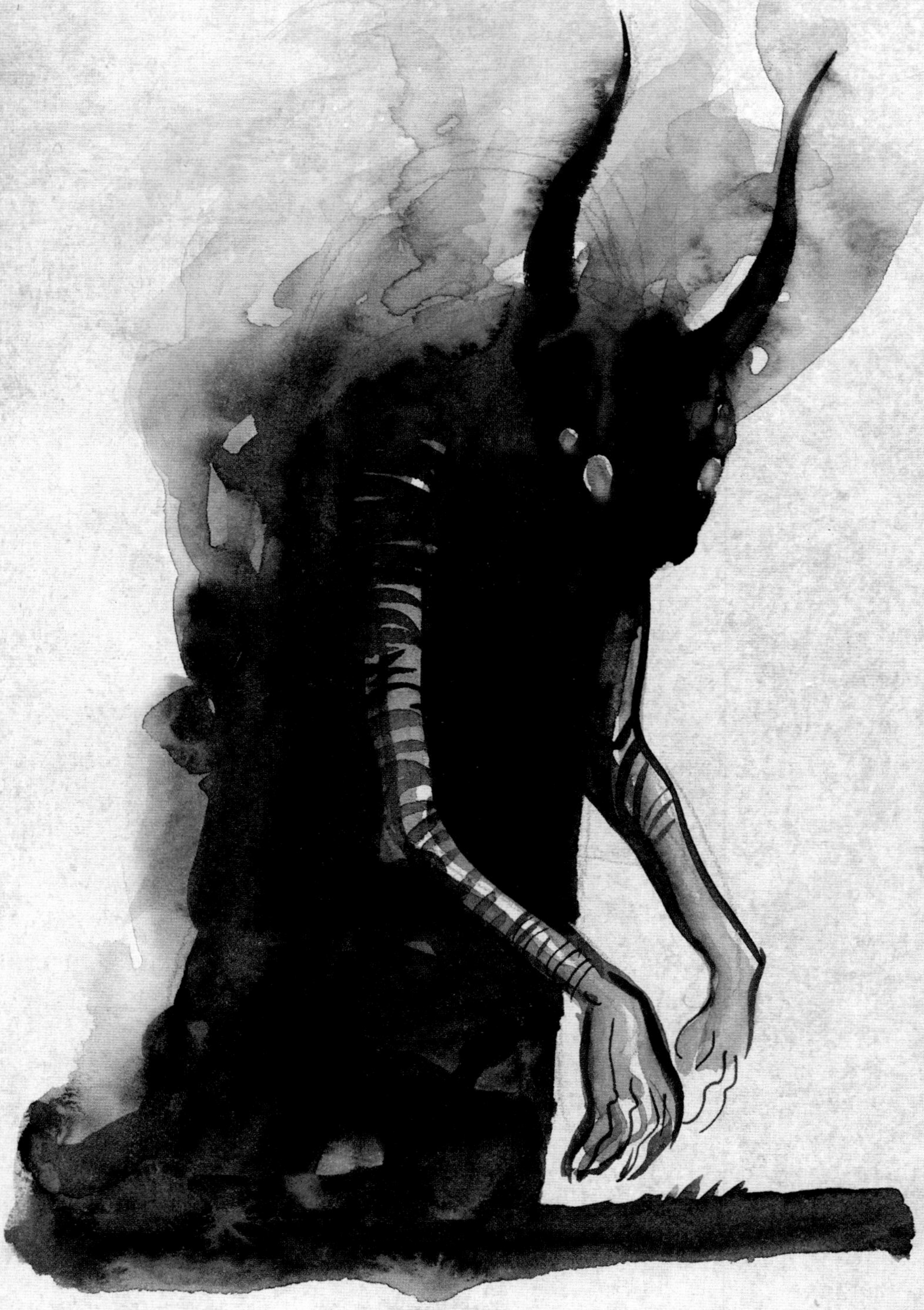

· KINDA A SMOKE MONSTER
· ALTERNATES BETWEEN PURE BLACK
+ GREENISH BLUE
· CAN BE ANY SHAPE – HUMAN, ANIMAL, BLOB

CB: For me, the Abandoned's eyes were very important. I wanted them to look like the eyes of a goat. My parents had goats on their farm . . . and those sideways-hourglass eyes always gave me the creeps.

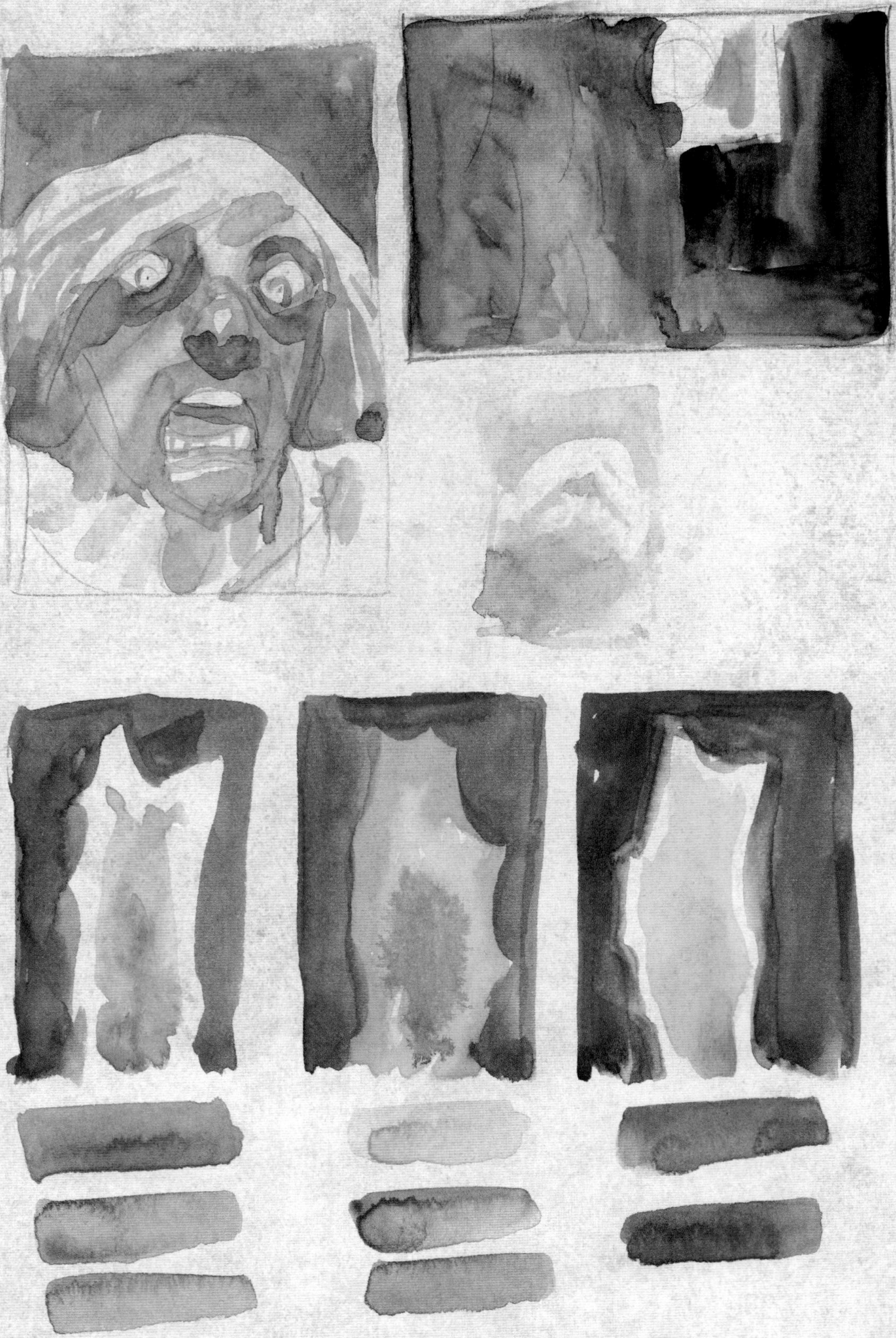

TC: The decision to color this book with watercolors makes for some interesting challenges. For one thing, there's no Undo like there is in Photoshop. Once I commit to putting color on the page, it's on the page for good. So I'll often test color combos on a scrap piece of paper before I start on the final page. These are a few of those tests.

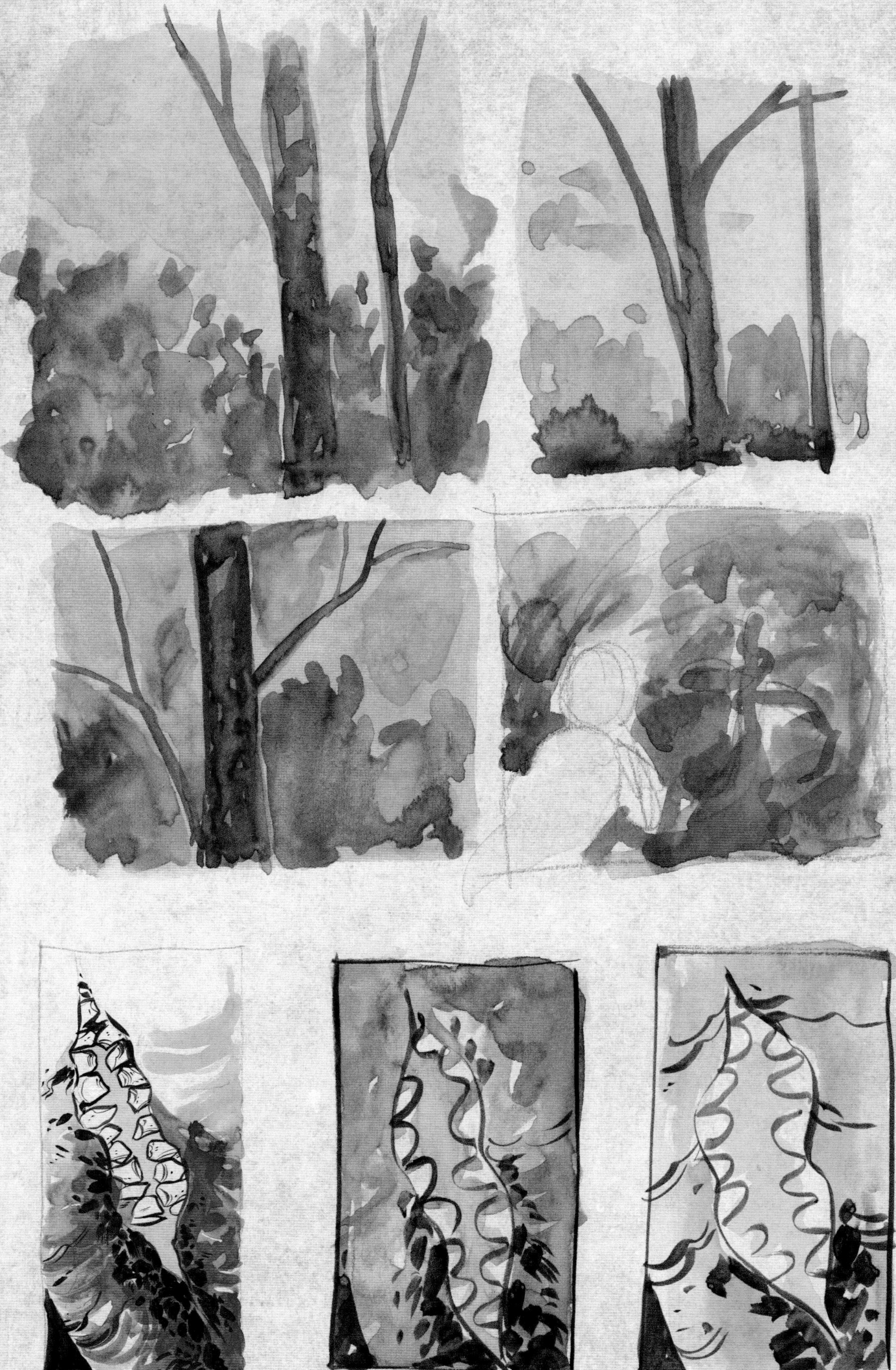

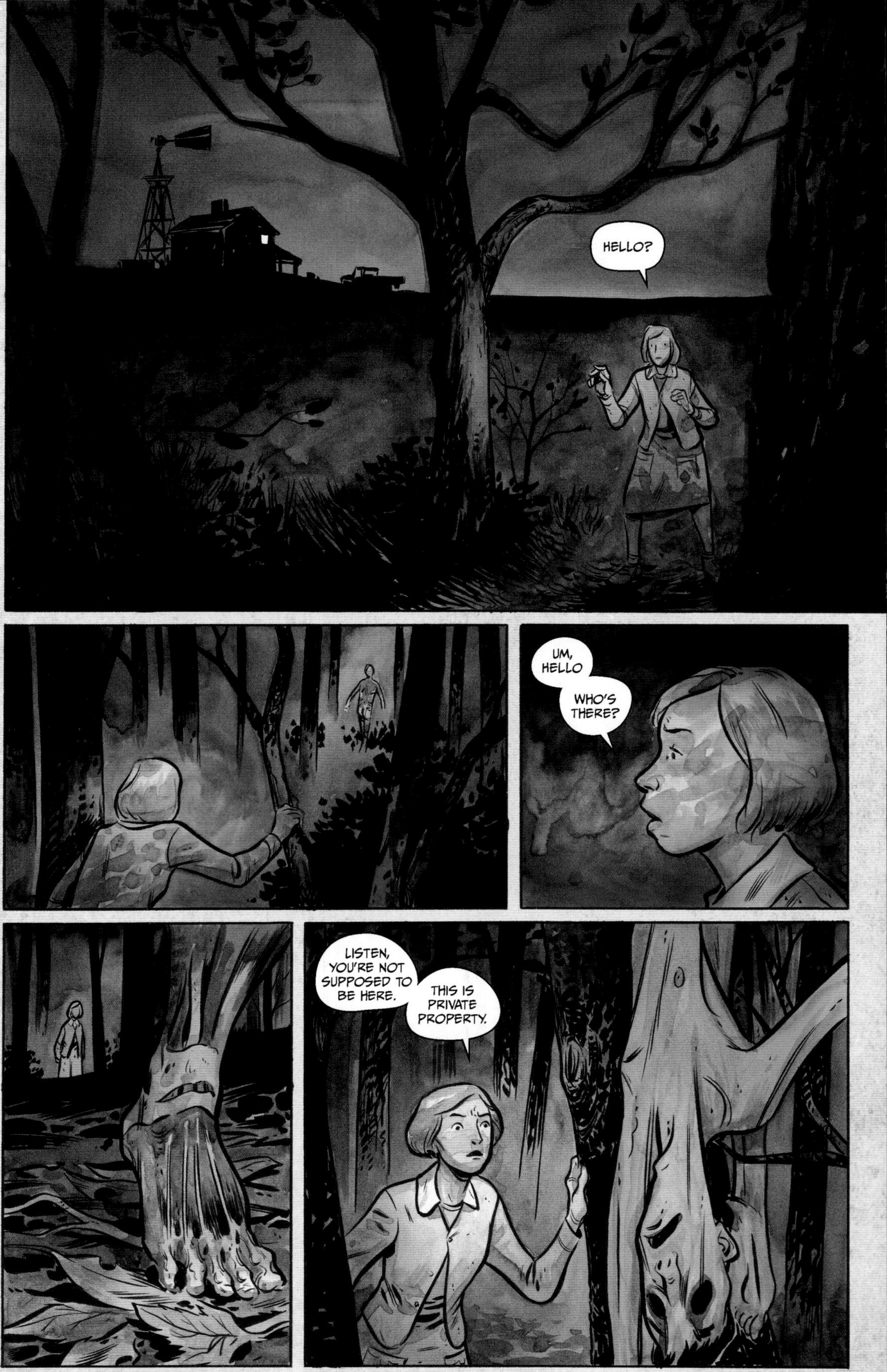
HELLO?
UM, HELLO
WHO'S THERE?
LISTEN, YOU'RE NOT SUPPOSED TO BE HERE.
THIS IS PRIVATE PROPERTY.

DANIEL CHABON: This page is the original art sample page that Tyler and Cullen cooked up to attach to their pitch for *Harrow County*.

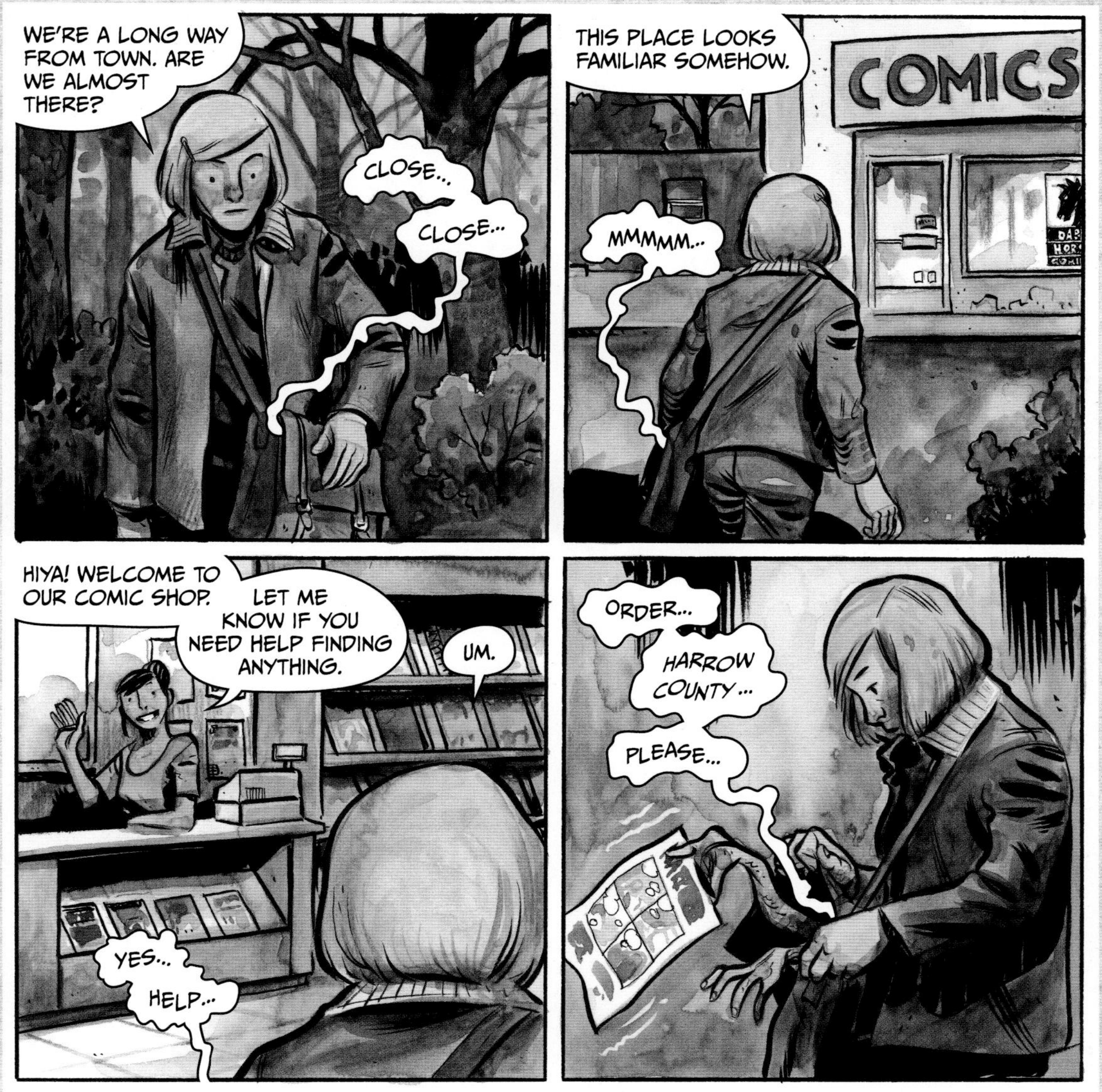
WE'RE A LONG WAY FROM TOWN. ARE WE ALMOST THERE?
CLOSE...
CLOSE...
THIS PLACE LOOKS FAMILIAR SOMEHOW.
COMICS
MMMMM...
HIYA! WELCOME TO OUR COMIC SHOP.
LET ME KNOW IF YOU NEED HELP FINDING ANYTHING.
UM.
YES...
HELP...
ORDER...
HARROW COUNTY...
PLEASE...

DC: ***Above,*** **art that Tyler created for a** ***Harrow County*** **#1 comics retailer order form.** ***Below,*** **more test art by Tyler.**

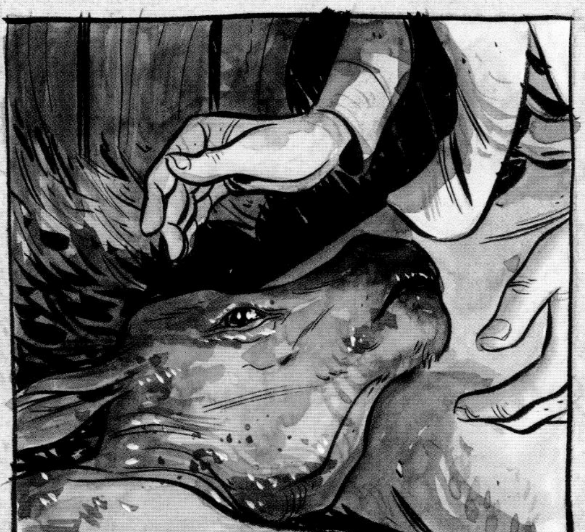

CONTÉ TEST
10/21

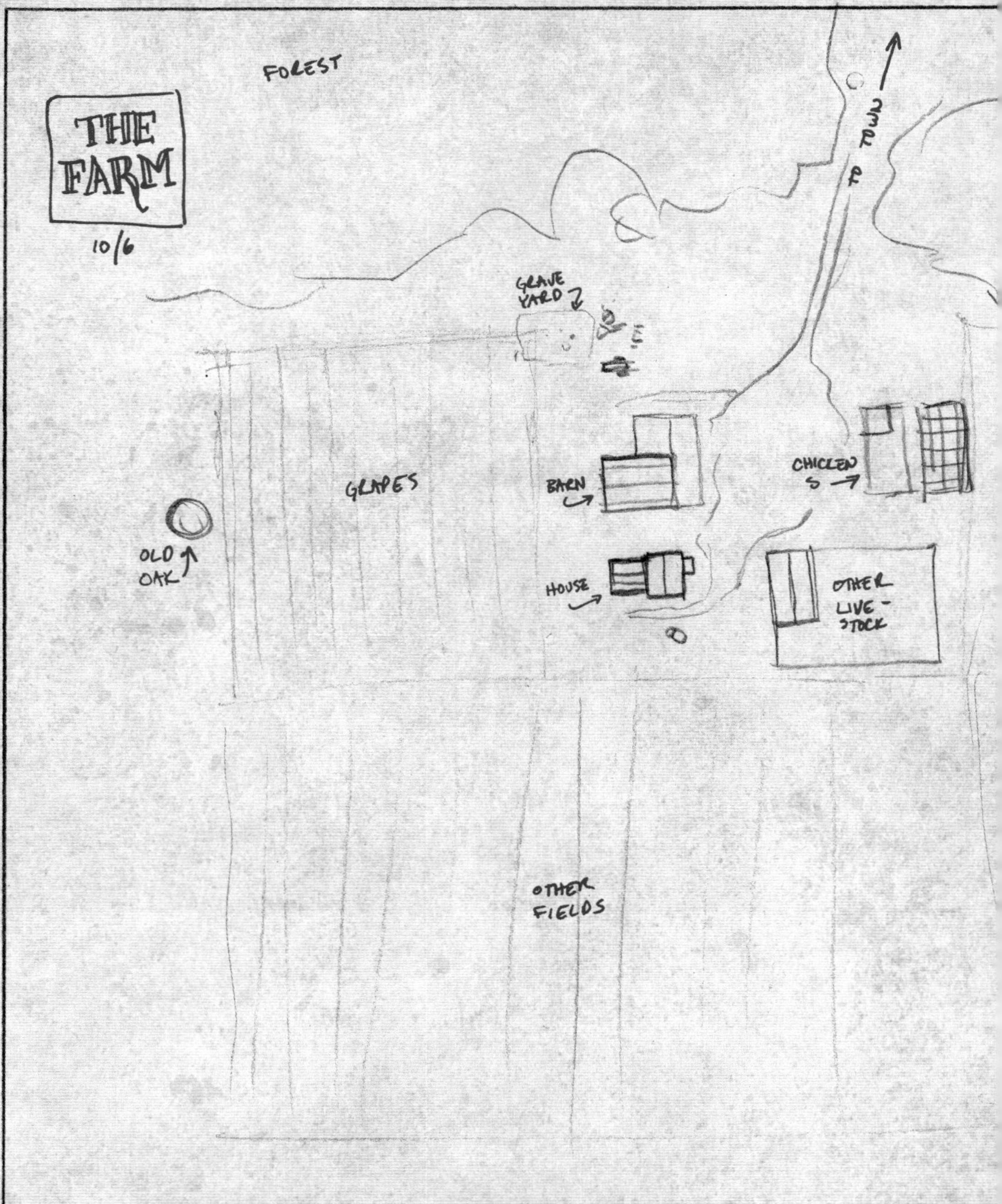
FOREST
THE FARM
10/6
GRAVE YARD
GRAPES
OLD OAK
BARN
HOUSE
CHICKEN S
OTHER LIVE-STOCK
OTHER FIELDS

TC: I started on this map to help me keep track of the farm's layout and plan different shots. But maps are too dangerous; they can paint you into a corner if you depend on them too much. So I stopped using it pretty quickly.

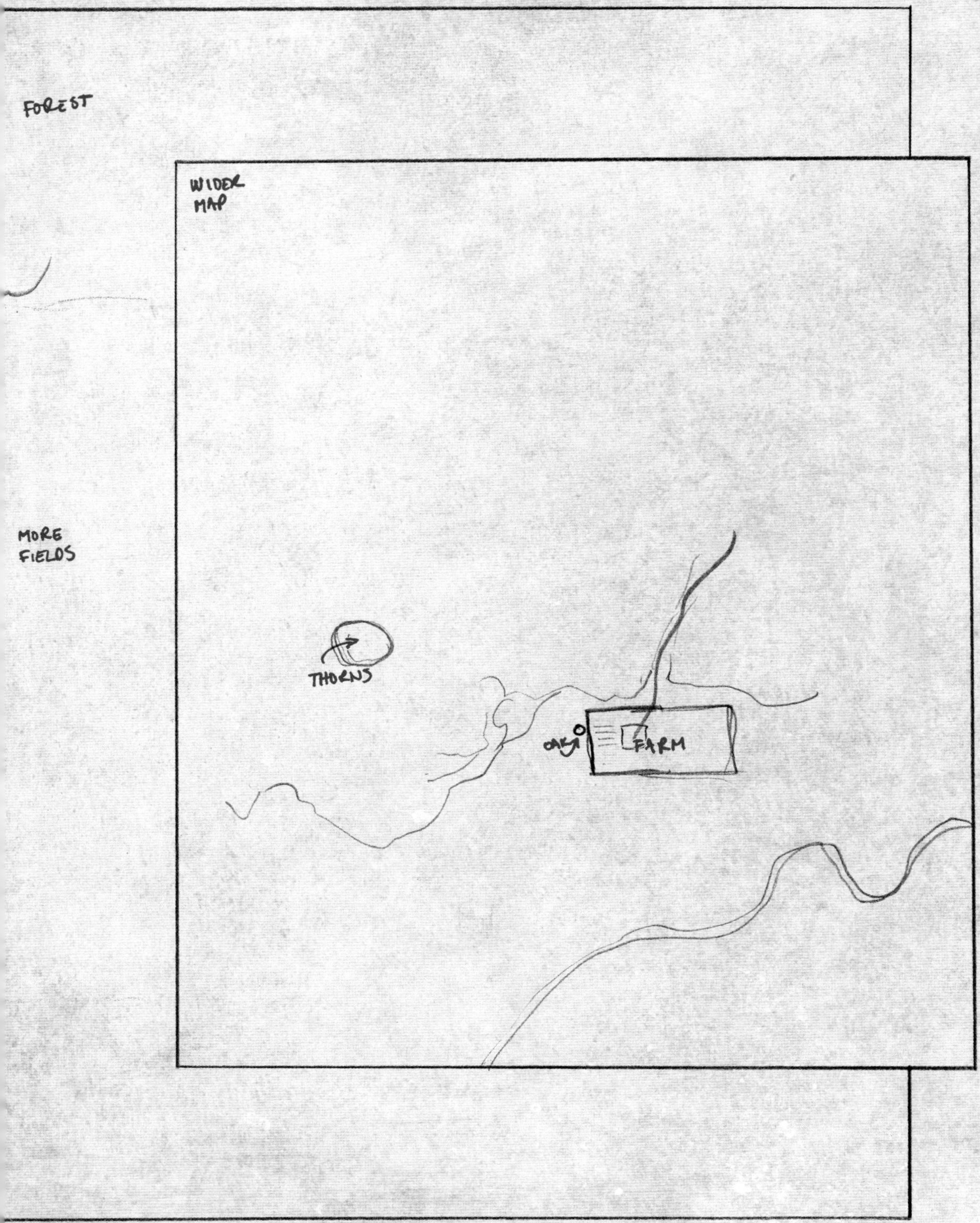
FOREST
WIDER MAP
MORE FIELDS
THORNS
OAK
FARM

CB: Tyler should have never shown me this map. Now I just want to expand it. I want to map out every corner of Harrow County . . . and the locale of every ghost story.

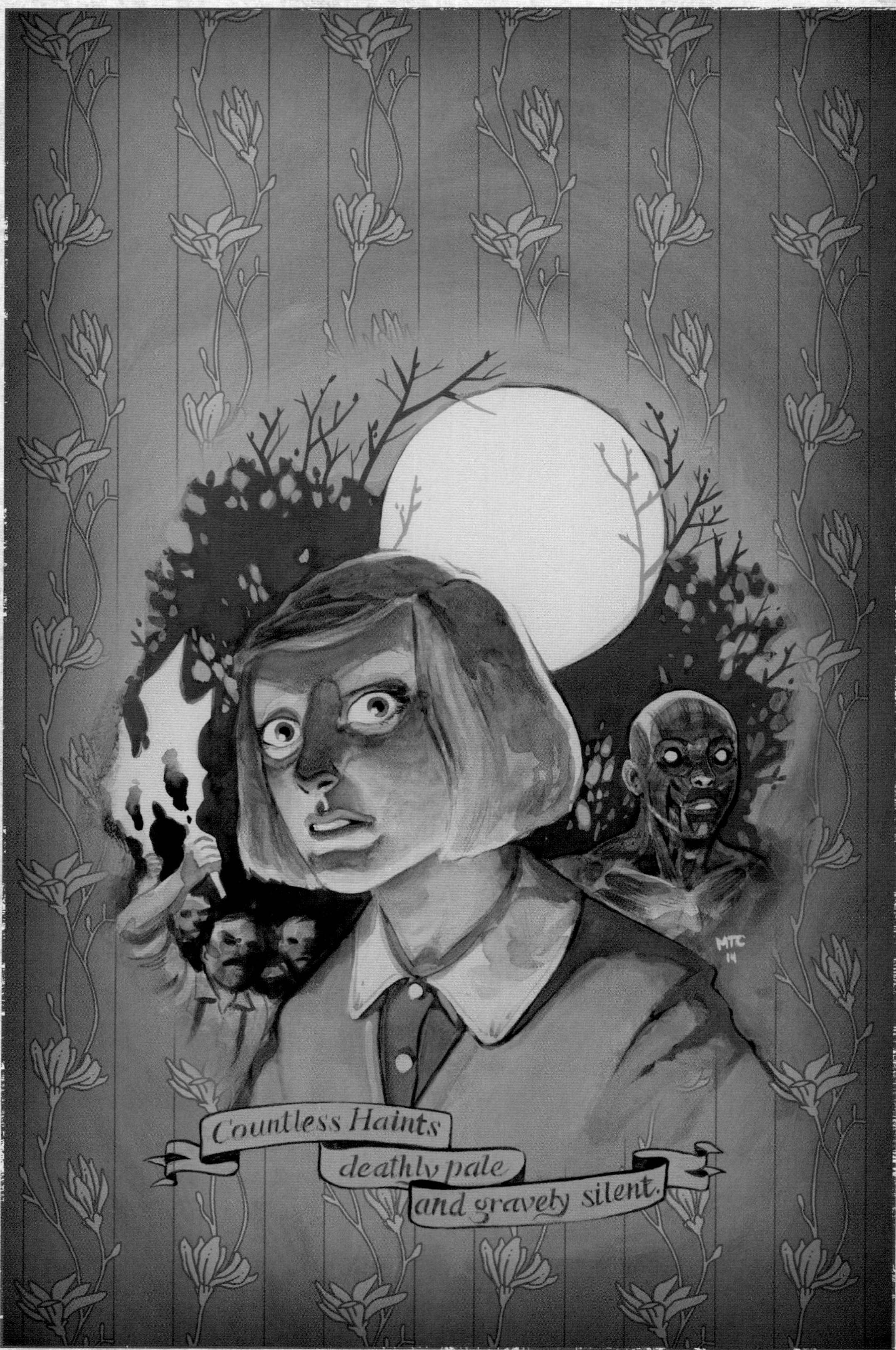
Countless Haints
deathly pale
and gravely silent.
MTC
14

TC: I had originally planned on doing all the covers in pastel colors. But we decided that was a bad idea. I always say that good drawings are easy; it's the mediocre drawings that take all the work. This cover is a good example of that. I fought and struggled with this cover, and it turned out terrible. The cover we ended up using (the skin in the drawer) felt almost effortless by comparison.

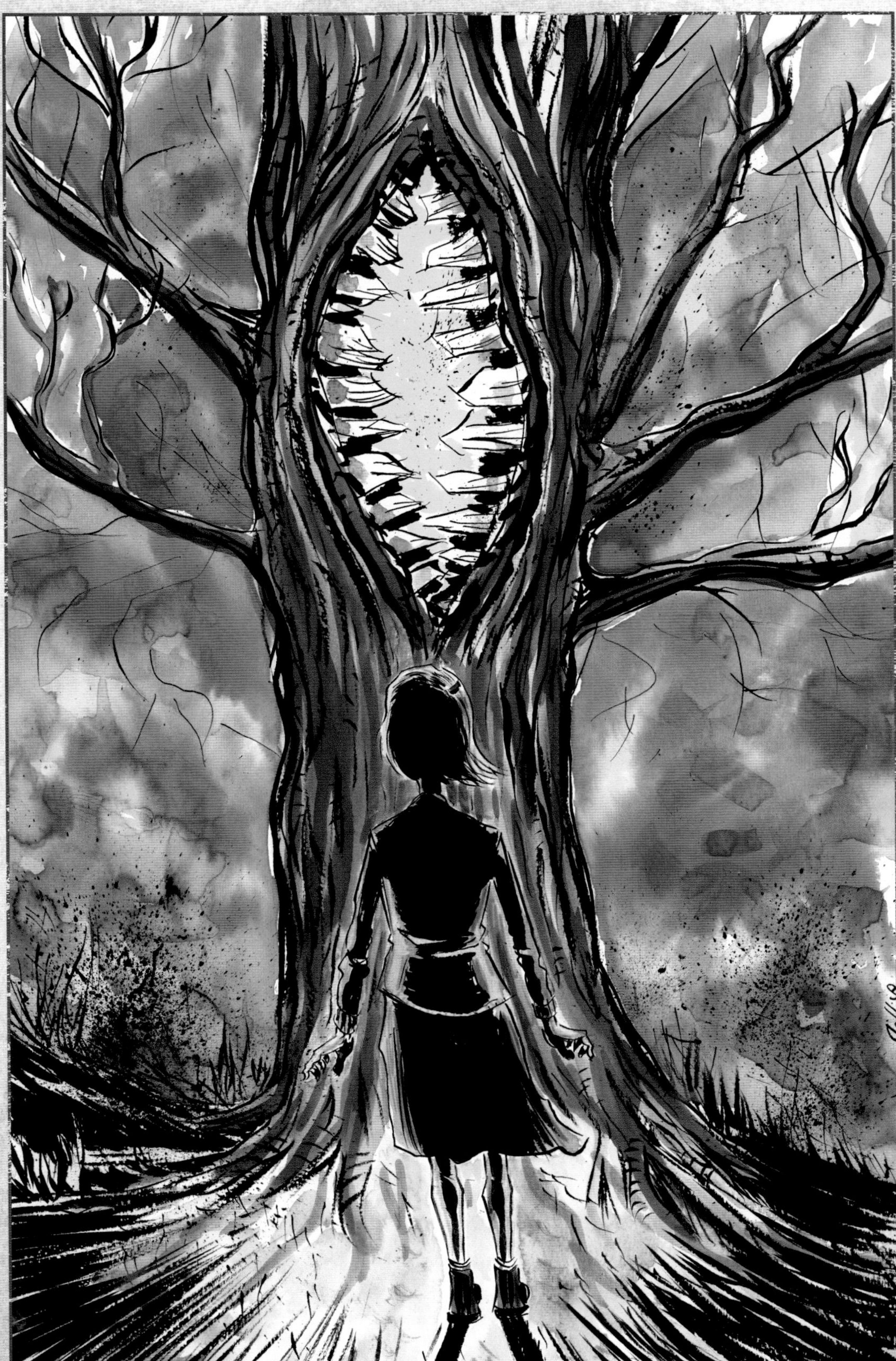

ARTWORK BY
JEFF LEMIRE

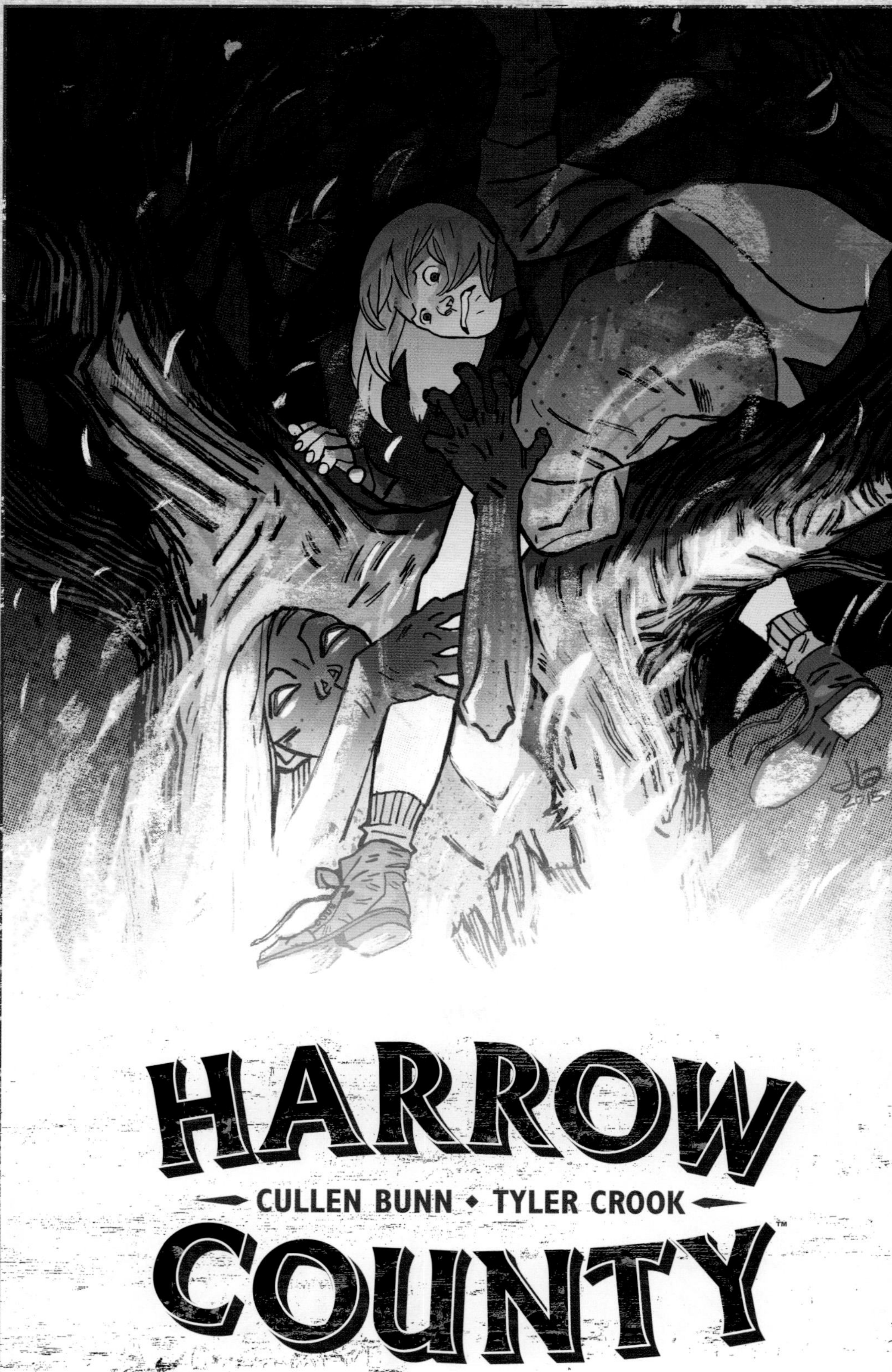
HARROW
CULLEN BUNN • TYLER CROOK
COUNTY™

ARTWORK BY
JASON LATOUR

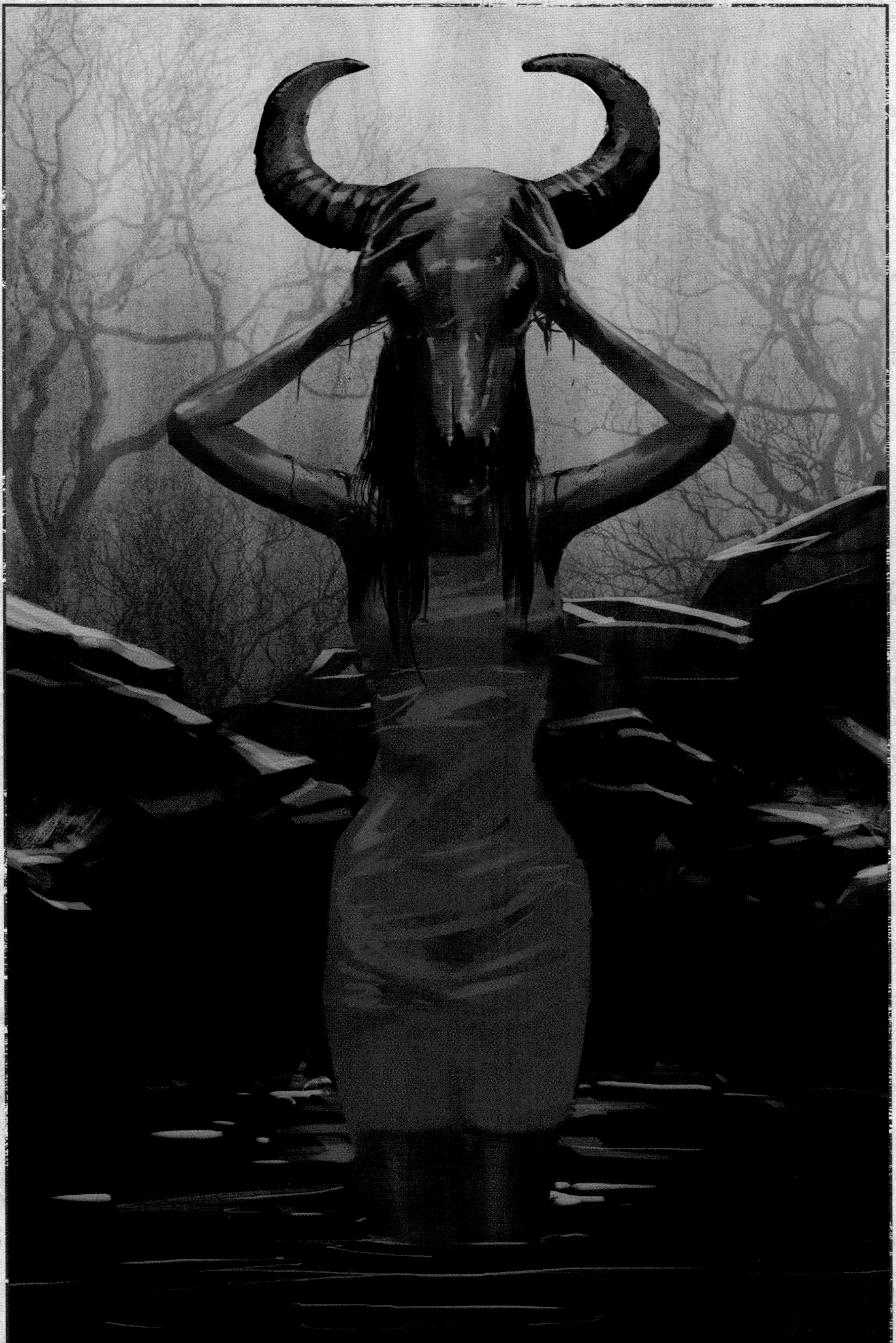

ARTWORK BY
SHANE WHITE

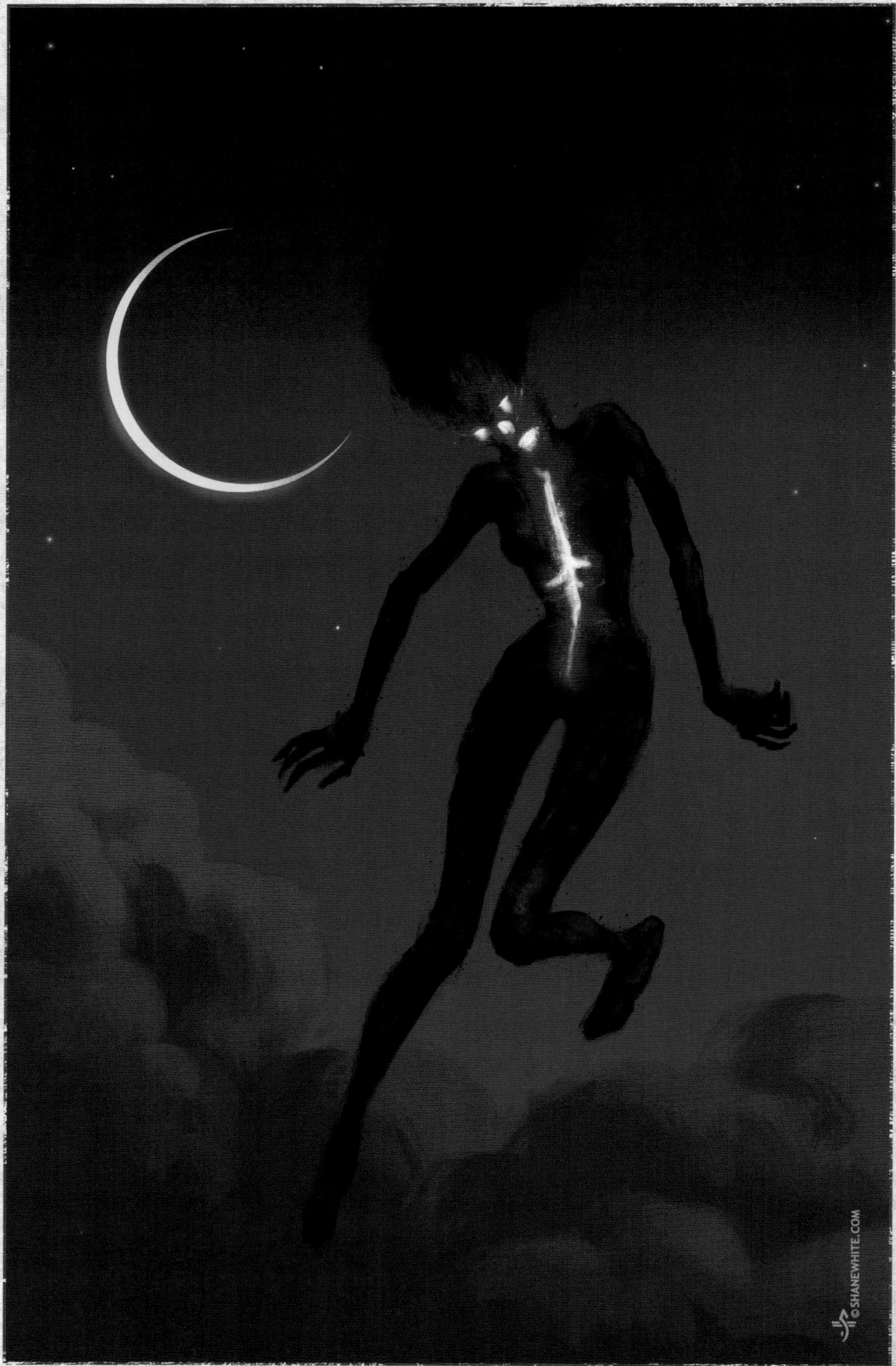
©SHANEWHITE.COM

ARTWORK BY
SHANE WHITE

ARTWORK BY
CAT FARRIS

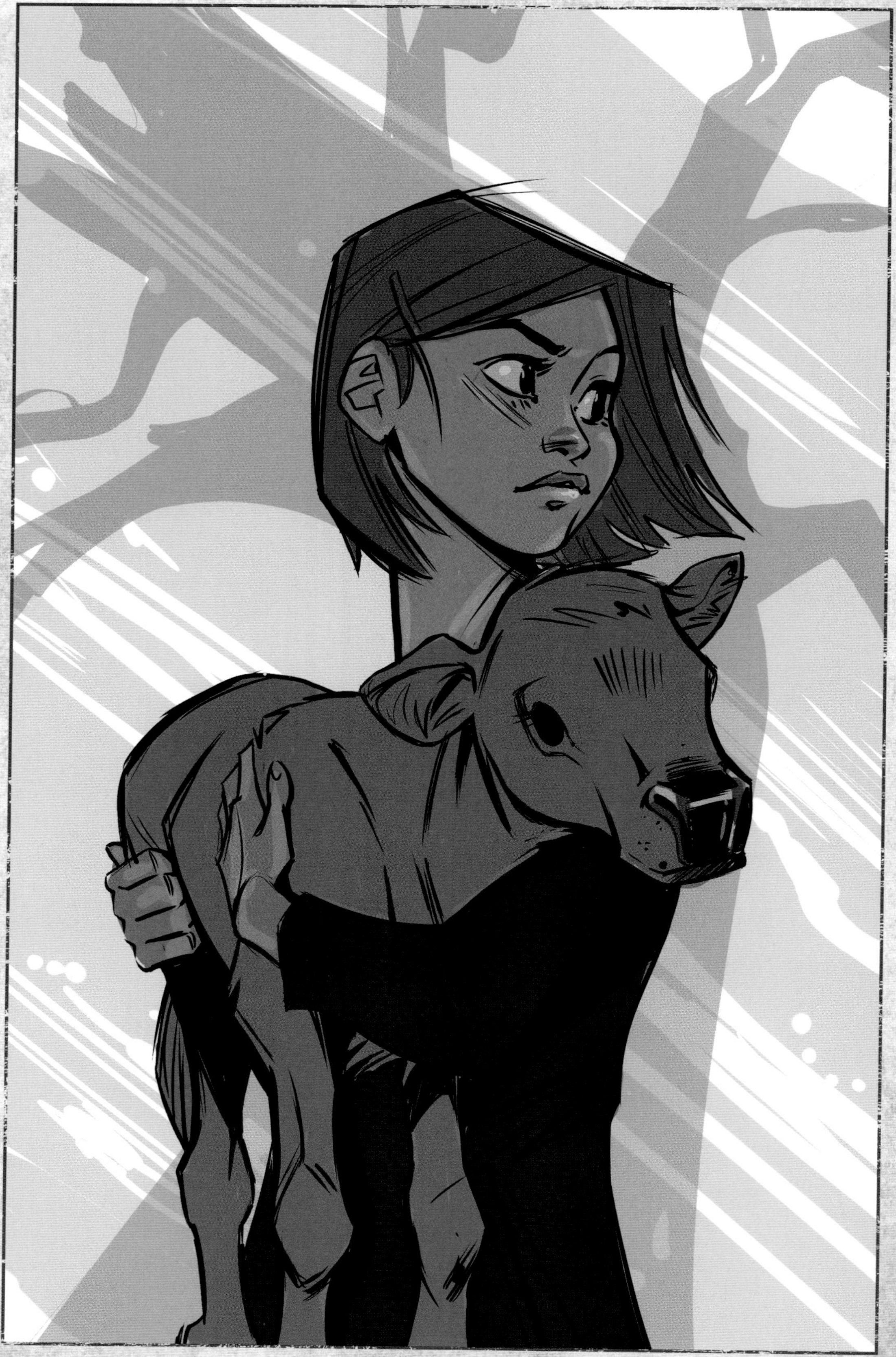

ARTWORK BY
JOËLLE JONES

CB: The original title of this book was *Countless Haints*, but we decided that *Harrow County* gave the series more scope. The earliest incarnation of this tale was a serialized novel I was going to put on my website. Presented here are the first few chapters of that novel. I think it's fun to look at the similarities ... and the differences. Straightaway, you'll notice we changed Madi to Emmy in the comic.

TC: I'm so glad Emmy's name isn't Madrigal anymore.

COUNTLESS HAINTS

CHAPTER ONE

Her earliest memories were of the taste of freshly turned earth and the bleating of goats.

"Pa?" Madrigal asked. "You know what tomorrow is, don't you?"

"Of course." Her father settled back in the creaking chair and placed his opened Bible upon his knee to hold his place. He drew deep on his pipe, and the sweet-smelling smoke plumed around his bald, sun-spotted head. "Can't say as I'd rightly forget."

Madi sat upon the hardwood floor, her legs drawn up close, her chin resting upon her knees. The house was silent, except for their voices, the groan of Pa's chair, and the ticking of the wall clock as it counted the seconds until ...

"I'll be almost a woman grown."

"Almost." Pa's eyes glittered in the lamplight. "You in such a hurry to grow up and leave your old father alone?"

"I ain't planning on leaving anytime soon. Where would I go? You reckon I should march down to Ahmen's Landing and marry me the first fisherman's son I fancy?"

"Say you won't."

"Don't fret." Madi smiled devilishly. "I'll go at least far as Nag's Head before I find me a fella."

"That's good." Pa nodded and returned to his Bible. "A girl ought to have standards."

Madi rolled her eyes at him, but let the matter drop.

The quiet rushed in to flood the house. The quiet. Madi sometimes thought of it as a living, breathing thing. And while the girl usually enjoyed being alone with her thoughts, tonight she felt as if the silence might smother her. The room, the house, the entire farm seemed too small.

Tomorrow, she would be seventeen. There would be no celebration, no gifts or cake, but Pa would wish her a happy birthday come sunup and, if he followed suit from previous years, let her skip her chores for the day. Maybe she *would* take a walk into town, but probably not to look for boys. She wanted a love like she read about in her books—something straight out of *Wuthering Heights* or *Pride and Prejudice* or *Romeo and Juliet*—and she doubted any one of the dirt- or salt-crusted young men from around these parts would be able to oblige. But she wouldn't mind seeing the sights Ahmen's Landing had to offer. She knew there were bigger and more exciting places in the world, but to a girl who almost never set foot off the farm on which she was born, even a tiny fishing village seemed exotic and fanciful.

But she knew better than to entertain the thought for long. Joking aside, Pa would never let her go into town by herself. She doubted he would approve of her going into town on any occasion or under any circumstances.

She watched him from across the dimly lit room. His face was lean and weathered, with deep creases in his flesh that seemed to snare the shadows and hold them prisoner. His eyes were deep set and weary. His lips trembled as he quietly read his scriptures, just as he did every night before bed. Sometimes, when Madi looked at him, she barely recognized him, as if she couldn't believe she was his own flesh and blood.

Her mother, on the other hand, had died when Madi was only a baby, and the girl didn't remember her at all.

"Pa?" she said. "I've been thinking."

"Yes?" He placed the Bible upon his knee again. "What is it, Madi?"

"I been thinking . . . about a name for the new calf."

"Uh-huh."

"I like the name Hanan."

"What's that now?"

"Hanan." Madi smiled. "The name's kinda—"

"Where'd you hear o' that? Ol' man Riah been talkin' on?" He was off his seat—his face pale and his hands knotted into fists—and the good book fell to the floor with a thump. "Well, out with it!"

Madi's eyes lingered on the fallen book.

". . . The Bible. It's a name from the Bible, Pa." She looked down and fell silent. She didn't know why her father, normally so soft spoken and gentle, had grown so angry. She'd certainly seen him agitated on occasion. It was a hard life, a farmer's, and sometimes it took its toll, but never before had his ire been directed at her.

"The Bible." He, too, looked at the book, and a splash of mottled red washed his cheeks. His shoulders slumped. His voice softened. "The Bible. That's it?"

"Yes, Pa."

"Well . . ." He licked his lips and spoke carefully. He was obviously embarrassed by not recognizing a name straight from the pages he read so often. "That ain't the point. The point is, ya gotta stop naming every blessed livin' thing on this farm. A cow don't need a name, especially a bull. You wouldn't go a-naming the grapevines, would ya, nor the shrimp we net, and them things are a sight more important to us than a cow or a hen. Sometimes creatures are best left to their ways. No sense in making 'em out like something they ain't."

"Yes, Pa. I didn't mean . . ."

"It's done and over now." His bones popped as he leaned over and grabbed the Bible from the floor. "Let's not worry on it any longer."

Madrigal dreamed of the tree upon the hill.

Shrouded in runaway scuppernong vines, the tall, gray oak cast its bent shadow across the valley and scratched with spindly branches at the sky. Years ago, or so Madi had been told, the oak had been struck by lightning during one of the summer squalls that blew in from the east. The tree had not grown an inch since, and a rotting hollow now yawned in the trunk. The cavity had been filled to keep the blight from spreading, but the effort had proven futile, the decaying wood pulling away from the concrete filling like gums receding from old, blunted teeth.

In the dream, the maw trembled and smacked, the tree groaning and spitting out mouthfuls of crumbling cement.

In the dream, Madi tried to gather up the bits of rubble, all the while muttering, "Oh no, no, Pa will be so angry."

But the tree, its mouth no longer gagged, did not care if the old farmer was angered or not. The draping grapevines rustled with a sound like whispered secrets, the oak's grit-encrusted lips quivered, and the mouth, running up and down rather than side to side, opened and closed and growled.

"Lies," the tree said. "Lies."

In the dream, lightning sizzled across the blackening sky, bright as witch's fire.

Madi woke and sat up in bed. Even though the night was warm and the cramped room was stuffy, she drew the patchwork blanket up close. Moonlight trickled in through the bedside window, painting the room in an eerie blue haze—the color, or so she'd always thought, of haints. They were all around her, crowding close to her bed, watching her. Countless haints.

She looked out the bedside window and gathered the covers even closer.

The vineyard's wire trellises, already heavy with leaves and grape clusters, climbed the hill. At the summit stood the crooked oak in stark silhouette, its black branches spread out and vanishing into the night, as if growing into the darkness itself.

She hated that tree, and she feared it, too.

Feared its secrets.

An echo of the dream rattled around in Madi's head, and she spoke the words in a hushed whisper.

"Lies."

CHAPTER TWO

The woods stretched away from the farm and into forever.

Madi grabbed a crooked switch from the ground and swatted at weeds and spider webs as she followed the pine straw–carpeted trail. Trees—mostly pines, but oaks and black walnut and white ash, too—loomed on either side of the path, taller even than the silent, lightning-scarred sentinel upon the hill. She wondered if the blighted oak had once been part of the forest, separated from its ilk when the farm was raised. If the oak had not been struck by lightning, would it have grown as large and strong as the rest of the woods? The trees here were healthy and proud, not twisted and mean spirited and cruel. They needed not to whisper secrets and were silent save for the rush of breeze through the leaves.

Soon, she heard the gurgling of the creek, and she quickened her pace. The worn footpath cut toward the cold, rushing creek and a rickety wooden bridge from which she sometimes fished or tossed skipping stones. For as long as she could remember, Pa promised he was going to repair the old, rotting bridge. "Sooner or later," he said, "someone's gonna fall straight through, down into the creek, I don't take hammer and nail to that bridge soon." But the creek water was so shallow in places that Madi imagined it could be crossed on foot without worry, and few people ever crossed the bridge, anyway, except maybe the grizzled trader man who brought canned food and tools and clothing loaded onto his mule-drawn wagon.

Riah.

Pa didn't like the old man much, even though he bartered with him from time to time when he came round. It was a way of doing business most folk didn't believe in anymore, Pa said, especially when they could just hop in the truck and drive to Walmart for the supplies they needed. Pa said Riah followed other old customs—old beliefs—and he didn't want the trader man talking to Madi. On more than one occasion, Pa had run Riah off when he tried to share a few whispered words with the girl, but the old man always returned a few weeks later, leading his creaking wagon out of the woods.

Madi stepped upon the bridge and crossed to the midpoint. The feel of the splintered wood beneath her bare feet was comforting in a way. Familiar. Between the planks of the bridge she saw the water below. She leaned upon the rail and looked over the edge. The creek wound past heavy stones and the roots of trees exposed by the washing away of soil. The water was so clear she could see a few skinny fish darting back and forth, and if she had set her mind on the task she could have counted the smooth creek bed pebbles. Water striders sliced lines across the surface, and dragonflies danced in the air.

Dragonflies—snake doctors, Pa called them. Whenever you saw one, you could be sure a copperhead or water moccasin lurked nearby.

But she didn't see a snake as she peered over the edge of the bridge.

Instead, she saw a boy.

Her breath caught in her throat.

"Hey, down there," Madi called.

Was he ever handsome! Madi gasped at the sight of him and felt both ashamed and excited by the feeling. The boy looked to be around her age, maybe a year older or younger, but no more than that. His jeans and T-shirt were wash worn and faded and threadbare, but he had refined, delicate features—the unkempt blond hair and large blue eyes of a fairy-tale prince.

He stood just inside the tree line, and shadow dappled his smooth, pale skin like shifting bruises. He watched the creek water run past, staring intently, as if he expected to see something of great value sweep through the cold current at any moment.

"Hey, down there," Madi called again. Her cheeks and the back of her neck felt warm, and she felt the corners of her mouth raise into a smile she just couldn't help. "Didn't you hear me?"

The boy looked up, squinting and raising a hand to shade his eyes from the sun. A smile played upon his lips for just a moment, then slipped away, as if washed away by the rushing of the water. He took a step back, letting the shadows fold around him.

"What's your name?" Madi asked. "I'm—"

He whirled around and scurried into the woods.

"Wait!" Madi shouted. "Where you going?"

She rushed to the other side of the bridge and down the sloping bank.

"Why are you running? Please wait."

She slipped in the damp earth and skidded down the muddy bank, her feet slipping into the creek. The water felt cold as ice. She scrambled in the mud, clawing her way up the bank. Dark mud spattered the hem and painted an outline of her legs and behind on the dress. Pa would tan her hide for sure when she got back home, but it was too late to worry about that now.

She reached the top of the bank, and saw the boy duck beneath a tangle of brush. He didn't follow the path, and branches slapped at him as he pushed through.

"Wait!" she cried. "You ruined my dress. Least you can do is talk to me."

If he heard her, he didn't react. Twigs and brush crunched beneath his feet. He dipped his head and vanished into a wall of tangled thorns.

"Careful!" Madi raised her voice. She no longer saw him, but could hear him struggling through the thickets up ahead. She didn't know why he was running, and she didn't reckon she'd ever see him again to ask. "That way's overrun with thornbushes."

Dozens of thick, thorny vines crisscrossed before her. Not impassable, but growing thicker every inch of the way. She'd never follow the boy's path without at least a few cuts and scrapes.

Old Man Riah once told her a tale of a young boy who had been chased through the briars by a pack of wild dogs. Nearly scared to death by the ravenous, nipping animals, the boy had plunged into the briars, ignoring the pain of hundreds of needle-sharp stabs. The dogs didn't dare follow, but by the time he emerged on the other side, he was nearly ripped to shreds, blood oozing from hundreds—if not thousands—of tiny cuts over his hands, neck, and face. He collapsed to the ground, weeping, his tears burning in his open wounds. And then he heard something padding up through the brush ahead of him. Weak from losing so much blood, he looked up to see the dogs loping through the brush. They'd circled around the briar patch and tracked the scent of his blood. He was too weak to run, and as they fell upon him, he couldn't even muster a scream.

Madi didn't believe the old man's story, of course. Riah was always spinning one story or another, almost all with gruesome ends. But she couldn't help but think of the frightened boy racing through the vines as they ripped and tore into his flesh.

I can make it if I'm careful, she thought. She cautiously crawled beneath the first of the overhanging briars.

She saw no sign of the boy, but she heard him, moving up ahead, slowly now to avoid the briars as best he could.

"Can you hear me?" she called.

No answer.

"What's wrong with you? You got beans in your ears?"

She pressed forward—carefully—avoiding the slicing thorns. The briars snagged her dress, ripping at the fabric. Tears burned in her eyes as a jagged thorn drew a dotted line of red across the back of her hand. She looked away. More than anything, she hated the sight of—

Blood.

Everywhere. Spattered across the thick carpet of pine straw and dead leaves. Glistening upon a gray-barked tree trunk. Dripping from a dozen or more thorns.

The boy had left a spattered trail of his own blood through the briars.

"You all right?" Madi cried.

She followed, her eyes tracing the bloody track. She moved even more slowly. She no longer heard the boy, but *something* rustled up ahead. She wondered if the thickets in this place were moving of their own accord and dark thoughts, like the old tree, whispering secrets in her dreams.

A half dozen thorns tore at her flesh, and tears ran freely down her cheeks. She looked back the way she had come, and saw the path of blood behind her. How much of it was the boy's blood? And how much of it was her own? Her stomach turned.

A copper-pot stink flooded her nostrils, and she covered her nose as she took another step. The forest floor was wet and warm and sticky beneath her feet.

Another step.

So much blood.

Another, and a briar stabbed into her cheek. She flinched away, and her hair became tangled in the grasp of one of the vines. She winced free.

There, lying in a crumpled heap, was the boy's threadbare clothes. The cloth was stained glistening red.

Another step.

And she saw the boy again.

Except, it wasn't him.

"Only the skin," Madi whispered.

All that was left of the boy was strung up between several barbed vines like wet clothes from the wash. His arms dangled loosely, the fingers flapping. His legs and feet trailed the ground, stretched out and twisted like old socks. His eyes and mouth sagged and gaped, empty.

Madi felt ashamed as her eyes strayed below the boy's waist, where the skin was ripped and shredded. Her face flushed, and she quickly looked away.

Her breath caught in her throat.

A trail of glistening, bloody footsteps continued through the forest, vanishing into the brush.

"Hhhhhh . . ."

Madi jumped and stepped away from the tattered skin dangling before her like a sheet phantom.

"Hhhhhh . . ."

The boy's torn lips twitched and the empty mouth tried to form words.

His breath reeked like a slaughterhouse.

CHAPTER THREE

A pair of tire tracks wound around the edge of the forest, leading in one direction toward the highway, and in the other toward the farm. Wiry grass grew tall and wild between the ruts, and a half dozen grasshoppers sprang through the brush, leaping ahead of Madi as she made her way home.

The bottoms of her feet felt swollen from briar sticks, and tiny cuts covered her ankles and calves, like a swarm of angry wasps knitted into a pair of stinging socks. She'd stopped at the creek to clean up as best she could, but her now-tattered dress was covered in mud . . . and tiny splashes of blood where the thorns had stabbed through the fabric and into her flesh. She didn't like the way the sodden cloth stuck to her legs. Her face was hot, and sweat burned her eyes and dribbled down the bridge of her nose. She mopped damp hair from her face with the back of her left forearm. Under her right arm, she carried the boy's skin, folded up neat as Sunday wash.

"Be still," she hissed.

The skin felt feverish. Madi could have sworn it was sweating, too. It squirmed under the crook of her arm as if trying to shimmy free.

"I said *be still*, or I swear I'll wrap you round a stone and chuck you in the creek."

The boy's hide stopped moving and, within seconds, grew cool as old leather.

She could hardly believe what she'd found in the woods.

A haint.

And on her birthday, too.

She knew plenty about haints. The hollows and the salt marshes crawled with them, deathly pale and gravely silent. Pa didn't like to talk about such things, but Riah told stories about the restless ghosts of pirates protecting long-buried treasures . . . or the wandering specters of Confederate soldiers who searched by moonlight for body parts severed by saber or cannonball . . . or older, darker spirits that had never been alive at all, at least not as people recognized the difference between life and death. He said Ahmen's Landing was infested with ghosts, sometimes two or three to a house, and no matter where you went in town, spectral eyes followed you.

"*And on certain nights,*" the old man had whispered, "*the mists roll in from offshore, thick as cotton, creeping into every crevice and corner, reeking like dead things washed in with the tide. The breath of drowned men, grown restless in the deeps. Phantom's breath.*"

Madi liked the stories. She liked being scared. But deep down she'd always known the yarns about ghouls and goblins and phantom's breath were nothing more than bunkum. But now—

She'd found a haint. A real, live haint.

She chuckled at herself. A *live* haint. Wasn't that a silly thing to think?

"Wouldn't be much of a ghost," Madi said, "if you were still alive."

The boy's skin did not answer.

As she walked along, she heard something following her in the forest scrub, like a bobcat stalking her, waiting to pounce. She pretended to ignore the sound, but every now and again she risked a glance at the trees. She saw nothing, but the sound stopped every time she peered into the brush. She knew something watched her from the woods. She could *feel* wild eyes upon her. She quickened her pace.

Rounding the bend, she saw her house. Chickens milled about the yard, pecking at bugs, and Madi felt a hint of guilt for driving the grasshoppers in their direction. The cows, including the new calf, stood in their fenced pasture, chewing vacantly on grass and weeds. The vineyard's wire trellises climbed the hill, already heavy with leaves and drooping grape clusters, and the sharp scent of the scuppernongs was thick in the air. At the summit of the hill stood the old tree in dark silhouette.

Madi saw no sign of her father, but she guessed he was a-wandering through the trellises, inspecting the vines.

She dashed across the yard and up the sagging front porch steps. When she reached the top step, she paused to watch the tree line. She discerned no sign of whatever had been shadowing her through the woods, but she figured it was out there even now. Watching. She rewarded the watcher's vigilance with a shrug, and she went inside.

The screen door creaked open and snapped shut. The house was gloomy and stuffy, and dust motes danced in the weak beams of sunlight streaming in from the open windows. The warm, still air smelled faintly of Pa's pipe smoke, with maybe a hint of the morning's breakfast— pork steaks and scrambled eggs—lingering about for good measure. The heat and the smells seemed to paw at Madi, and her skin felt greasy and sticky. During the winter months, she couldn't wait for warmer days, but now that summer was settling down upon the farm, autumn couldn't get here fast enough for Madi's tastes. The here and now was never good enough for the girl, and she would have been the first to admit it.

Madi went straight to her room, pulled the door closed, and drew the window shade down. She gently unfolded the skin and spread it out upon the bed. The skin looked like something out of the funny papers, like a comic strip character who'd been smashed flat by a falling boulder or piano. Only, in the funny papers, there was never blood.

"I don't know if you can see or not, since you don't have eyes." Madi tugged the covers back from the bed and threw them over the haint's flattened face. "But I know enough about boys to know that even without eyes, you'd find a way to peek at me if you could."

She quickly changed out of her sweaty, muddied dress and hid the garment under the bed until she could try to wash it proper. She opened her dresser drawers and chose a fresh, clean pair of denim cutoffs and a T-shirt. The garments were old, well worn, and soft, and they hugged her body with a familiarity that only comes from being worn over and over again throughout the years. Madi pouted a little. She knew it was a ridiculous idea, but she'd halfway believed the clothes wouldn't wear the same now that she was "all grown up."

As she dressed, she heard the heavy tread of her father's boots on the front porch. The screen door whined as he wrenched it open. She quickly grabbed the castoff skin, crumpled it up, and threw it into the dresser. She closed the drawer and quickly straightened her bedclothes.

Pa was talking to someone. His voice sounded muffled and hushed, but Madi had a knack for hearing the subtlest sigh or whisper. She held her breath and listened.

"... Of course I know what it means," he said. "You think I haven't been expecting this day for the past seventeen years?"

"Well, then you know what has to be done." Madi recognized the second voice. Old Man Riah. "You've known since the day you took up in this house."

Madi tiptoed to the door for a better listen.

"But I'm telling you, it ain't like that," Pa said. "I've been watching her."

"She's growing up."

"But she ain't showing any signs." Pa raised his voice. "Not like you and the others said she would."

"She will, though. That's the way of it."

"Don't act as though you don't care." Madi could tell from Pa's tone of voice his face was growing red. "You've watched her grow up, same as me."

"But I still remember the pact," Riah said.

"Maybe it's easier for you, because you ain't her father."

Madi nearly squeaked in shock at what Riah said next.

"Neither are you."

Madi's heart thudded in her chest. She couldn't breathe. The rush of blood in her ears nearly drowned out the conversation between the men. Madi thought she heard her father snap back at the trader man, but she couldn't make out the words. What did Riah mean? Surely she had misunderstood him. The men were arguing, and she caught only a few words here and there—*pact* and *grave* and *birthing* and . . .

She gasped as if splashed with a bucket of ice water.

Witch.

CHAPTER FOUR

Riah was right. And wrong.

Madi *was* curious, probably too much so for her own good, and she'd gotten herself into trouble more than once by snooping where she didn't belong. But she wasn't stupid, and—contrary to what Riah might have said—the threat of death was plenty to keep her from following her father to the Gathering.

Whatever that might be.

For the rest of the day, Madi avoided Pa, partly because she didn't want him to suspect anything (he could read her expressions and tone of voice the way he read that Bible of his) and partly because she knew she'd never be able to look him in the eye. His words echoed in her brain.

"*Maybe it's easier for you,*" Pa had said, "*because you ain't her father.*"

And Riah had answered, "*Neither are you.*"

What could that have meant? Madi wanted to believe she hadn't heard the men clearly. She wanted to believe Riah was "talking on," as her father might say, spinning a wild yarn with about as much weight in the real world as any one of his haints. Only, his voice had sounded different—more serious somehow—and Madi knew that he was speaking what he believed to be the truth. And, after all, haints were a little more real than she had believed when she crawled out of bed that morning. She felt as if the whole world was unraveling around her, and sooner or later it would all come undone and spill into . . . nothingness.

Around suppertime, Pa knocked on the door to her room.

"Madi, your supper's gonna get cold, girl."

She sat on the edge of her bed, quietly. He still sounded the same, but at the same time, she barely recognized his voice. Tears blurred her vision. She squeezed her eyes shut.

"Madi?" The doorknob turned. The door started to creak open. "Supper's—"

"I'm not hungry," Madi snapped. She jumped to her feet and took a step away from the door. If she could have kept walking, through the wall, into the shadows, into the nothingness, she might have done so. Instead, she faced the corner, not looking toward the door. If Pa entered the room, she wouldn't look at him. She couldn't. Even though she wanted to beg him to explain what she'd overheard, she knew the words would never crawl from her throat, and she didn't know if she'd ever be able to face him again.

The door did not open. Pa's footsteps, as he walked down the hall, were slow and shuffling.

Madi's stomach growled. No matter what she said, she was starving. She hadn't eaten a bite since breakfast, but it hadn't crossed her mind until she smelled pan-fried potatoes, okra, and cornbread. Pa almost never cooked a meal, but tonight he was either cooking in honor of his daughter's birthday, or he was feeling guilty. Either way, the food smelled delicious. Madi's mouth watered, but she refused to set foot outside her room. If she was lucky, there'd be something left over, and she could sneak to the kitchen for a bite after Pa was . . .

Gone.

The thought settled on her like an early frost across the grass. She wanted Pa to be gone. Gone. Because she couldn't face him. Gone. Because of his secrets and his lies. Gone. Because he wasn't her father anyway, and she didn't care if he ever returned.

The frost turned to darkness, and Madi's thoughts became bloody.

And surely there's a way to get rid of him and make sure he stays gone. Forever.

Her breath caught in her throat.

No, she thought. *No. No.*

She spoke the word—"No!"—to give it form, to make it real.

The frost—the darkness—receded, leaving an emptiness in its wake. Shock and shame and sadness filled the void, and when it overflowed, Madi started crying.

That isn't me, she thought, as she threw herself onto the bed and buried her face in the pillows. *That isn't who I want to be.* And yet the thought had come so naturally to her. In the moment she began to wish her father harm, it felt *right.* It terrified her that she could even think such thoughts—let alone relish them. She wept into the pillow, her sobs racking her body. She cried until there were no tears left. At last, she slept.

And she did not dream.

Pa opened the door just a crack. The creaking hinges, the light spilling into the darkened room, roused Madi. Her eyes fluttered open, but she didn't move. She didn't speak.

"You awake?" Pa asked. His voice, barely a whisper, trembled.

Madi's back was to the doorway, but she imagined Pa standing there, watching silently, chewing the inside of his mouth the way he did when nagging thoughts worried him. Madi pretended to sleep, and after several minutes Pa pushed the door closed and retreated down the hall. Still, Madi didn't move a muscle until she heard the whine and snap of the screen door, the heavy tread of Pa's boots on the front porch steps. Only then did she sit up in bed.

She couldn't be sure what time it was, but she guessed it was late, maybe close to midnight or later. The house was still and quiet, and the darkness was deep and thick, not the tentative shadows of the early hours, but a rich blackness that only came as evening matured into night.

Madi's eyes burned and the skin of her cheeks felt stiff from dried tears. She still felt sleepy, but she didn't want to close her eyes again. When she had awakened, the most awful thought had popped into her head—that her father and Old Man Riah and a half dozen faceless men were stealing into her room to spirit her away. Her heart still raced, and she drew the sheets up and squeezed the blankets in her fists. Her stomach flipped and turned. She felt weak and lightheaded, and she thought she might throw up.

"What's the point of that?" she muttered. "Ain't nothing in my belly anyway."

The bottom drawer of her dresser rattled.

"You have something to say?" Madi asked.

The drawer shook as if unseen hands were struggling to yank it open.

Madi hopped out of bed. A wave of dizziness swept over her. She closed her eyes and took in a couple of gulps of air to steady herself, then crossed the room. Kneeling, she pulled the drawer open.

"What do you want?" she asked.

Within the drawer, the boy's skin squirmed and crawled, like an enormous, fleshy flatworm. She reached in—the skin was warm to the touch once more—and pulled the haint out. The skin unrolled before her, and she laid it out across her chair. It looked almost as if the boy sat across from her now, only he was flat as a board, and the eyes that stared back at her were gaping holes. A tremor passed over the boy's lips.

"Window," he hissed.

"What about it?" Madi looked at the window beside her bed. The shade was drawn. "Something out there I'm supposed to see?"

"Tree . . ."

"Hate to disappoint you, but I've seen that old tree darn near a million times."

"Hhhhhh . . ."

The skin breathed in frustration, then said:

"Tree . . . Lies . . ."

"What's that?" Madi took a step away from the haint. "What's that about lies?"

"*Window . . .*"

"All right. All right." Madi turned to the window and pulled the shade. "Don't know what's so fascinating for you, anyway. You can't see a thing—"

Several figures stood beneath the branches of the old tree. Madi couldn't see them very well, but she counted at least eight, men and women alike. They carried torches that flared and guttered in the wind.

"That's them," she whispered. "The Gathering."

Another figure climbed the hill toward the tree. From the way his shoulders slumped and feet dragged in the dirt, the torch he carried might have weighed a couple of hundred pounds. Despite the darkness and the distance between the house and the figure, Madi recognized the man.

"Pa." She glanced at the boy's skin. "How'd you know? How'd you know they were out there?"

Thunderheads crawled across the night sky, blanketing the stars. The muted glow of the moon struggled to pierce the haze. On warm afternoons, Madi could wile away hours watching the sky, picking out the shapes of unicorns and castles and butterflies in the clouds. But she didn't like the shapes she saw looming out of the vapors tonight—and the old oak tree reached out to them like a beckoning hand.

As Pa reached the top of the hill and joined the other torchbearers, Madi couldn't help but think she might never see him again.

"*Avrum Creed . . .*" the boy's hide wheezed.

Madi snapped her head toward the speaking skin. "How do you know my pa's name?"

"*The pact . . .*" The haint ignored her, but continued to hiss. "*. . . Years . . . Seventeen years . . .*"

"What are you talking about?"

"*No signs . . . Just a child . . .*"

Madi couldn't make any sense of the haint's gibbering. She leaned close to the window, her breath fogging the glass. She couldn't tell Pa from any of the other people crowding around the trunk of the tree.

"*Time has come . . . Terms of the pact . . . Killed her . . . Killed the witch . . .*"

"Would you just pipe down?" Madi said. "I'm trying to think."

"*Not her . . . Raised her . . . I'm her father . . .*"

Madi gasped.

"Are you trying to tell me you can hear what they're saying way out there?" she asked the skin. "How can that be?"

And then she knew.

Something dark and spindly was crawling in the branches of the old tree. The people gathering upon the hill didn't see the creature, even as it clambered through the tangled limbs toward them, leaning in close, listening. In the light of the torches, its naked flesh glistened. Madi remembered the bloody footprints trailing through the brush, leading away from the spot where she had found the boy's skin. She remembered the eerie feeling of being followed and spied upon.

"The . . . rest of you is out there, isn't it?" Madi said. "Your body, your eyes, your ears. It's out there, in the tree, and whatever it sees and hears, so do you."

"*Witch,*" the haint continued. "*Witch.*"

Madi couldn't help but smile as she gazed upon the hill. She had her own personal spy, one who could tell her anything—

Her smile faltered when the boy's skin next spoke.

"*Decided . . . It's decided.*"

Her throat grew dry. Her blood ran cold.

"*The girl . . . must die . . .*"

***

CHAPTER FIVE

She ran.

She didn't know what else to do, and she didn't have much time to think about it. Even as she pulled herself away from the window, she saw the congregation of torchbearers disbanding. They scattered in every direction, the light of their fires snapping in the night's gusts, shadows shrinking away from them as if afraid. The thing crouching in the tree watched them with baleful, glimmering eyes. Pa—at least she assumed it was her father—loped toward the farmhouse, his steps hesitant and labored.

He's going to kill me, Madi thought.

Maybe she was letting her imagination get the best of her, but she didn't plan on waiting around to find out. She grabbed a musty bag from under her bed. With a snap of her wrist, she sent the dust bunnies that had been nesting on the bag flying. Throwing open the dresser drawers, Madi packed several untidy handfuls of clothes.

"You're coming with me, too," she said as she bunched up the boy's skin and shoved it into the satchel along with the garments.

Madi took one last look around. She didn't know if she'd ever see her room—let alone the house or the farm or her father—again. She drew in a shuddering breath to steel her courage. She wasn't afraid Pa might catch her. She knew she could duck out into the night before he so much as suspected she was gone. But she was afraid of what else might be waiting for her . . . out there in the dark. More than that, she feared leaving the only home she had ever known behind.

It dawned on her that the boy's skin might have been lying. It might have been trying to trick her into leaving the safety of her house and rushing into danger, like fool's fire dancing over a bog. The raw flesh and bloody bones of the boy's body might have been waiting in the darkness to pounce on her and eat her alive.

And maybe Pa was on his way to choke the breath from her lungs right this very moment.

She couldn't trust anything or anyone except herself, and she didn't put much faith in her own mind anymore. The dark thoughts surfacing in her head didn't feel right. It felt as though she was losing touch with the person she had always been.

Old Man Riah said something about me changing, she thought. *Maybe he was right. Maybe this is what he was talking about. Maybe whoever it is I'm becoming doesn't deserve to live.*

But it didn't matter what she deserved. She didn't want to die. At least, not tonight. Not by her father's hand.

She barely remembered racing through the house, crashing out the front door, and jumping from the porch without so much as touching a single step. One second, she stood trembling in her room. The next, the night air was whipping past her. She dashed through the yard, past the animal pens, and into the wood. She stopped and crouched in the brush, watching the house.

Pa rounded the corner. He tossed the torch to the ground and stomped upon it until it went out. Wisps of smoke rose around him in tangles. His eyes scanned the woods, and Madi flinched and hunkered down, even though there was no way his old eyes could have picked her out in the darkness. He climbed the steps and went inside.

If he stays inside, Madi thought, *that means he didn't mean me any harm. It means he went straight to bed without so much as looking in on me. But if he comes back out—*

The front door couldn't have been closed more than a minute before it swung open again. Pa strode onto the porch. He leaned against the railing. His hands were clenched into fists. His knuckles were pale white.

"Madi!" he called. "Where are you, girl?"

Madi crept backward, trying not to make a sound. When the branches obscured her view of her father, she turned and scrambled through the thickets.

CHAPTER SIX

Madi knew those woods just as well as she knew her own bedroom. She'd been exploring the wilds all her life—the hollows where she chased squirrels, the muddy swimming holes where she cooled off on hot days, the brooks where she skipped stones on lazy afternoons—but the places she knew seemed a distant memory. Now—in the dark . . . with her father chasing her . . . with her father possibly wanting to *kill* her—*nothing* seemed familiar.

The ground dipped and rolled, and Madi tripped through the thickets as she pressed on at a breakneck speed. The darkness was as thick and syrupy as tree sap, and the sweet smell of honeysuckle was redolent of decaying funeral wreaths. She crossed a fallen, moss-covered tree and skirted a dry, winding creek bed. She wasn't sure where exactly she was heading. She only knew that she had to get *away* . . . away from her father and all the other men and women who had gathered under the blight-ridden oak tree to proclaim her a witch and decide her fate.

"The girl must die," they had said.

Hearing movement in the brush behind her, Madi quickly hunkered down behind a tree trunk to spy the source of the sound. Peering out from around the tree trunk, she saw nothing. But she knew that someone—something—scrabbled through the woods after her. She heard the snap of breaking twigs, the rustle of something passing through the underbrush, a stirring among the branches.

In the satchel at her side, the boy's skin squirmed and wriggled as if wanting to crawl out on its own.

Madi clutched the bag tight, and the boy's hide grew still.

She waited, holding her breath, watching.

Whatever it was, it loped through the woods in a kind of herky-jerky gait, stopping and keeping still for several seconds at a time, then lurching forward without caution. Something about its movement reminded Madi of a spider, lying in wait upon its web, still as death in anticipation of a fly crossing its path, then pouncing with ruthless speed.

Not her pa . . .

At least, she didn't believe so.

Whatever followed her, it moved like an animal—like a predator tracking prey.

And then, just as she thought she might have spotted a shadowy form moving through the brambles, the sound stopped. The forest was still once more. Madi's eyes darted back and forth as she tried to once again discern the strange, crouched shape she had seen just seconds earlier. Whatever she had seen—or imagined she had seen—it was gone now. Shadows rushed in like black, freezing water to obscure Madi's vision.

She was alone.

"Not . . . alone . . ."

The voice, little more than a feeble hiss, came from the satchel, from the skin within.

"I know," Madi said. "I know. You're here, too, for all the good it does me."

"Not alone."

She wondered if maybe it was the boy's skinless body that was following her through the forest. The thought did little to comfort her.

Knowing her pa was somewhere out there, maybe not too far behind her, Madi didn't wait long before setting out again. She knew he'd find her soon enough. Pa was an excellent hunter and tracker. He'd find her trail if he hadn't done so already, and—

Startled by a sudden commotion, birds—sparrows and towhees—erupted out of the brush and took flight through the darkness. Something crashed through the trees. At first, Madi thought her father had found her and was leaping through the foliage to grab her up. She realized soon enough, though, that the sound was moving away from her.

"Not alone," the boy's skin rasped once more.

"That was you," Madi said to the haint, "wasn't it? I mean, it was the other you. And it's making another trail for Pa to follow. It's covering my tracks."

The haint released a rasping sigh.

"Hhhhhhhh . . ."

"How did you . . . How did it know what I was thinking? How did it know I was worried about Pa tracking me?"

But the haint did not respond.

Confused and frustrated, Madi set out through the woods once more. Her surroundings grew more and more strange, more foreboding. The air smelled of rich, earthworm-ridden soil freshly turned for a crop, but Madi couldn't imagine anything wholesome growing in this place. The trees were tall and twisted and clustered together in gnarled tangles, the trunks knotted with fat, black growths and veined with pale vines.

She moved past the trees the way a small child might move through a room full of tall strangers. She watched them nervously, as if she feared they might reach out, snatch her up, and rip her to bits with their gnarly branches.

Her foot struck something hard, and she tripped, sprawling to the ground. The fall knocked the wind from her lungs, and it took her a moment to recover. She pushed herself up and brushed her hands clean. She looked to the ground, and saw a chunk of white rock jutting up out of the leaves and pine straw. Turning, she realized she had entered a small clearing, and she saw dozens of taller stones all around.

"Not alone," the boy's skin hissed.

Dozens of grave markers stood before her.

She had stumbled into a cemetery.

CHAPTER SEVEN

The tombstones were so old that the epitaphs—if the graves had ever borne epitaphs—had been worn down to nothing by time and the elements. The pale markers looked like ancient bones only partially uncovered. Madi imagined that if she dug, she'd find that the cold stones stretched deep into the earth, like roots.

Tears burned in Madi's eyes.

This was a lonely place. Madi might have been the first living soul to set foot in the cemetery for decades. The people who were buried here were forgotten by their family and friends. Looking out across the bare gravestones, Madi felt a terrible sadness weighing her down, as if her bones were frozen and caked with ice.

Up until now, Madi had not noticed the mist. A cool, shifting cloud of vapor crawled between the twisted trees surrounding the clearing. It rolled in from all sides, as if moving with intent. Thick fingers of fog scrabbled silently along tree trunks and across the ground. The mist oozed slowly around the headstones, inching closer.

"On certain nights," Madi remembered, "the mists roll in, thick as cotton, creeping into every crevice and corner, reeking like dead things."

Phantom's breath.

The air grew suddenly colder, and as Madi gasped, mist erupted from her lips, uncurling into the night air to mix with the fog. She clasped her hands over her mouth. She feared that if the mist tasted her breath, it might try to draw more of it from her until it hungrily ripped it from her lungs, suffocating her.

She took a step, ready to bolt for the trees.

The fog seemed to react to her movement. It withdrew, pulling away from her for a second, then billowed out again, coming ever closer, closing in around the girl.

"Not alone."

The voice of the dead boy's skin hissed.

Something moved in the fog. At first Madi thought it might be a trick of the weak moonlight playing through mist. As she watched, though, figures started to take shape. The hazy outline of men and women and boys and girls materialized in the gloom. Their "flesh" was the color of the fog, and their bodies . . . their faces . . . were featureless. They moved silently and with an ease that told Madi that their feet did not touch the ground. The fog carried them, carried them out of the darkness, carried them into the graveyard. The faceless creatures drifted closer, and as they reached the graves, each one took a spot looming behind a tombstone.

These were their graves, Madi realized, and as the names and epitaphs had faded from the stones, so too had the faces of the poor souls buried here faded away. Madi wondered if the spirits even remembered who they once were.

Although they had no eyes that could be seen, Madi knew that the ghosts were looking at her. She felt their fathomless gazes piercing her to the very core of her being. The faceless grave wights watched her silently, their heads shifting slightly, curiously, as if waiting for the girl to speak.

"Not alone," the dead boy hissed.

Madi took a breath, and she felt cold mist rushing down her throat.

"Never alone."

CHAPTER EIGHT

Faceless and silent, the ghosts stood behind the grave markers, one spirit for every stone.

They reminded Madi of schoolchildren waiting patiently for their teacher's instruction. Of course, Madi had never set foot in a real school. She'd been educated mainly by her pa, who read to her from the Bible, and by Miss Cora, the teaching woman who used to visit her twice a week. Madi had liked Miss Cora, who always brought a bag full of books and old magazines and learning games. But Miss Cora had stopped visiting more than four years ago. Pa said she had met a fella, married him, and moved to West Virginia.

Now, with everything she thought she understood crashing down around her ears, Madi wondered if even that had been true. Maybe Miss Cora had run afoul of the congregation that had gathered under the branches of the twisted oak.

Or maybe Miss Cora had been among their number.

Madi had never seen a real classroom, although she could guess what one looked like. She had never had a real teacher, but she had learned just the same. She had never had a real father, and the man she thought was her pa was chasing her through the woods, intent on killing her.

If the ghosts, lurking behind the weather- and time-worn headstones, sensed Madi's growing confusion—her mounting panic—they showed no sign. They simply stood there, watching. They made no sound, and their faces were as barren as the grave markers behind which they stood. Madi wondered if the ghosts had once worn faces . . . faces with eyes and noses and ears and mouths . . . faces that friends or family might recognize . . . faces that had faded away and been forgotten as the epitaphs on the gravestones had dulled with unkind years.

"You don't want to hurt me, do you?"

Although little more than a whisper, Madi's words seemed to thunder in the darkness.

The grave wights offered no answer.

"Way I figure it," Madi said, "if you wanted to do me harm, you would have gotten it over with already. There ain't much I could do—now is there?—to protect myself from ghosts."

In their silence, the spirits agreed.

"So maybe you just want to scare me." Madi felt her face flush with quickening anger. "Is that it? Now that you're dead, you ain't got nothing better to do than spook people?"

A ripple seemed to pass through the spirits, like a gust of wind through the mist, like the long-dead souls sensed Madi's anger.

And feared *her*.

And *that* might have chilled Madi's blood more than anything she'd seen or heard tonight.

"I . . ."

She started to speak, and as she did so, the spectral figures shifted again, a furrow of subtle movement passing through them, the way goose flesh might spread across living skin.

"I'm going now."

Madi took a step to move around the tiny cemetery. But as she inched to the side, several of the featureless grave wights swept out from behind stones to block her path. They didn't reach for her with icy, dead fingers. They didn't whisper of ill tidings, curses, or doom. They stopped short of touching her. Instead, they simply barred her path so if she took another step forward, she would walk through their misty forms.

She moved to the left, and the spirits moved to block her. She ducked to the right, and the spirits darted that way as well.

"What do you want?" Madi asked.

The grave wights said nothing.

Madi knew that she had to keep moving. Pa was out there—somewhere not far behind—looking for her. She couldn't go back the way she had come.

A growl formed in her throat.

"Move," she said.

And—just like that—the grave wights recoiled from her, the mist rolling back like waves turned away by breakers. The ghosts flowed back to their positions behind the grave markers and simply . . .

Watched.

Madi looked back at the spirits as she took one slow, tentative step after another. As she cleared the cemetery, her pace quickened, and soon she was running again, not looking back.

Later, she would realize that the grave wights were trying to protect her from what lay ahead.

But by that time, they wouldn't be there to help her.

CHAPTER NINE

Madi thought she was farther away from home than she had ever been before.

That wasn't true, of course. Every now and then, Pa had taken her into the nearby town of Ahmen's Landing. Usually, she just sat in the truck while he ducked into the feed store or the hardware supply. She would sit there, watching the townsfolk—the women chatting as they exited the beauty shop, the men gathering outside the diner, the kids her age laughing and goofing off as they strolled past. Once, one of the boys had looked her way and smiled, even though he was walking close to a girl who must have been his girlfriend. Madi felt her face flush and she gasped aloud. In the instant when their eyes met—in that second before Madi forced herself to look away—she felt like the prettiest girl in all the world . . . and she was certain that he was the most handsome boy that ever lived. And then he was gone, continuing on his way, throwing his arm around his girl, talking loudly and boisterously with his friends.

A couple of times, Madi had accompanied her father to the grocery store. The small store with its crowded, dusty shelves and rumbling refrigeration units seemed like a magical place to the girl. She could have spent hours browsing those shelves, but Pa always hurried along, like he didn't want to be seen with her. Madi had to admit, some of the other customers looked at her strangely, not with malice or distaste, but with a glimmer of familiarity. Madi always left the store with a couple of bags of groceries, a tattered paperback book or a few out-of-date magazines, and the distinct impression that the townsfolk *wanted* to talk to her . . . but they were afraid.

Ahmen's Landing.

How far away was town? At least a few miles, she guessed, maybe as many as a couple of dozen. On foot, with someone chasing her through the woods, it might as well have been on the other side of the—

"Madi!"

Pa's voice cut through the night—loud and clear and close. The sound of it sent a shock wave through Madi's bones, and she stumbled and almost lost her footing.

She whirled around, scanning the darkness. For a few dreadfully slow seconds, she saw nothing, heard nothing, and she wondered if her mind might have been playing tricks on her, if the sounds of the forest weren't coming together in such a way as to make her think she'd heard her father.

"Madi! Stop right there!"

As he called out again, Madi spotted him in the shadows. He threaded his way through the trees, a shadow among shadows, moving toward her quickly.

"Don't move!" he cried.

Madi had never known her father to have a quick temper. He had never been a cruel or mean-spirited man. But she had seen him angry from time to time, not necessarily with her, but maybe with life in general. She recognized the knife-like edge of anger in the man's voice when she heard it.

And she heard it now.

Pa was angry.

"Run."

From the satchel at her side, the boy's skin hissed.

"Run!"

And she ran, turning away from her father and scrambling into the darkness, slipping in the leaves and pine straw and almost falling face first to the ground, but pushing herself forward, through the trees, down a hillside, over a cluster of large rocks that pushed their way out of the forest floor. She heard her father behind her—his bellowing cry, his breath coming in ragged gasps, his heavy footsteps coming closer, but she didn't dare look back. She willed her legs to pump faster, and the world around her seemed to blur into nothing but mist and gloom and the painful sting of branches slapping at her, scratching her face, trying to drag her down.

"Stop!" Pa called, and it sounded like he was just a couple of steps behind her. He no longer sounded like himself, though. Instead, his voice was deep and rough and bestial. "Madi! Listen to me!"

His fingertips grasped at her shoulders, and she almost fell again. His hand caught hold of her arm, jerking her to a stop. Madi cried out in pain. It felt like he had ripped her arm out of its socket. The satchel fell from her shoulder, thumping to the ground, as Madi was forcibly yanked around to face her father. She tried not to scream, tried not to sob, but she couldn't help herself.

"Dammit, girl!"

His face was a mask of anger, and sweat dripped from his nose. His breath came in hot blasts that washed across Madi. He grabbed her—hard—by both shoulders and pulled her close. She knew he was going to kill her right then and there. He was going to put his big, sweaty hands around her throat and squeeze until he choked the life out of her.

"Dammit!" he spat again. "Why make this any harder than it has to be?"

"Please," Madi whined, "I don't want to—"

"Don't you say it! Don't you dare say another word! You think anyone wants to die? You think anyone—least of all me—wants to do what has to be done?"

"Why?" Madi tried to pull away, but her father only seemed to draw her in closer. His hands moved up to her throat, his fingers crawling across her skin. His touch seemed to sear her flesh. "Why are you doing this?"

"It's good that you don't know, girl." Pa's chin trembled as if he was on the verge of weeping. "It's good that you'll be gone before you realize what you are."

His fingers closed around her throat.

He squeezed.

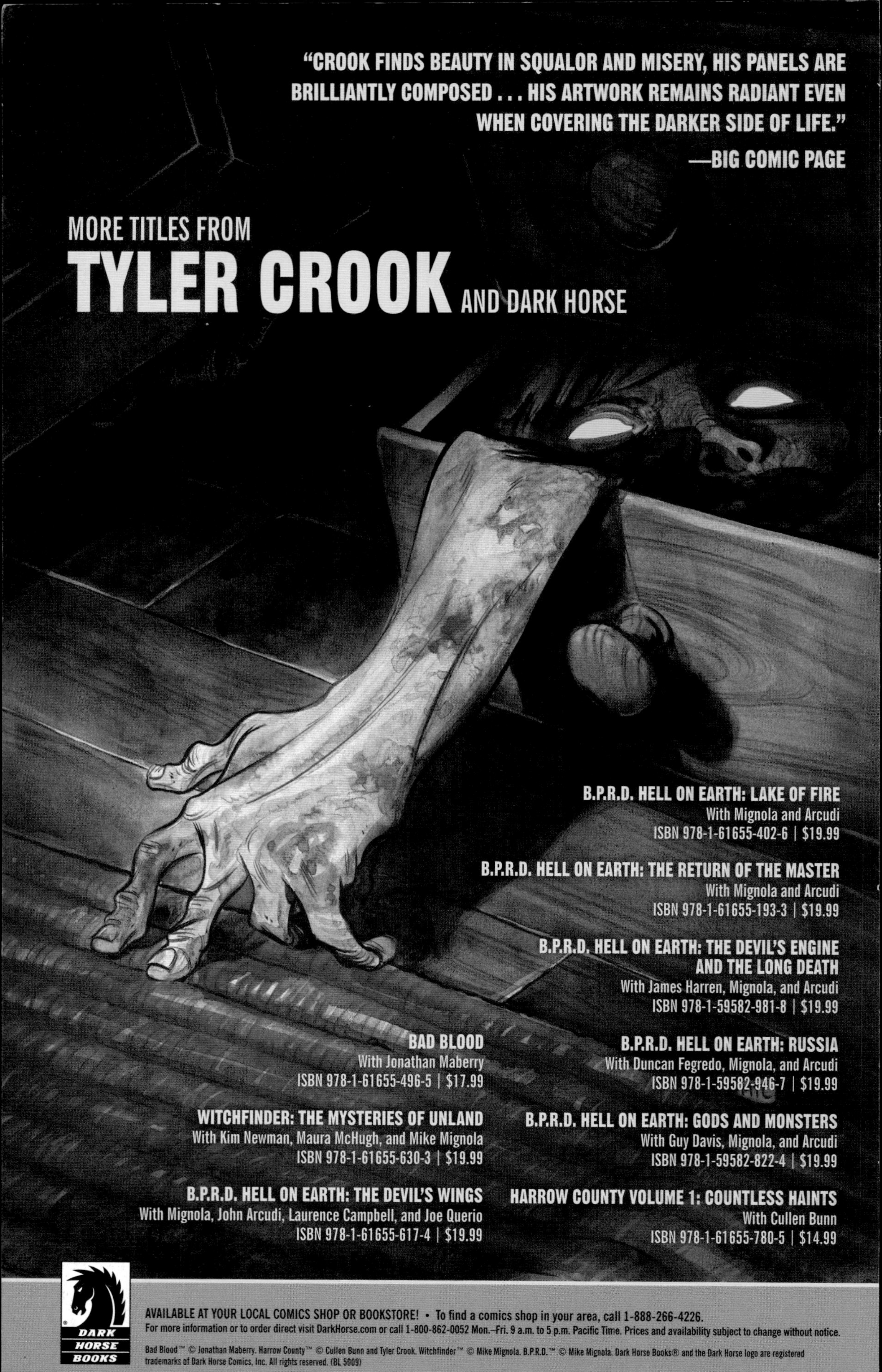

"CROOK FINDS BEAUTY IN SQUALOR AND MISERY, HIS PANELS ARE BRILLIANTLY COMPOSED . . . HIS ARTWORK REMAINS RADIANT EVEN WHEN COVERING THE DARKER SIDE OF LIFE."
—BIG COMIC PAGE

MORE TITLES FROM
TYLER CROOK AND DARK HORSE

B.P.R.D. HELL ON EARTH: LAKE OF FIRE
With Mignola and Arcudi
ISBN 978-1-61655-402-6 | $19.99

B.P.R.D. HELL ON EARTH: THE RETURN OF THE MASTER
With Mignola and Arcudi
ISBN 978-1-61655-193-3 | $19.99

B.P.R.D. HELL ON EARTH: THE DEVIL'S ENGINE AND THE LONG DEATH
With James Harren, Mignola, and Arcudi
ISBN 978-1-59582-981-8 | $19.99

BAD BLOOD
With Jonathan Maberry
ISBN 978-1-61655-496-5 | $17.99

B.P.R.D. HELL ON EARTH: RUSSIA
With Duncan Fegredo, Mignola, and Arcudi
ISBN 978-1-59582-946-7 | $19.99

WITCHFINDER: THE MYSTERIES OF UNLAND
With Kim Newman, Maura McHugh, and Mike Mignola
ISBN 978-1-61655-630-3 | $19.99

B.P.R.D. HELL ON EARTH: GODS AND MONSTERS
With Guy Davis, Mignola, and Arcudi
ISBN 978-1-59582-822-4 | $19.99

B.P.R.D. HELL ON EARTH: THE DEVIL'S WINGS
With Mignola, John Arcudi, Laurence Campbell, and Joe Querio
ISBN 978-1-61655-617-4 | $19.99

HARROW COUNTY VOLUME 1: COUNTLESS HAINTS
With Cullen Bunn
ISBN 978-1-61655-780-5 | $14.99

DARK HORSE BOOKS

AVAILABLE AT YOUR LOCAL COMICS SHOP OR BOOKSTORE! • To find a comics shop in your area, call 1-888-266-4226.
For more information or to order direct visit DarkHorse.com or call 1-800-862-0052 Mon.–Fri. 9 a.m. to 5 p.m. Pacific Time. Prices and availability subject to change without notice.